Shakespeare in Ten Acts

Shakespeare in Ten Acts

Edited by Gordon McMullan and Zoë Wilcox

First published in 2016 by
The British Library
96 Euston Road
London NW1 2DB

On the occasion of the British Library exhibition
Shakespeare in Ten Acts
15 April–6 September 2016
Curated by Zoë Wilcox, Tanya Kirk and Greg Buzwell

British Library Cataloguing-in-Publication Data
A catalogue record for this book is available from the British Library

ISBN 978 0 7123 5631 2 (paperback)
ISBN 978 0 7123 5632 9 (hardback)

Shakespeare in Ten Acts was supported by the British Library's Patrons
and has been made possible by a gift in memory of Melvin R. Seiden.
We gratefully acknowledge their generosity. The loan of photographs
from Peter Brook's 1970 production of *A Midsummer Night's Dream*
(RSC) was supported by Mrs Felicia Crystal.

Designed by Andrew Shoolbred
Picture research by Sally Nicholls

Printed in Hong Kong by Great Wall Printing Co.

Contents

Preface

It is four hundred years since Shakespeare died; four hundred years in which his plays have been revived and revised, remixed and recast, traded and translated. The history of Shakespeare in performance has been one of constant reinvention. This is hardly surprising, given that Shakespeare himself and his fellow actors in the King's Men company kept reinventing the plays – the differences between the two early authoritative versions of *King Lear,* the three early versions of *Hamlet,* each attests to the changes that took place in the performance history of plays even within a few years of the first night. Each suggests not only that no performance is ever quite the same as another, even in the same run, but that the unparalleled success of the Shakespeare canon in performance across the centuries is the result of never-ending revision, reimagining and reshaping.

It is this history of rediscovery and innovation that we celebrate in this book and in the exhibition it accompanies. We offer 'Shakespeare in Ten Acts' – that is, we have chosen ten landmark performances across the centuries from the first performance of *Hamlet* in the Globe Theatre to a digital-age deconstruction of the same play in very different circumstances. They are not necessarily the ten 'best' performances of Shakespeare's plays (after all, each generation believes its own actors to be the greatest, the most 'natural', compared with the stiff hams of the previous eras); rather, they are ten moments in history that express profound changes in our culture and in the way we see the world.

Each performance has been chosen to characterise the era in which it took place. The first professional stage appearance by a woman in 1660 and the first black actor to play Othello in 1825 were momentous occasions for society, and close inspection of the way they were received at the time and of what they have come to mean since can make a huge difference to our understanding both of Shakespeare and of our own moment in history. While some of our chosen performances highlight how technological innovation has invigorated Shakespearean performance (*The Tempest* at Shakespeare's new indoor theatre in the early 1600s and The Wooster Group's multimedia *Hamlet* at the Edinburgh Festival in 2013), others tell of a desire to strip back the visual excesses of the stage and liberate the audience's imagination (Peter Brook's modernist *A Midsummer Night's Dream* at the Royal Shakespeare Company in 1970 and Shakespeare's Globe's 'Original Practices' production of *Twelfth Night* in the twenty-first century). Still others are examples of increasing reverence for all things Shakespeare, such as the controversial forgery staged at Drury Lane in 1796 and the return of Shakespeare's *King Lear* in 1838 after an absence of almost 150 years. And, since no account of Shakespeare's afterlife can ignore his worldwide popularity, we also re-examine the evidence for what has been widely believed to be the performance that started global Shakespeare: *Hamlet* on board an East India Company ship off the coast of Africa in 1607.

Together, the chapters of this book chronicle the most extraordinary sea-changes in Shakespeare's reputation; it is a reputation that is still in the process of being constructed today. We can only guess at what future generations will make of him.

Notes on Contributors

Judith Buchanan is Professor of Film and Literature and Director of the Humanities Research Centre at the University of York. She writes widely on Shakespeare and performance and is the author of, *inter alia*, *Shakespeare on Silent Film: An Excellent Dumb Discourse* (2009), *Shakespeare on Film* (2005) and the edited collection *The Writer on Film: Screening Literary Authorship* (2013). Her current project is entitled *Shakespeare Beyond Words*. She is co-Director of the York International Shakespeare Festival and Director of Silents Now (silents-now.co.uk).

Greg Buzwell is Curator of Contemporary Literary Archives and Manuscripts at the British Library and a co-curator of the *Shakespeare in Ten Acts* exhibition. He was also a co-curator of the British Library's *Terror and Wonder* exhibition, which explored 250 years of Gothic literature, and has edited a collection of ghost stories by the Victorian author Mary Elizabeth Braddon. His main area of interest is the Gothic literature of the late Victorian era.

Ian De Jong is a doctoral student at the University of Nevada. His scholarship centres on the cultural construction of Shakespeare. His work has appeared in *Shakespeare Quarterly* and he is a contributor to the British Library's *Discovering Literature* project.

Peter Holland is McMeel Family Professor in Shakespeare Studies in the Department of Film, Television and Theatre, and Associate Dean for the Arts, at the University of Notre Dame. He is editor of *Shakespeare Survey* and co-General Editor of *Oxford Shakespeare Topics* with Stanley Wells (OUP) and of *Great Shakespeareans* with Adrian Poole (Arden Shakespeare). In 2015 he was appointed co-General Editor of the Arden Shakespeare fourth series. He has edited many Shakespeare plays, including *A Midsummer Night's Dream* for the Oxford Shakespeare series and, most recently, *Coriolanus* for the Arden Shakespeare third series. He has published over 100 articles in many areas of Shakespeare studies as well as on David Garrick, pantomime, twentieth-century British drama and other topics outside Shakespeare.

Tony Howard is Professor of English Literature at the University of Warwick. His has written widely on the relationship between politics, theatre and the mass media. He is lead investigator on the Multicultural Shakespeare Project, which explores the contribution of BAME artists to British understanding of Shakespeare. His publications include *Women as Hamlet* (2007).

Kathryn Johnson has been Curator of Theatre Archives and Manuscripts at the British Library since 1999, with special responsibility for the Lord Chamberlain's Plays collection. She catalogued the archives of Laurence Olivier, John Gielgud and Ralph Richardson, and is currently working on an annotated handlist of plays refused a licence by the Lord Chamberlain between 1900 and 1968.

Farah Karim-Cooper is Head of Higher Education and Research at Shakespeare's Globe, Visiting Research Fellow of King's College, London, and Chair of the Globe Architecture Research Group. Her major publications are: *Cosmetics in Shakespearean and Renaissance Drama* (Edinburgh University Press, 2006; 2012); *Shakespeare's Globe: A Theatrical Experiment*, co-edited with Christie Carson (Cambridge University Press, 2008); *Shakespeare's Theatres and the Effects of Performance*, co-edited with Tiffany Stern (Arden/Bloomsbury, 2012); *Moving Shakespeare Indoors: Performance and Repertoire in the Jacobean Playhouse*, co-edited with Andrew Gurr (Cambridge University Press, 2014); and *The Hand on the Shakespearean Stage: Gesture, Touch and the Spectacle of Dismemberment* (Arden/Bloomsbury, 2016).

Gordon McMullan is Professor of English and Director of the London Shakespeare Centre at King's College, London. He is Academic Director of Shakespeare400. He is a general textual editor of the new *Norton Shakespeare*, third edition, and a general editor of Arden Early Modern

Drama. His publications include *Shakespeare and the Idea of Late Writing* and *The Politics of Unease in the Plays of John Fletcher*, and he has edited *Henry VIII* for the Arden Shakespeare and both *1 Henry IV* and *Romeo and Juliet* for Norton Critical Editions. He has also edited or co-edited several collections of essays, including *Women Making Shakespeare, Reading the Medieval in Early Modern England* and *Late Style and Its Discontents: Essays in Art, Literature and Music*.

Hannah Manktelow is a PhD student working on a Collaborative Doctoral Award with the University of Nottingham and the British Library. Her research uses the Library's playbill collection to explore Shakespeare performance in the English provinces from 1769 to 2016, and examines the connection between national and regional identity and the stage. She has worked as an academic advisor to the BBC, and is the author of *The Bard in Brief: Shakespeare in Quotations* (British Library, 2016).

Sonia Massai is Professor of Shakespeare Studies in the English Department at King's College, London. She has published widely on the history of the transmission of Shakespeare on the stage and on the page, focusing specifically on the evolution of Shakespeare's texts in print before 1709 and on the appropriation of Shakespeare across different languages, media and cultures in the late twentieth and early twenty-first centuries. Her publications include *Shakespeare and the Rise of the Editor* (Cambridge University Press, 2007), collections of essays on *Shakespeare and Textual Studies* (Cambridge University Press, 2015) and *World-Wide Shakespeares: Local Appropriations in Film and Performance* (Routledge, 2005), and critical editions of *The Paratexts in English Printed Drama to 1642* (Cambridge University Press, 2014) and John Ford's *Tis Pity She's a Whore* for Arden Early Modern Drama (2011).

Lucy Munro is a Reader in Shakespeare and Early Modern Literature at King's College London. Her research interests include the performance and reception of Shakespeare and other early modern dramatists, editing and textual scholarship, literary style and genre, and childhood and ageing. She is the author of *Children of the Queen's Revels: A Jacobean Theatre Repertory* (Cambridge University Press, 2005) and *Archaic Style in English Literature, 1590–1674* (Cambridge University Press, 2013), and her edition of Dekker, Ford and Rowley's *The Witch of Edmonton* is forthcoming from Arden Early Modern Drama in 2016.

Eric Rasmussen, Foundation Professor and Chair of English at the University of Nevada, is co-editor of the award-winning Royal Shakespeare Company's edition of *William Shakespeare: The Complete Works* and of the catalogue raisonné *Shakespeare's First Folios: A Descriptive Catalogue* and its companion volume *The Shakespeare Thefts: In Search of the First Folios*.

Zoë Wilcox is Lead Curator of the *Shakespeare in Ten Acts* exhibition. She trained as a theatre designer and worked for the National Theatre Archive and Trinity Laban Conservatoire of Music and Dance before qualifying as an archivist in 2009. Since joining the British Library she has catalogued the archives of Peggy Ramsay, Mervyn Peake and Keith Waterhouse and co-curated the exhibition *The Worlds of Mervyn Peake*.

Acknowledgements
Prologue: With thanks to Ian De Jong and Arthur Evenchik
Chapter 1: With thanks to Arthur Evenchik and Eric Rasmussen
Chapter 3: The author would like to thank several colleagues who have provided invaluable feedback on this essay. Among them, special thanks are due to Zoë Wilcox, Antonia Moon and Tanya Kirk for helping to hunt down some of the exciting British Library collection items.
Chapter 4: The author would like to thank Clare McManus for her invaluable guidance on early modern female performers and Peter Kirwan for his comments on an earlier draft.
Chapter 9: The author would like to thank Mark Rylance, Claire van Kampen and Jenny Tiramani for their guidance and support.

The editors gratefully acknowledge the advice and assistance of the exhibition advisory group: Judith Buchanan, Andrew Dickson, Michael Dobson, Gabriel Egan, Andrew Gurr, Tony Howard, Farah Karim-Cooper, Peter Kirwan, Clare McManus, Sonia Massai and Eric Rasmussen. Special thanks are due to the exhibition's co-curators, Tanya Kirk and Greg Buzwell, and to the many other curators who assisted with research and object selection, especially Eva del Rey, Tim Pye, Andrea Clarke, Sandra Tuppen, Steve Cleary and Stella Wisdom. Gordon wishes to thank Jamie Andrews, the British Library's Head of Culture and Learning, for being so supportive of Shakespeare400 and everyone at King's College, London, involved in facilitating the season.

Mr. WILLIAM
SHAKESPEARES

COMEDIES,
HISTORIES, &
TRAGEDIES.

Published according to the True Originall Copies.

Martin Droeshout sculpsit London.

LONDON
Printed by Isaac Iaggard, and Ed. Blount. 1623.

Prologue

Beginnings of a Life in Performance

Eric Rasmussen

The publication of the Shakespeare First Folio in 1623, seven years after Shakespeare's death, was an extraordinary event. The prestigious folio format had previously been used only for books by leading theologians, philosophers and historians, although Ben Jonson included nine plays in his complete *Workes* (1616) – and was mocked by contemporaries, who joked that he seemed not to understand the distinction between 'work' and 'play'. A folio devoted entirely to drama was unprecedented before the publication of this 900-page collection of his thirty-six plays: *William Shakespeare's Comedies, Histories, & Tragedies*. For those devoted to Shakespeare's memory – or, perhaps, his myth – the First Folio became, and remains, something of a sacred text. The title-page purports to be definitively authentic, claiming sources in 'the True Originall Copies'. It provides our only certain image of Shakespeare, the iconic engraving by Martin Droeshout. Moreover, in their introductory epistle 'To the Great Variety of Readers', the assemblers of the folio, John Heminges and Henry Condell (two of Shakespeare's fellow actors in the King's Men theatre company), lay the foundations for the bardolatry that would sweep England through the following centuries. They claimed (among other things) that Shakespeare's expressive skill was such that he never crossed anything out in his writing: 'We have scarce received from him a blot in his papers'. They close their effusive praise with a warning: if you don't like his plays, there is probably something wrong with you: 'And if then you do not like him, surely you are in some manifest danger, not to understand him'.

OPPOSITE
Title-page of the First Folio, 1623. This copy is one of only four in the world which feature the first state of the famous portrait by Martin Droeshout, printed before the engraved plate was recut to alter some of Shakespeare's features.
British Library C.39.k.15

Heminges and Condell were by no means the first to fashion an image of Shakespeare. Throughout the playwright's career – even before he was a household name in London and a dominant force in London's professional theatre community – his contemporaries, well-wishers and rivals were attempting to construct identities for him. As a result, much of what we think we know about Shakespeare's life may in fact be obscured by the editorialising pens of his contemporaries. Given this ambiguity, attempts to understand who Shakespeare was must also rely upon official documents – church registries, governmental financial records, legal contracts and the like.

The volume of such evidence is regrettably rather slim. We know that William Shakespeare was born in 1564 in Stratford-upon-Avon. His father, John, made gloves for a living and served as an alderman; his mother, Mary, came from a local land-owning family. The Shakespeares had roots in the community, and it is likely that Will spent his boyhood in Stratford. Stratford had a grammar school, the King's New School, and much of Shakespeare's work demonstrates a familiarity with grammar-school material. Unfortunately for us, the school's records have perished. Indeed, no definitive record of Shakespeare's life exists between his christening on 26 April 1564 and his marriage in November of 1582. The marriage documentation itself may hint at some youthful drama. In 1582, Shakespeare was 18 years old – young to be married by today's standards, but not necessarily by the standards of the time. His wife, Anne Hathaway, was 26. Their first daughter was born the following May – less than seven months after the wedding. Did Will and Anne marry quickly to avoid scandal?

In 1585, Anne Shakespeare gave birth to twins, Hamnet and Judith, who were duly christened. From then until 1592, we have no records of Shakespeare's activities save for a mortgage action in 1589 relating to a local property in Stratford. It is hard to believe that during this period he was static, idle. We want to imagine him in situations where he could observe human nature and human interaction, experiment with language and nurture the seeds of genius in his bosom. Some early biographers argued from slender evidence that he was a schoolmaster; others claimed he was writing ballads against political enemies or holding theatregoers' horses in London. In 1587, the travelling acting troupe known as the Queen's Men visited Stratford-upon-Avon, where they found themselves unexpectedly shorthanded when one of their actors was killed by another player in a drunken fight. Perhaps this was the moment at which Shakespeare got his start in the theatre.

In truth, we can deduce only one fact about Shakespeare's 'lost years', as they are called: at some point before 1592, he gained entry to London's professional theatre community. Did he start out as an actor? A jobbing writer? A supplier of gloves, a costumier, a holder of horses? No one can say. But by 1592, Shakespeare had begun writing for the London stage – at the very least, he had written a play or two about King Henry VI. What is more, his confidence and skill had begun to irk some of his more established contemporaries. We know this by means of the first extant printed reference to

Shakespeare – one which marks the beginning of the process of public, collaborative and polyphonal construction of 'Shakespeare'.

This earliest surviving reference is decidedly inauspicious. Robert Greene's 1592 pamphlet, *Groatsworth of Wit, Bought with a Million of Repentance*, does not mince words:

> there is an upstart Crow, beautified with our feathers, that with his *Tiger's heart wrapped in a Players hide*, supposes he is as well able to bombast out a blank verse as the best of you: and being an absolute *Johannes fac totum* [jack of all trades], is in his own conceit the only Shake-scene in a country.

The publisher of the pamphlet characterises *Groatsworth* as the valediction of an established, well-reputed and linguistically and intellectually sophisticated writer. The introductory epistle, 'To the Gentlemen Readers', praises it as a 'Swanne like song', alluding to the notion that a swan sings sweetly immediately before its death. Presented to the public as a posthumous work, *Groatsworth* functions both as a redemption of Greene's putative literary failings and as the triumphant culmination of a profitable career. However, the fact that *Groatsworth* was entered into the official register of books 'upon the perill of Henrye Chettle' has led many to believe that Chettle – a young writer who would go on to have a prolific though not necessarily popular career as a dramatist and pamphleteer – was its author. Chettle himself claimed that he had only copied Greene's unreadable final papers. If in fact Chettle took the opportunity to ventriloquise the voice of the older, more established cultural critic, it certainly enabled him to say some fairly inflammatory things.

Groatsworth's famous jab at Shakespeare occurs in a farewell section addressed to 'those Gentlemen his Quondam [former] acquaintance, that spend their wits in making Plaies'. The author indicates that these former colleagues have forsaken him in his later life; though he never identifies them by name, he clearly tailors his advice to specific individuals. His third exhortation is directed to one 'no lesse deserving than the other two, in some things rarer, in nothing inferiour; driven (as my selfe) to extreme shifts'; he bemoans the perceived poor treatment that his unnamed addressee has received at the hands of their compatriots, then warns him against the new generation of theatre professionals. Among the 'burres', 'Puppets', 'Anticks', 'Apes' and 'rude grooms', he singles out a particular 'upstart Crow' who has borrowed the (superior) 'feathers' of his contemporaries. In the author's mind, Shakespeare and his cohort of up-and-comers commit three related sins: they overestimate their own abilities; masquerade as those more skilful than they are; and downplay the contributions of their betters. *Groatsworth* offers no antidote to this cocktail of arrogance, deception and disrespect, and Greene's advice to his mysterious ill-treated interlocutor is to leave the profession. If he could prescribe a remedy to the 'rude grooms', he might recommend humility, originality and deference – subjugation to the old guard, submission to cultural conservatism.

Shakespeare was famously referred to as an 'upstart Crow' in *Greenes Groatsworth of Wit* by Robert Greene (1592).
British Library C.57.b.42

The Shakespeare of whom we read in these few lines of *Groatsworth* is surely filtered through Greene-coloured glasses. To derive a portrait of the man or the artist from this brief passage must be more an exercise in conjecture than in true deductive biography. That said, the 'feathers' comment suggests that Shakespeare was already cultivating his talent for borrowing, recasting and improving his source material. This talent could very well have alienated Shakespeare's theatrical elders, especially when he began appropriating contemporary drama. Perhaps even more fascinating than this image of Shakespeare's creative identity is the hint of psychological biography. Did Shakespeare carry himself confidently? Did he vigorously defend the merits of his budding *oeuvre*? Did he speak out in the company of more experienced theatre professionals? Although we cannot answer any of these questions conclusively, we may venture that Shakespeare was not a timid participant in the theatrical community. He thought of himself as belonging to it – or at least behaved as if he thought he belonged. And despite the author's discomfort with Shakespeare's position – and positioning – within that community, the 'upstart Crow' had only just begun to spread his wings.

While Shakespeare was being attacked in print, other events were taking place that would have a bearing on his reputation and legacy. Shakespeare's fellow playwright, Christopher Marlowe, was physically attacked on the evening of 30 May 1593: Ingram Frizer stabbed Marlowe just above the eye, killing him instantly. Only three days earlier, a government informant named Richard Baines, who had spent some time with Marlowe in the Low Countries, provided sworn testimony accusing Marlowe of advocating homosexuality and atheism, and concluded with the sinister line: 'I think all men in Christianity ought to indevor that the mouth of so dangerous a member may be stopped'. Although the Queen's Coroner attributed the killing to a quarrel over the dinner bill – 'the reckoning' – Baines may have been part of a covert campaign to end the life of this promising dramatist. Queen Elizabeth I's spymaster, Sir Francis Walsingham, had prescribed that playwrights produce patriotic dramas about English history, wholesome Protestant morality plays written in rhymed couplets. Marlowe had flown in the face of these instructions by writing in blank verse about a foreign infidel, Tamburlaine, who repeatedly commits heinous acts and yet is never struck down by the hand of divine justice. Were Marlowe's plays considered to be so subversive by the authorities as to warrant his murder?

Marlowe and Shakespeare were exact contemporaries: both were born in 1564. However, by the late 1580s, Marlowe had already written several masterpieces, all of them massive commercial successes, whereas Shakespeare had produced only a handful of plays. As a result, there is a widespread tendency to stereotype the two dramatists, as does the 1998 film *Shakespeare in Love*, valorising Marlowe as a gifted superstar and dismissing Shakespeare as a slow-to-learn fledgling. Given that the two almost certainly interacted during their formative years, however,

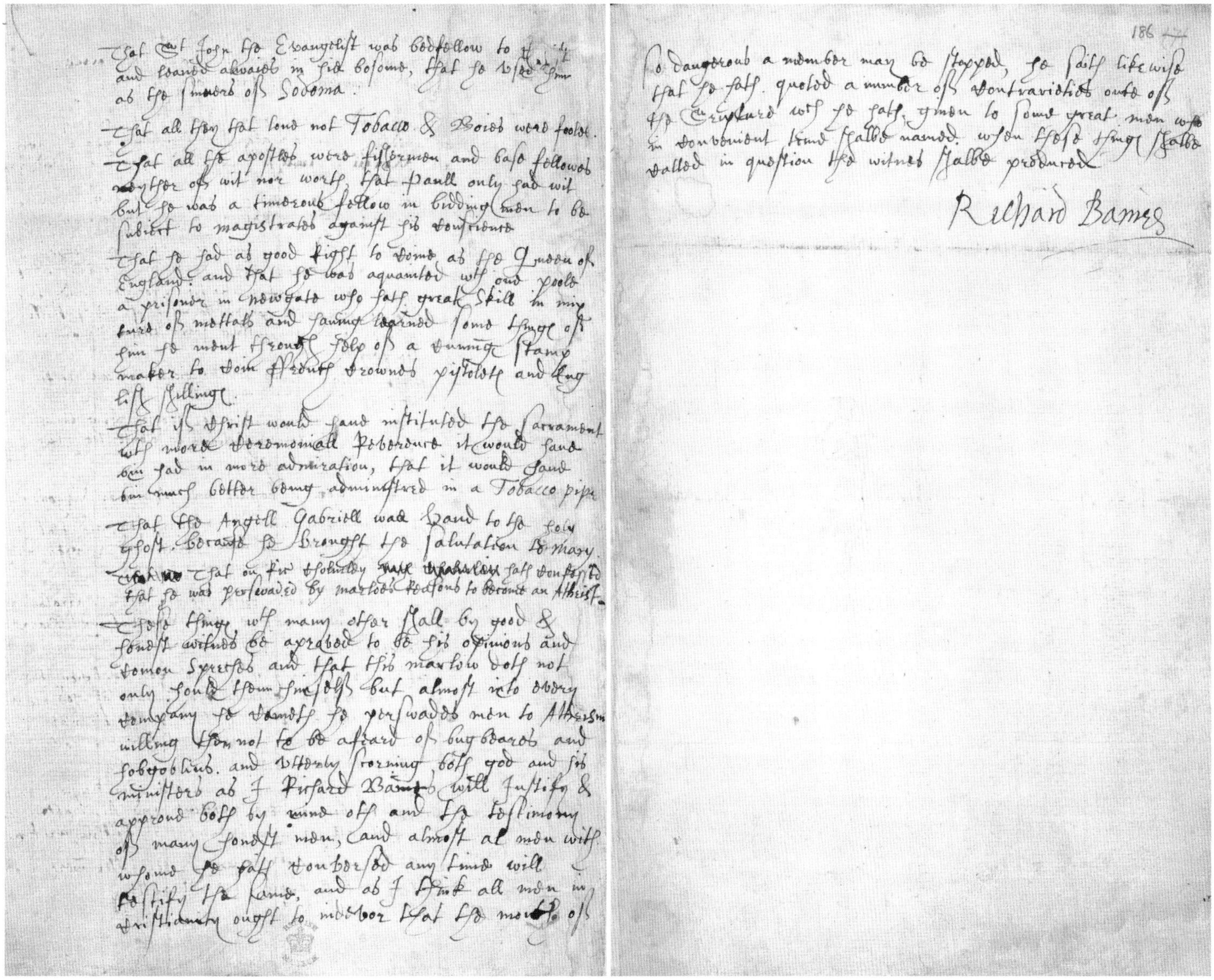

a more nuanced understanding of their relationship can be teased out: in *Tamburlaine* Marlowe invents blank verse, which Shakespeare admires and adopts for *Henry VI*. Marlowe, in turn, admires Shakespeare's ability to defer to Walsingham's wishes by writing about an English king while simultaneously subverting them by choosing a weak and ineffectual one. Marlowe then imitates this by choosing as the subject for his next play King Edward II, who neglects his kingdom and is overthrown by his barons. Shakespeare then continues the theme by writing about the overthrow of Richard II. Given this mutually beneficial working out of their craft, one is left to wonder why Marlowe may have been targeted by the authorities while Shakespeare was not. Marlowe's death broke this mutuality, and Shakespeare soon enough found his own distinctive way, not only with the Marlovian genres of history and tragedy but also with the full range of possibilities encompassed by the term 'comedy'.

The spy Richard Baines's accusations against Christopher Marlowe, 1593. The fateful line, 'I think all men in Christianity ought to indevor that the mouth of so dangerous a member may be stopped' begins at the bottom of the left-hand page.

British Library Harley MS 6848

VENVS AND ADONIS

Vilia miretur vulgus: mihi flauus Apollo
Pocula Caſtalia plena miniſtret aqua.

LONDON.

Imprinted by Richard Field, and are to be ſold at
the ſigne of the white Greyhound in
Paules Church-yard.
1594.

TO THE RIGHT HONORABLE
Henrie VVriotheſly , Earle of Southampton,
and Baron of Titchfield.

Ight Honourable , *I know not how I ſhall offend in*
dedicating my vnpoliſht lines to your Lordſhip,
nor how the vvorld vvill cenſure me for chooſing
ſo ſtrong a proppe to ſupport ſo vveake a burthen,
onely if your Honour ſeeme but pleaſed, I account
my ſelfe highlie prayſed, and vow to take aduantage of all idle
houres , till I haue honoured you vvith ſome grauer labour . But
if the firſt heyre of my inuention proue deformed, I ſhall be ſory it
had ſo noble a god-father : and neuer after eare ſo barren a land,
for feare it yeeld me ſtill ſo bad a harueſt , I leaue it to your Honou-
rable ſuruey,and your Honor to your hearts content,vvhich I wiſh
may always anſwere your owne vviſh , and the vvorlds hopefull
expectation.

Your Honors in all dutie,

William Shakeſpeare.

In the year of Marlowe's murder, the theatres were closed because of an outbreak of the plague. As a result, Shakespeare had to look elsewhere for financial security. His first known publication, *Venus and Adonis*, appeared in 1593 with a dedicatory epistle addressed 'TO THE RIGHT HONORABLE Henrie VVriothesly, Earle of Southampton, and Baron of Titchfield' and signed 'Your Honors in all dutie, William Shakespeare'. (Elizabethan printers often purchased their supplies of type from French founders; the absence of 'W' in the French alphabet meant that they had to use two 'Vs' to create the letter.) Artistic patronage in the early modern period operated like a sort of pre-emptive product placement: creators would dedicate their work to nobles, gentlefolk and even royalty in the hope that the dedicatee would reciprocate with a gift. The seventeenth-century author and historian Thomas Fuller claims that Edmund Spenser, author of *The Faerie Queene*, received £100 from Queen Elizabeth I for his fine poetry, and King Edward III famously granted Geoffrey Chaucer a lifetime allowance of wine, disbursed in (sizeable) daily increments. Shakespeare's decision to solicit Southampton's patronage was a shrewd one. If the gambit succeeded, he would be able to stay in London, continue writing and broaden his already

Title-page and
dedication of
Shakespeare's first
known publication,
the narrative poem
Venus and Adonis.
It first appeared in
1593, but proved very
popular and was
reprinted the
following year.
British Library G.11180

respectable reputation. Even more shrewdly, Shakespeare's self-deprecatory epistle promises a 'graver labour', another, putatively better, poem to come after *Venus and Adonis*. Just as today's franchise-hungry film studios set up sequels in the closing moments of big-budget films, Shakespeare intimates that bigger and better things will follow this first foray into narrative poetry. *Venus and Adonis* apparently pleased the earl sufficiently to spur Shakespeare to keep his promise: *The Rape of Lucrece*, published in quarto in 1594, was also dedicated to Southampton.

By 1598, Shakespeare's reputation was firmly established, according to Francis Meres's glowing report in his book of commonplaces, *Palladis Tamia*. According to Meres, who compiled lists of accomplished poets, Shakespeare had taken his place among exalted literary peers, including Edmund Spenser and Philip Sidney. Among dramatists, Meres praises Shakespeare's versatility in comedy and tragedy as well as his verbal skill. He calls Shakespeare 'mellifluous and hony-tongued', refers to his 'fine filed phrase', and claims that, thanks to Shakespeare among others, 'the English tongue is mightily enriched and gorgeously invested in rare ornaments and resplendent abiliments'. Although they have vastly different goals, Greene (or Chettle) and Meres adopt similar rhetorical strategies: they each construct a version of Shakespeare through florid characterisation. But whereas the author of *Groatsworth* asks his readers to accept more or less on faith the claims he makes about the character of Shakespeare the man, Meres offers evidence for his claims about the skill and reputation of Shakespeare the artist. Meres mentions thirteen plays, two narrative poems and an unspecified number of 'sugred Sonnets [distributed] among his private friends' – an impressive body of work, given that Shakespeare's writing career was not even half over. It was an achievement Meres attributed to diligence, conscious diversification and genius.

The year 1598 also saw the first appearance of Shakespeare's name on the title-pages of his printed plays. The quarto of *Love's Labour's Lost*, the earliest first edition of a play to bear his name, was advertised as '*By W. Shakespere*'. From the moment *Love's Labour's Lost* hit the bookstalls, Shakespeare's standing – in the community of theatre professionals, in artistic circles and in London itself – advanced to a higher level. Shakespeare had paid his dues, having spent between eight and twelve years as a sort of journeyman. During that period, his name had not appeared on title-pages; he had been publicly insulted by established practitioners in his field; and he had had to tailor his creative output to fill his purse. By 1598, this period was effectively over. To be sure, Shakespeare would still face challenges, but those challenges would be of a different sort for the rest of his career.

Still, increasing fame brought with it a new round of resentment, and forced Shakespeare's rivals to be creative in their ridicule. Since outright attacks had failed, the anti-Shakespeareans apparently decided to fight fire with fire, and set out to humiliate Shakespeare using dramatic poetry. The result was the *Parnassus* plays, a trilogy performed at Cambridge University during the 1590s.

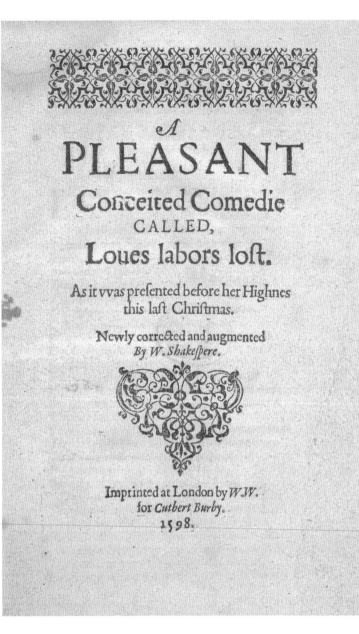

A

PLEASANT

Conceited Comedie
CALLED,
Loues labors loft.

As it vvas prefented before her Highnes
this laft Chriftmas.

Newly corrected and augmented
By *W. Shakefpere.*

Imprinted at London by *W.W.*
for *Cutbert Burby.*
1598.

Title-page for *Love's Labour's Lost*, 1598, the earliest first edition of a play to bear Shakespeare's name. This page also records the fact that Shakespeare had found royal favour, the play having been performed in front of Elizabeth I 'this last Christmas'.
British Library C.34.l.14

Parnassus includes multiple slighting references to Shakespeare – attempts to distance his work from what were perceived as the more artistically sophisticated creations of university-educated playwrights. The 'University Wits' saw the material being created for the popular stage as unpolished, unartistic and generally undesirable. Believing themselves more qualified to shape the intellectual culture of their time than the common herd of London dramatists, they encouraged disdain for theatre professionals. Naturally, then, Shakespeare's skill and popularity were an affront to them. The *Parnassus* trilogy attempts to dampen enthusiasm for Shakespeare's work by putting praise of Shakespeare in the mouths of ridiculous characters with little intelligence and less discrimination. By mocking the judgement of the London masses who flocked to Shakespeare's plays, the trilogy reinforces the prejudices of the elitist audience for whom it was performed. It constructs a 'Shakespeare' who appeals only to philistines, an unsophisticated creator of vulgar entertainments. This denigration of Shakespeare did not change the fact that he had become a major draw.

In what may have been the earliest attempt to capitalise on Shakespeare's reputation, the publisher William Jaggard (who would later print the 1623 First Folio) in 1599 brought out an anthology of poems entitled *The Passionate Pilgrim*. Although he claimed that the entire collection was 'By W. Shakespeare', only five of the twenty poems included are Shakespearean: three were extracted from the *Love's Labour's Lost* quarto, and two would eventually appear as numbers 138 and 144 in the 1609 quarto of Shakespeare's Sonnets. How Jaggard got his hands on the two sonnets is anyone's guess. Meres's reference to Shakespeare's 'sugred Sonnets among his private friends' suggests a coterie of readers among whom Shakespeare circulated poems never – or not yet – intended for publication. Perhaps one of those 'friends' decided to break the unspoken coterie-bond and profit from the sonnets' sweetness. If nothing else, *The Passionate Pilgrim* corroborates Meres's claim that Shakespeare was writing sonnets at least ten years before they appeared in quarto in 1609. The volume also provides us with a sense of the demand for 'Shakespeare' of one sort or another: even Jaggard's cobbled-together *bricolage* of dubious provenance sold well enough to merit two further editions.

It is not clear whether Shakespeare himself ever saw any profit from *The Passionate Pilgrim*, but the chances are not good. Apparently, though, he did not need the money: by 1597, he was sufficiently well off to buy a house in Stratford-upon-Avon. New Place, as the house was called, was a large, conspicuous residence whose previous inhabitants included a Lord Mayor, a surgeon and a lawyer whose son, William Underhill, sold it to Shakespeare. The ink on the deed was barely dry when Underhill was murdered by *his* son, Fulke, who himself died almost immediately thereafter. But Fulke was the heir, a fact that complicated Shakespeare's claim to New Place, and in 1602 Shakespeare had to renegotiate the deed in order to acquire the property free and clear, as is recorded in documents held by the National Archives and the Folger Shakespeare Library.

By 1600, Shakespeare was a pre-eminent figure in London's literary scene, both in terms of market share and in terms of artistic output. He was well on his way to ruling the community of theatre professionals. His fortune was more or less made, though he never stopped investing. Only one arena remained for Shakespeare to conquer: the complex, not-quite-codified but inflexible social order. Today, in many cultures, financial success is the only requirement for entrée into elite circles, but Shakespeare's route to becoming 'gentle' demanded rather more than that. His family had no claim to nobility. John Shakespeare had tried to buy his way into 'gentle' status by applying to the College of Heralds for a coat of arms in the mid-1570s, but something went wrong, and the application was ignored for roughly twenty years. Then, in 1596, something went right, and John's bid for social elevation was reviewed and accepted. It is not clear why, after two decades, the application should have been revived, especially since John had fallen on hard times by the 1590s.

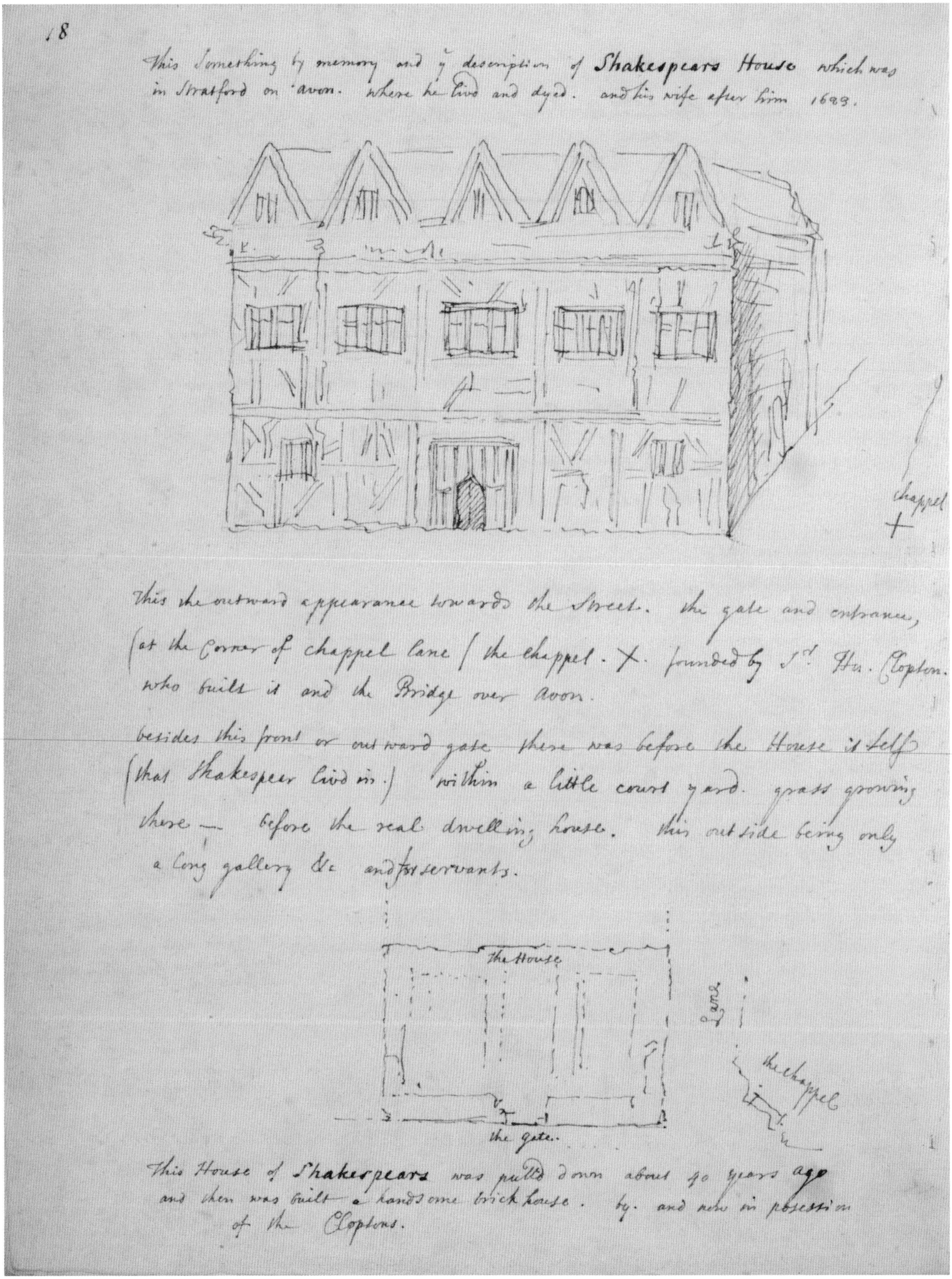

This Something by memory and y description of **Shakespears House** which was
in Stratford on 'Avon. where he lived and dyed. and his wife after him 1623.

chappel
+

this the outward appearance towards the Street. the gate and entrance,
(at the corner of chappel lane) the chappel. X. founded by S: Hu. Clopton.
who built it and the Bridge over Avon.

besides this front or outward gate there was before the House it self
(that Shakespeer lived in.) within a little court yard. grass growing
there — before the real dwelling house. this outside being only
a long gallery &c and for servants.

the House

Yard

the gate.

the chappel

this House of **Shakespears** was pulled down about 40 years ago
and then was built a handsome brick house. by. and now in possession
of the Cloptons.

Prevailing wisdom suggests that it was William who restarted the review process.

However, the story does not end with the acceptance of the application. In 1602, Ralph Brooke, a herald of York whose eye was as jaundiced as it was sharp, complained that William Dethick – the head of the College of Heralds, the Garter King-of-Arms – had granted coats of arms that should never have been awarded, including the grant to John Shakespeare. Dethick responded, summarily, that the awarding of nobility to John Shakespeare had been justified, and the case was closed. Why did Brooke raise his objection in the first place? John Shakespeare had died in 1601; surely there was no need to safeguard the social order against a dead glover. Brooke's actual target, then, must have been William Shakespeare. He had seen through William's play for social status, and he wanted to preserve the status quo.

For his part, William Shakespeare certainly believed his father's claim (and, by extension, his own) to be just. Stephen Greenblatt has pointed out the latent truculence of the motto Shakespeare chose for the coat of arms: *Non Sanz Droict*, 'Not without Right'. It's possible that Ben Jonson's play *Every Man out of His Humour* pokes fun at Shakespeare's coat of arms in the character of Sogliardo, who boasts a crest with the motto 'Not without Mustard'.

If the 1590s have left us with enough evidence to piece together the blistering beginning to Shakespeare's career, the early years of the seventeenth century have left us with something perhaps even more precious: the only surviving literary manuscript in Shakespeare's hand. 'The Book of Sir Thomas More' ('Book' being the technical term for the copy of the play that was used by the bookholder to direct the actors in performance) is a manuscript playbook in which the handwriting of seven distinct authors can be identified. Around the year 1600, Edmund Tilney, the Master of the Revels, who ensured that the theatres were producing politically and socially acceptable entertainment, returned the draft play manuscript to its authors, Anthony Munday and Henry Chettle, with several passages censored, and instructed them to

> leave out the insurrection wholly and the cause thereof, and begin with Sir Thomas More at the Mayor's sessions, with a report afterwards of his good service done being Sheriff of London upon a mutiny against the Lombards, only by a short report, and not otherwise, at your perils.

So a variety of collaborators and assorted theatre professionals, Shakespeare among them, were recruited to help. The extant manuscript gives us a fascinating glimpse of Shakespeare's creative process and collaborative practice. His three-page scene, in which Sir Thomas More quells a potential riot, stands out from the rest of the play in terms of artistic merit, leading some critics to argue that Shakespeare was called in to 'punch up' a less-than-enthralling play, not merely to help address the censor's concerns. If, in fact,

OPPOSITE
The antiquarian George Vertue's 1737 sketch of New Place, the house in Stratford-upon-Avon that Shakespeare bought in 1597.
British Library Add MS 70438

Shakespeare functioned as a script doctor, it seems clear that he did not linger in the collaborative milieu. He repeatedly refers to characters as 'other', leaving it to a theatrical scribe to fill in the appropriate speech prefixes. Shakespeare was apparently willing to write a chunk of a play without familiarising himself with the material surrounding it.

Even more provocatively, Henry Chettle seems to have been perfectly willing to work with Shakespeare. Were Chettle's objections to the 'upstart Crow' articulated in *Groatsworth of Wit* overruled by others on the project, or did he overcome his own misgivings? Interestingly, Chettle's *Kind-Heart's Dream* (1592) contains an apology to an unnamed playwright for the treatment he received in *Groatsworth*:

> I am sorry as if the original fault had been my fault, because my self hath seen his demeanour no less civil than he excellent in the quality he professes: besides divers of worthship have reported his uprightness of dealing, which argues his facetious grace in writing.

The apology may be directed specifically towards Shakespeare.

Some of the various Shakespeares we have sketched in the preceding pages – drawn by Greene, Chettle, Meres, the University Wits and Jaggard – may indeed resemble elements of the real glover's son from Stratford, the man who wandered the sordid streets of London, played before nobility and royalty, and drove himself to conquer every arena of public life available to him. And yet, one may well continue to feel that we do not have a handle on the real man. Perhaps our image of Shakespeare is just as constructed, just as much the 'Shakespeare' we want to imagine, as theirs.

ABOVE
The head of the College of Heralds' justification for the granting of arms to Shakespeare's family, written in 1602 in response to a challenge from another herald, Ralph Brooke.

College of Arms MS W.Z. f276v

OPPOSITE
The only surviving literary manuscript in Shakespeare's hand: part of the scene he wrote for the co-authored play *Sir Thomas More*. Shakespeare's rewrite probably dates from the early years of the reign of James I, *c.* 1603–4.

British Library Harley MS 7368

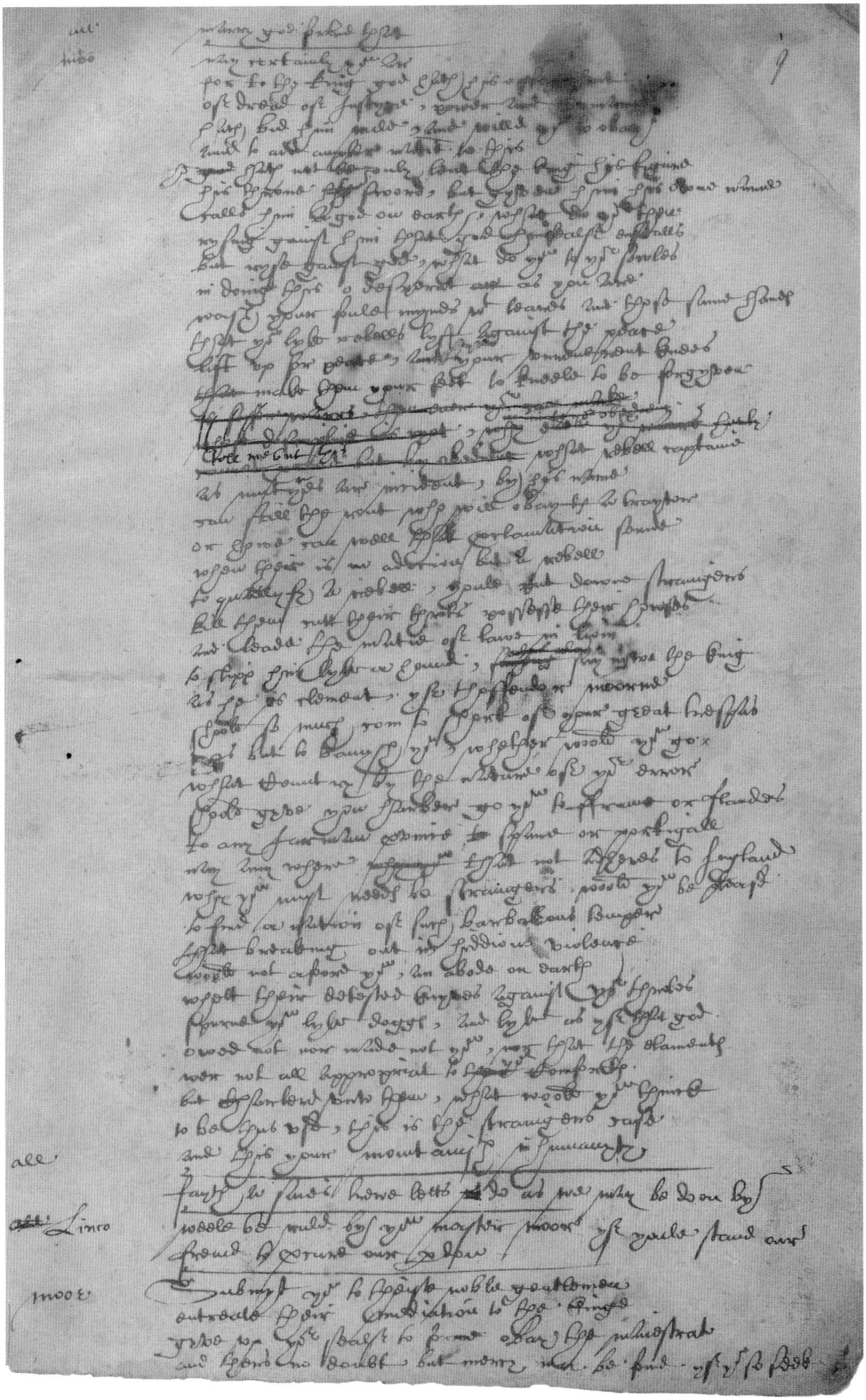

'A hit, a very palpable hit': *Hamlet* at the Globe, *c.* 1600

Ian De Jong

At some point late in the reign of Queen Elizabeth I, a new play was performed in London, using a human skull as a stage property for the first time in recorded history – and an icon was born. The first audience may have recognised the play's title; its subject matter may have stirred dim memories of a Ghost shrieking for revenge; its star actor was well known; its supporting players had established themselves in London's professional theatre community. But despite the audience's familiarity with elements of this play, its initial performance at the Globe Theatre lit the fuse of a cultural bombshell whose shock waves still reverberate today. *The Tragical History of Hamlet, Prince of Denmark*, by William Shakespeare, would inspire allusion, imitation, commentary, diatribe, reproduction and possibly even a performance on board ship off the coast of Africa during Shakespeare's lifetime. And Hamlet holding up the skull – 'Alas, poor Yorick!' (Act 5, scene 1) – would become one of the most famous moments in the history of drama.

Hamlet at the Globe

The exact date of *Hamlet*'s premiere is unknown, but the first printed text of the play provides some important clues about its early performance history. This first quarto edition (Q1), a slim volume about the shape and size of a modern comic book, was not discovered until the early nineteenth century. Only two copies are known to exist and neither is complete: the copy now in the

The Tragicall Historie of

HAMLET

Prince of Denmarke.

Enter two Centinels. {*now call'd Bernardo & Francisco —*}

1. STand: who is that?
2. STis I.
1. O you come most carefully vpon your watch,
2. And if you meete *Marcellus* and *Horatio*,
The partners of my watch, bid them make haste.
1. I will: See who goes there.
                Enter Horatio and Marcellus.
Hor. Friends to this ground.
Mar. And leegemen to the Dane,
O farewell honest souldier, who hath releeued you?
1. *Barnardo* hath my place, giue you good night.
Mar. Holla, *Barnardo*.
2. Say, is *Horatio* there?
Hor. A peece of him.
2. Welcome *Horatio*, welcome good *Marcellus*.
Mar. What hath this thing appear'd againe to night.
2. I haue seene nothing.
Mar. *Horatio* sayes tis but our fantasie,
And wil not let beliefe take hold of him,
Touching this dreaded sight twice seene by vs,

                        B   There-

Huntington Library lacks the final page, whereas the copy in the
British Library lacks the title-page. The unique Q1 title-page of the
Huntington Library copy is dated 1603 and tells us that the play 'hath
been diverse times acted ... in the City of London: as also in the two
Universities of Cambridge and Oxford, and elsewhere'. The text of
the play in this first edition presents a number of puzzles. It appears
to have been reconstructed from memory by one of the actors who
played a bit part, perhaps as a gift for a friend, which was known
to be a common practice. Although the Q1 text differs substantially
from later textual versions, it includes some unique stage directions
– such as the details that the Ghost appears *'in his nightgown'* and that
the mad Ophelia enters *'playing on a lute, with her hair down, singing'*
– which give us some tantalising glimpses of the play in its first
performance.

Shakespeare wrote *Hamlet* for his acting company, the Lord
Chamberlain's Men, and the tragedy was probably first performed

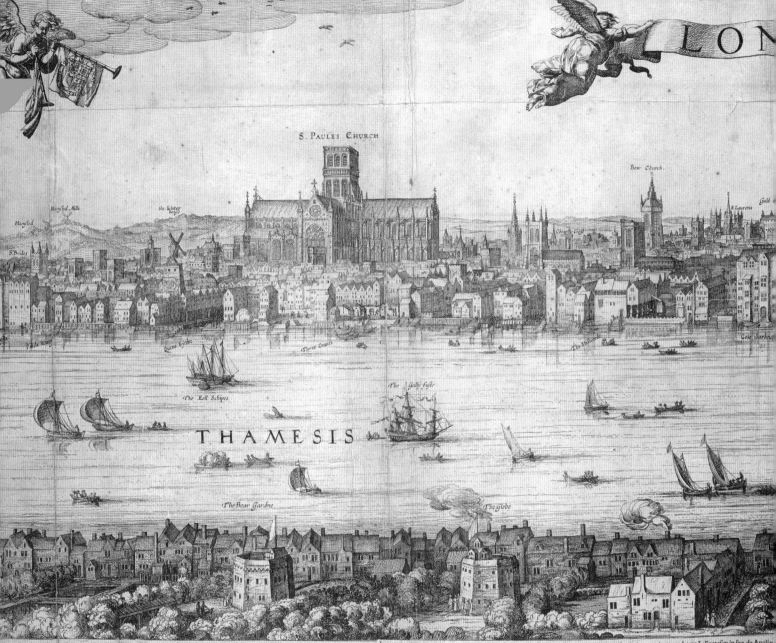

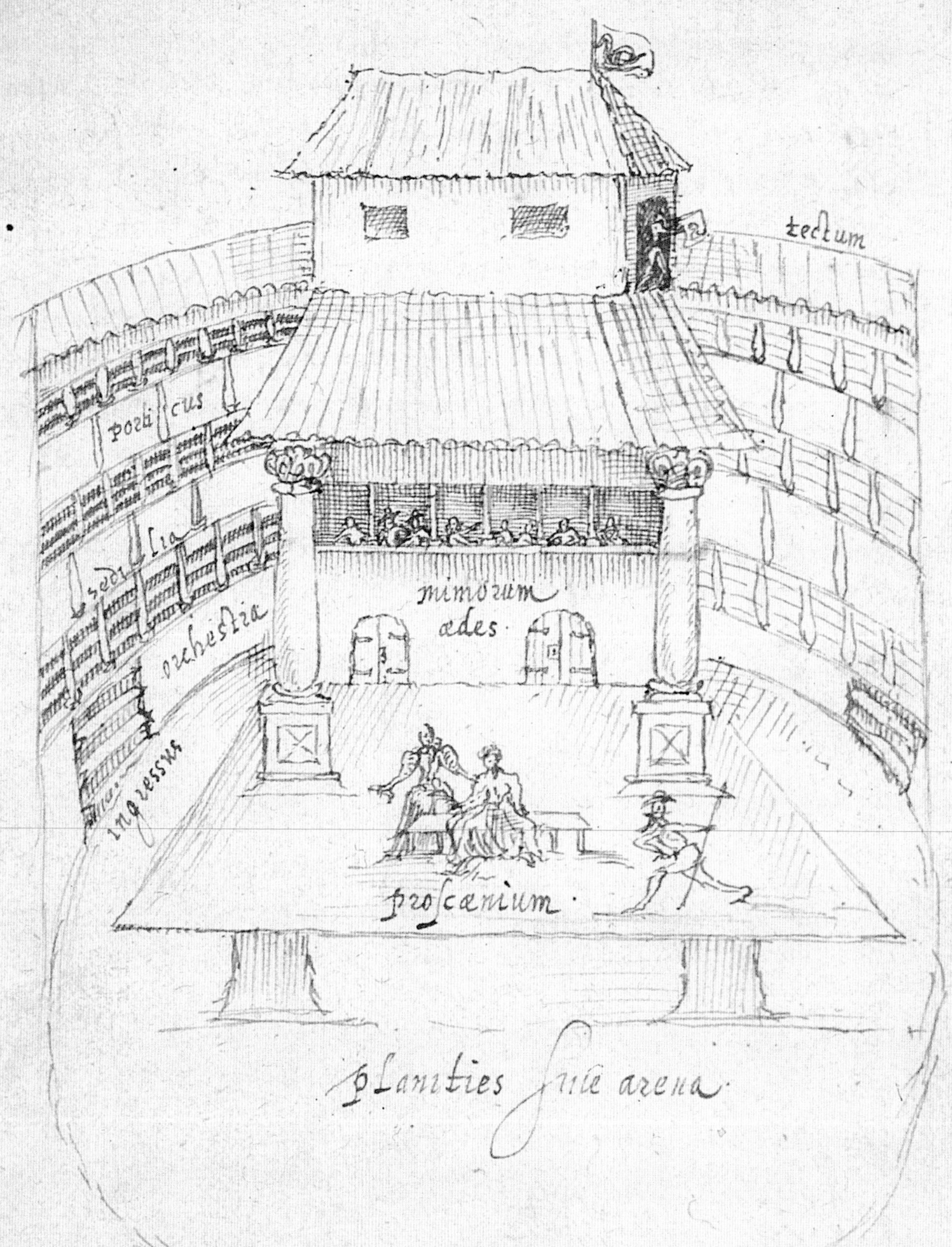

tectum

porticus

sedilia

orchestra

ingressus

mimorum aedes

proscænium

planties sive arena

quintum sed dispari et structura, bestiarum concitati
oni destinatum, in quo multi ursi, tauri, et stupenda
magnitudinis canes, distinctis caueis et septis aluntur, qui
ad

in a playhouse with which they were associated. Until 1597, the Chamberlain's Men played at the Theatre in Shoreditch; the building belonged to the company, but they leased the land that it stood on. When their lease expired, their landlord sought to appropriate the building as well as the land, and so the Chamberlain's Men played temporarily at the Curtain Theatre. Then, on a frosty night in 1598, three days after Christmas, a carpenter and several men associated with the company secretly dismantled the Theatre and removed the timbers. In the spring, they ferried the timbers across the Thames and used them to build a larger theatre in Southwark: the Globe. To cover the cost of the new construction, the owner, James Burbage, sold shares in the building to Shakespeare and four other actors in the company. The Globe opened in 1599 – probably featuring the new plays *Henry V* and *Julius Caesar* – and provided a leading dramatic venue for the next fourteen years. In 1613, however, during a fateful performance of *Henry VIII*, a stage cannon ignited the thatched roof and the Globe burned to the ground 'all in less than two hours', according to a contemporary account, 'the people having enough to do to save themselves'. Years before this calamity, the Globe was probably the site of *Hamlet*'s premiere.

On the strength of evidence such as a copy of a drawing of the Swan Theatre made by Johannes de Witt, a Dutch visitor to London in 1596, scholars have been able to deduce a number of features of the Globe. While every playhouse in London differed slightly from the rest, most playhouses shared similar traits. De Witt's drawing provides us with a general sense of the layout of the average playhouse, and archaeological research at the Globe's original site has confirmed these conjectured similarities between Globe and Swan. The 'wooden O' of the Globe was roughly 30 metres (more than 98 feet) in diameter and could accommodate an audience of 3,000, with standing room in the yard for the 'groundlings' and levels of seating for more wealthy patrons. The stage protruded into the standing area, so when players were downstage they would be surrounded on three sides by the groundlings, who were presumably talking, belching, eating nuts and sometimes engaging in discussions with the actors onstage. There was a trapdoor to a cellar beneath the stage; when ghostly or demonic characters appeared, they would emerge from the cellar, accompanied perhaps by smoke, noise, or other special effects. The ghost of Hamlet's father – who may have been played by Shakespeare himself – probably entered through the trapdoor in the play's first performance, startling groundlings and seated patrons alike. From the cellar, he bellowed 'Swear!' resoundingly and repeatedly. Complementing the hell-space, the Globe had a heaven-space, a cloud-painted roof over the back of the stage. Below the heavens, a balcony held musicians and provided a space from which characters could survey the action below (perhaps the royal audience sat there during the play-within-the-play in *Hamlet*), and very important members of the audience might be seated there as well. There was probably a curtained alcove beneath the balcony, the 'discovery space', which may have provided the arras, or tapestry, through which Hamlet stabbed Polonius.

OPPOSITE
The interior of the Swan Theatre in 1596, copied by Aernout van Buchel from a sketch by Johannes de Witt, a Dutch traveller who visited London. This is the only reliable illustration of the interior of an outdoor playhouse in Shakespeare's time, and gives us an idea of how the inside of the Globe Theatre may have looked.
Utrecht University Library Add MS 842.1

The many warm, perspiring, probably unwashed, possibly intoxicated bodies crammed into a relatively confined theatre space would get mighty hot, mighty fast, so when Francisco complains of the bitter cold in the opening scene of *Hamlet*, one wonders how the audience reacted. Would the afternoon daylight and the smelly humidity of the playhouse prompt them to laugh at the incongruity of the sentinel's lines? Or were those thousands of people so conditioned to suspend their disbelief that they imagined themselves transported from the pervasive dampness of Southwark to the frigid battlements of Elsinore?

We can be certain that Shakespeare's audience included veteran playgoers. In 1576, James Burbage had constructed the Theatre, the first purpose-built playhouse in Europe since the fall of the Roman Empire. In the years that followed, Londoners had become accustomed to the existence of a flourishing industry producing professional drama, with widely varying new plays frequently available to them for reasonable prices, relatively near to where they lived and worked. Theatre was more accessible than ever before, and Londoners of all classes, both men and women, flocked to the playhouses. The government, concerned that these tightly packed venues propagated the plague, shut down the whole industry for nearly two years from 1592 to 1593. Elizabethan theatre, however, seems to have been an unstoppable juggernaut, shrugging

Portrait of Richard
Burbage, painted in
the early seventeenth
century by an
unknown artist.
Dulwich Picture Gallery

off government obstruction, infectious disease, religious objections, infighting and condescension from intellectual elites as it rose to cultural dominance.

The audience members who attended the first performance of *Hamlet* at the Globe brought with them a knowledge of individual actors in the Lord Chamberlain's Men, especially the company's star performer, Richard Burbage. Apparently born to a life in the theatre, Richard was the son of James Burbage. The 'plot' of a play known as *The Dead Man's Fortune* dating from around 1590 records that Burbage played the part of a messenger, but he was soon playing major Shakespearean roles such as Richard III, Othello and Lear, and taking leading parts in plays by Ben Jonson, Francis Beaumont and John Fletcher, and John Webster. An elegy written upon his death claims that Burbage also played 'young Hamlet'. A pamphlet published in 1605 about the notorious highwayman Gamaliel Ratsey corroborates the claim in an episode in which Ratsey advises the leader of a group of touring players to perform in London, where his Hamlet will rival Burbage's.

Then as now, popular actors were often the subjects of gossip, and Burbage was no exception. Indeed, a theatregoer named John Manningham recorded in his diary a salacious story about Burbage and Shakespeare:

> Upon a time when Burbage played Richard III there was a citizen who grew so far in liking with him that before she went from the play she appointed him to come that night unto her by the name of 'Richard III'. But Shakespeare, overhearing their conclusion, went before, and was entertained and at his game before Burbage came. Then message return to be made [that is, Shakespeare sent a message to Burbage] that William the Conqueror was before Richard the Third.

Manningham provides the explanatory gloss, 'Shakespeare's name William'.

No doubt the audience at the opening of *Hamlet* welcomed Burbage's appearance and expected a high-quality performance. On the other hand, they may have been somewhat disappointed when, later in the play, two clowns entered to jest and gibe and dig a grave, and neither of them was Will Kemp. Kemp's place on the Elizabethan stage mirrored Burbage's: while audiences knew Burbage as an imposing, multi-talented, somewhat dark figure of noble tragedy, they knew Kemp as a witty extemporaneous clown, gifted physically with agility, control and strength. This familiarity had developed throughout the 1590s, when Kemp played roles such as Dogberry in *Much Ado About Nothing*, Nick Bottom in *A Midsummer Night's Dream* and, possibly, Falstaff, one of Shakespeare's finest and most complex clowns. But although Kemp owned a share in the Globe, he severed his association with the Lord Chamberlain's Men before the new theatre was finished, and divided his share among the other shareholders. Scholars have puzzled for centuries over

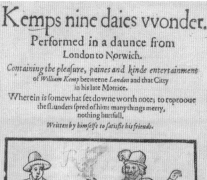

Will Kemp's record of his 100-mile morris dance following his departure from Shakespeare's company: *Kemps nine daies wonder* (1600).

Bodleian Library, University of Oxford

THE
Hiftory of the two Maids of More-clacke

VVith the life and fimple maner of IOHN
in the Hofpitall.

Played by the Children of the Kings
Maiefties Reuels.

VVritten by ROBERT ARMIN, feruant to the Kings
moft excellent Maieftie.

LONDON,
Printed by N.O. for *Thomas Archer*, and is to be fold at his
fhop in Popes-head Pallace, 1 6 0 9.

Woodcut of Robert
Armin, who joined the
Lord Chamberlain's
Men in 1599, shown
here on the title-page
of his play *The History
of the two Maids of
More-clacke* (1609).
British Library C.34.c.1

Kemp's abrupt departure; audiences similarly puzzled by *Hamlet*'s
lack of Kemp might have detected some annoyance in the prince's
complaint about improvising clowns who 'speak more than is set
down for them', thereby drowning out 'some necessary question
of the play then to be considered' (Act 3, scene 2). It is possible that
similar real-life tensions between the company's clown and its
leading dramatist may have precipitated Kemp's departure. In any
event, Kemp literally took his act on the road, famously performing
a morris dance from London to Norwich, a distance of 161 kilometres
(100 miles), which he then celebrated in the autobiographical
pamphlet *Kemp's Nine Days Wonder*.

　　After Kemp withdrew from the Chamberlain's Men, Robert
Armin was brought in as his replacement. Though Armin's new
position came with certain expectations, those expectations were
elastic, conforming to his skills. Whereas Kemp excelled in physical
entertainment – dancing and pratfalls – along with broad, bumbling,
often improvised humour, Armin seems to have specialised in
sensitive, complicated, intellectual comedy, and he had a pleasing

singing voice. Consequently, Armin reconfigured the role of the clown in Shakespeare's theatre. The playwright began writing parts such as Feste in *Twelfth Night*, Lear's Fool, and Autolycus in *The Winter's Tale* – all wise fools who sing – to capitalise on Armin's talents. In composing the Gravedigger's song for *Hamlet*, Shakespeare adapted lyrics from an early sixteenth-century poem, 'The Aged Lover Renounceth Love', by Lord Vaux.

The first audiences attending *Hamlet* would have registered the change from Kemp to Armin in the clown's role, and the play itself appears to memorialise the successions of theatrical clowns. Hamlet's rueful address to Yorick's skull has been seen by many as a reference to Richard Tarlton, the famed clown of the early English theatre. Tarlton had died in 1588, but his jokes would have been fresh in the minds of the audience in the wake of the publication of *Tarlton's Jests* in 1600. Like Yorick, Tarlton was 'a fellow of infinite jest', remembered for gambols, songs and 'flashes of merriment, that were wont to set the table on a roar' (*Hamlet*, Act 5, scene 1). With unexpected poignancy, Burbage and Armin place their hands on Yorick's skull while the melancholy Dane reflects on how mortality affects us all.

This dramatic moment has, of course, become iconic; representations of major Shakespearean actors holding the skull – such as the portrait of John Philip Kemble – are legion. Meanwhile, skulls of Yorick have enjoyed a colourful life in the theatre. A skull currently owned by the Furness Memorial Library at the University of Pennsylvania is signed on the cranium by nine major nineteenth-century actors who all used it while playing Hamlet, among them Edmund Kean, William Charles Macready, John Philip Kemble, Edwin Forrest and Charlotte Cushman. The novelist Victor Hugo gave a human skull to the French actress Sarah Bernhardt (1844–1923), inscribed with a verse, originally in French:

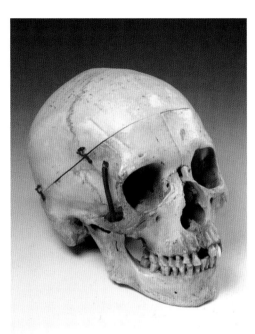

Human skull, presented by Victor Hugo to Sarah Bernhardt.
Victoria & Albert Museum

> Skeleton, what have you done with your soul?
> Lamp, what have you done with your flame?
> Empty cage, what have you done with
> The beautiful bird that used to sing?
> Volcano, what have you done with your lava?
> Slave, what have you done with your master?

When Bernhardt later played Hamlet, she used this skull in the graveyard scene. More recently, the concert pianist André Tchaikowsky on his deathbed in 1980 requested that his skull be sent to the Royal Shakespeare Company (RSC) to be used in a production of the play. After initial difficulties securing permission from the Human Tissue Authority to present the skull onstage, the RSC included it in its 2007–8 production starring David Tennant. When accounts of the origins of the skull began to overshadow Tennant's celebrity in the press, the RSC announced that it was replacing it with a plastic replica. At the end of the production's run, however, Artistic Director Greg Doran admitted that the skull had in fact been real all along.

The Spanish Tragedie:

OR,

Hieronimo is mad againe.

Containing the lamentable end of *Don Horatio*, and
Belimperia; with the pittifull death of *Hieronimo*.

Newly corrected, amended, and enlarged with new
Additions of the *Painters* part, and others, as
it hath of late been diuers times acted.

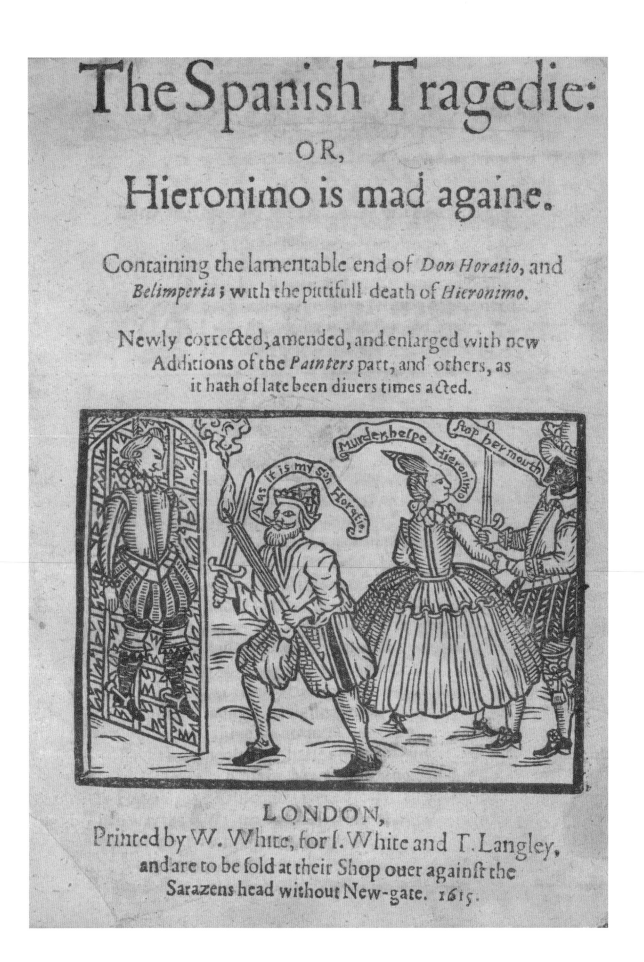

LONDON,
Printed by W. White, for I. White and T. Langley,
and are to be sold at their Shop ouer against the
Sarazens head without New-gate. 1615.

Hamlet **and Tragedy**

Although *Hamlet* is the earliest of the 'great tragedies' – with *King Lear, Macbeth, Othello* and *Antony and Cleopatra* still to come – it was not Shakespeare's first venture into the genre. Early in the 1590s, he wrote *Titus Andronicus*, a blood-soaked Roman play in the style of the classical dramatist Seneca. Furthermore, both *Richard III* and *Richard II*, which today we view as history plays, were labelled 'tragedies' on the title-pages of their quarto editions, and *Romeo and Juliet* 'an excellent conceited tragedy'. Thomas Kyd's early blockbuster, *The Spanish Tragedy*, had led the way for a flood of tragedies in the 1590s. Christopher Marlowe, for instance, with *The Jew of Malta* and both parts of *Tamburlaine*, created tragic dramas that satisfied audiences' lust for gore, while continually evolving both the genre of tragedy and the medium of publicly performed theatre. Thanks to the efforts of Marlowe, Shakespeare and others in the 1590s, the audience at *Hamlet*'s premiere would have had a fairly concrete set of expectations for what the upcoming tragedy would involve: there would be political strife, some sort of supernatural or paranormal element and piles of bodies. There would be blood.

Moreover, *Hamlet*'s first audience would almost certainly have known the story of a Danish prince whose uncle had murdered the king, his brother and the prince's father. The tale of Amleth and his mother Gerutha, from Saxo Grammaticus's *Historia Danica*, a twelfth-century Scandinavian text, was translated from the Latin into French in François de Belleforest's *Histoires tragiques*, which was published in 1570. The story even appears to have been dramatised before Shakespeare: the existence of a now-lost play, commonly called the *Ur-Hamlet*, can be deduced from an early reference by Thomas Nashe to 'whole Hamlets, I should say handfuls of tragical speeches' (1589) and another by Thomas Lodge to a 'ghost who cried so miserably at the Theatre like an oyster-wife, Hamlet, revenge!' (1596). Nashe and Lodge both participated actively in the London literary scene throughout the last two decades of the sixteenth century; if Amleth's tale had appeared in some form onstage in the 1580s, Nashe and Lodge would have known about it. Further, if we read their oblique hints correctly, and a version of the Amleth myth had previously been staged, most in the audience at the first performance of Shakespeare's *Hamlet* – readers of Belleforest and avid revenge-tragedy buffs alike – would have had certain expectations of what would happen, what would be said, who would die.

For more than a decade, audiences had been conditioned to expect a certain straightforwardness in the instigating trope of revenge tragedy: the need for revenge. Such plays had to get to the revenging fairly quickly, since revenging sold. In Thomas Kyd's *The Spanish Tragedy*, a character named Revenge – a literal embodiment of the trope – appears before the play's action even begins, to set the stage for what follows. Although Shakespeare's Hamlet promises the Ghost that he will 'sweep' to his revenge, the vengeance ultimately occurs only after thousands of lines of monologue and dialogue have

OPPOSITE
Thomas Kyd, *The Spanish Tragedie*, written *c.* 1587. The play features a personification of Revenge and established the genre of the revenge tragedy in English drama.
British Library C.117.b.36

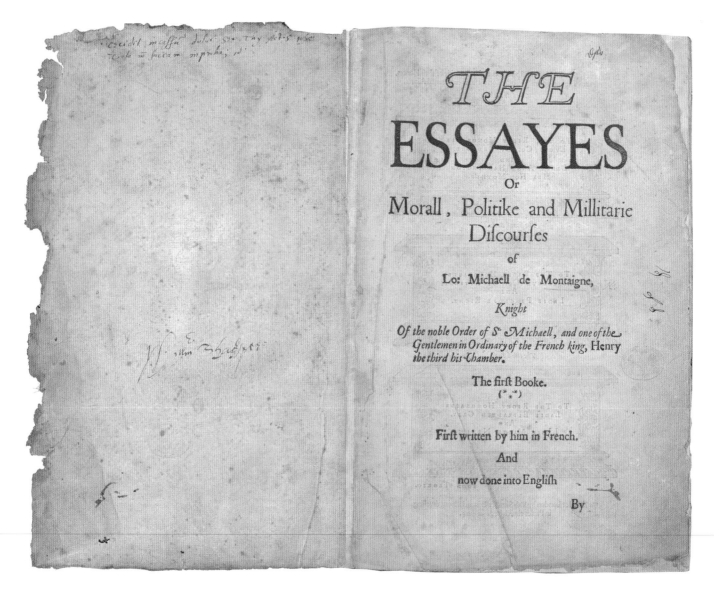

THE ESSAYES

Or

Morall, Politike and Millitarie Difcourfes

of

Lo: Michaell de Montaigne,

Knight

Of the noble Order of St Michaell, and one of the
Gentlemen in Ordinary of the French king, Henry
the third his Chamber.

The firft Booke.
(*.*)

Firft written by him in French.

And

now done into Englifh

By

been spoken. And this was Shakespeare's extraordinary innovation. In each of the first four acts, rather than engaging in the physical act of revenge killing, the avenging son has a lengthy soliloquy in which he articulates his innermost thoughts and feelings. Although one might expect that an Elizabethan audience, eagerly anticipating blood and action from a revenge tragedy, would have been disappointed by long speeches (and there is some indication that the company may have cut Hamlet's fourth soliloquy in performance, since it does not appear in the First Folio, which was apparently printed from the company's playbook), this innovation of psychological realism was an unexpected commercial success in the theatre. Indeed, in the wake of the triumph of *Hamlet*, it appears that Shakespeare was commissioned to update the script of *The Spanish Tragedy* by adding substantial soliloquies in which the play's avenging hero Hieronimo gives voice to his profound grief at the loss of his son.

The contemporary interest in interior monologues is reflected in the publication in 1603 – the same year as the first

Montaigne's *Essayes* translated by John Florio (1603). The signature opposite the title-page purports to be that of Shakespeare, but this is often disputed because of discrepancies between this and other, verifiable autographs. It is intriguing, however, as Montaigne's work almost certainly inspired aspects of *Hamlet*.
British Library C.21.e.17

quarto of *Hamlet* – of John Florio's translation of Michel Eyquem de Montaigne's *Essays* (which Shakespeare may have had access to in manuscript form before its publication). Shakespeare's debt to Montaigne is well attested. Indeed, there may be a direct link between Polonius's 'This above all: to thine own self be true' (Act 1, scene 3) and Florio's translation of Montaigne's essay 'Of the Institution of Education of Children': 'That above all, he be instructed to yield, yea to quit his weapons unto truth'.

Hamlet's Impact

How did the first audiences receive Shakespeare's *Hamlet*? The earliest recorded response comes to us, interestingly, via Geoffrey Chaucer. Chaucer was valorised as the father of English poetry, and his canon had been published in multiple editions. In 1598, the thirty-fourth edition of Chaucer's complete works was printed in London by Adam Islip; among its purchasers was a poet named Gabriel Harvey. Harvey was university educated and culturally sophisticated – Edmund Spenser was among his correspondents – and, as such, interacted gleefully with London's intellectual, artistic and public culture. He seems to have paid attention to what his peers thought of London's theatre scene, for he wrote in the margins of his copy of Chaucer that '[t]he younger sort takes much delight in Shakespeares Venus & Adonis: but his Lucrece & his tragedie of Hamlet, Prince of Denmarke, have it in them, to please the wiser sort'. There is some indication that Harvey's annotation was made before 1601, which adds another clue in helping to date the play. Moreover, Harvey provides evidence that *Hamlet* was being discussed after its first appearance, and that it had even then developed a patina of sophistication: the lusty *Venus and Adonis* was all very well for the concupiscent 'younger sort', but wiser – presumably older – heads preferred the high metaphysics of *The Rape of Lucrece* and *Hamlet*. Even at this early date, *Hamlet* was 'caviare to the general', as its titular character puts it (Act 2, scene 2).

This veneer of refinement may be due in part to a journey the play took shortly after it was first performed. Touring is now and has always been fundamental to theatre history. Long before the playhouse boom in the second half of the sixteenth century, touring productions of plays were crossing the length and breadth of England, with actors and luggage moving about the country in wagons, and this tradition continued even after permanent playhouses began to be built and repertory companies sprang up. The Lord Chamberlain's Men apparently took *Hamlet* on an early tour. As we have seen, the title-page of the first quarto claims that the play was acted 'in the two Universities of Cambridge and Oxford'. For a Shakespeare play to have been performed for university audiences was actually a major coup for the playwright and his craft; just six years before *Hamlet's* first quarto appeared, Shakespeare had been roundly mocked by university students in the *Parnassus* plays, a trilogy satirising popular London theatre. But time heals all wounds,

Heywoods prouerbs, with His, & Sir Thomas Mores Epigrams, may serue for sufficient supplies of manie of theis deuises. And now translated Petrarch, Ariosto, Tasso, & Bartas himself deserue curious comparison with Chaucer, Lidgate, & owre best Inglish, auncient & moderne. Amongst which, the Countesse of Pembrokes Arcadia, & the Faerie Queene ar now freshest in request: & Astrophil, & Amyntas ar none of the idlest pastimes of sum fine humanists. The Earle of Essex much commendes Albions England: and not vnworthily for diuerse notable pageants, before, & in the Chronicle. Sum English, & other Historical nowhere more sensibly described, or more inwardly discouered. the Lord Mountioy makes the like account of Daniels peece of the Chronicle, touching the Vsurpation of Henrie of Bullingbrooke. which in deede is a fine, sententious, & politique peece of Poetrie: as profitable, as pleasurable. The younger sort takes much delight in Shakespeares Venus, & Adonis: but his Lucrece, & his tragedie of Hamlet, Prince of Denmarke, haue it in them, to please the wiser sort. Or such poets: or better: or none.

Vilia miretur vulgus: mihi flavus Apollo
Pocula Castaliæ plena ministret aquæ: quoth Sir Edward Dier, betwene iest, & earnest. Whose written deuises farr excell most of the sonets, and cantos in print. His Amaryllis, & Sir Walter Raleighs Cynthia, how fine & sweet inuentions? Excellent matter of emulation for Spencer, Constable, France, Watson, Daniel, Warner, Chapman, Siluester, Shakespeare, & the rest of owr florishing metricians. I looke for much, aswell in verse, as in prose, from mie two Oxford frends, Doctor Gager, & M. Hackluit: both rarely furnished for the purpose: & I haue a phansie to Owens new Epigrams, as pithie as elegant, as plesant as sharp, & sumtime as weightie as briefe: & amongst so manie gentle, noble, & royall spirits meethinkes I see sum heroical thing in the clowdes: mie souerain hope. Axiophilus shall forgett himself, or will remember to leaue sum memorials behinde him: & to make an vse of so manie rhapsodies, cantos, hymnes, odes, epigrams, sonets, & discourses, as at idle howers, or at flowing fitts he hath compiled. God knowes what is good for the world, & fitting for this age.

apparently. For their part, the Lord Chamberlain's Men were so eager to please their Oxford audience that they may have changed the names of Polonius and Reynaldo, two mildly unpleasant characters, because they sounded too similar to those of Robert Polenius and John Rainolds, both Oxonians (the change is reflected in the first quarto, where the characters are called Corambis and Montano, respectively). So the play travelled north to Cambridge and northwest to Oxford, and when it came back, its patina of refinement glowed all the more brightly. Not only did *Hamlet* appeal to the wiser sort in London, it had also been played for the still wiser sort in the universities.

Hamlet's gathering momentum did not confine itself to the intelligentsia; it also had an impact on the theatrical community. *The Revenger's Tragedy* (1607) displays most clearly the influence *Hamlet* had upon subsequent plays. Possibly written by Thomas Middleton, it is an odd piece; at times it seems in deadly earnest, and at times its conceits are so extravagant as to be laughable. Whatever its intentions – whether it be a good-faith revenge tragedy or a parodic metacommentary – it demonstrates its debts to the genre throughout. Most strikingly, the play's opening action directly references what must by that time have already been one of *Hamlet's* distinguishing marks: a young man, wronged by a corrupt authority figure, sits on stage talking to the skull of one who was close to him. In *The Revenger's Tragedy* the skull belongs to the young man's betrothed, who was murdered by the Duke (the play's antagonist), but the image no doubt recalled to audiences' minds the image of Hamlet lamenting over Yorick's remains. The skull's intrusion into early Jacobean tragedy marks a critical point in the spread of *Hamlet's* dominion: that moment when it became a target for allusive popular appropriation. And thus has it been ever since.

OPPOSITE
Gabriel Harvey's copy of *The Workes of Chaucer* (published in 1598), with a note beside the stars in the margin stating that *Hamlet* is a tragedy 'to please the wiser sort'. This is the earliest known reference to Shakespeare's *Hamlet* and is evidence that the play was well received.
British Library Add MS 42518

'Into something rich and strange': *The Tempest* at the Blackfriars Playhouse, *c.* 1610–11

Gordon McMullan

When in 1610 or 1611 the audience climbed the great stone stairs of the Blackfriars to see Shakespeare's new play *The Tempest* performed in the candlelit theatre within the former monastery's dining hall, they would have found themselves participating in a magical theatrical experience. It will have been new in multiple ways for many in the audience, and certainly for any who had not previously attended this indoor playing space, newly reclaimed by the King's Men – the former Lord Chamberlain's Men, under royal patronage since the accession of James I in 1603 – to function as the winter counterpart to their long-standing open-air theatre, the Globe. As the earliest play we can be sure Shakespeare wrote with the Blackfriars in mind, *The Tempest* capitalises on performance possibilities that had not been available to the company before the occupation of its new theatre a couple of years earlier – and the brio with which Shakespeare exploits the potential of the space resonates down the centuries as each generation re-makes the play for a new time. There have been many extraordinary performances of *The Tempest* since 1611, but arguably none more so than that very first afternoon at the Blackfriars.

 The Tempest is a magical play, casting a spell over theatregoers and readers alike. Its protagonist, Prospero, is both a politician and a magician or male witch. He is haunted by the memory of another witch, Sycorax, the mother of Caliban, the only indigenous inhabitant of the island on which he finds himself exiled. Prospero deploys the magical powers he has learned from his books both

OPPOSITE
The Almeida Theatre's 2001 production of *The Tempest* opened with a spectacular deluge. A water tank built into the stage concealed a secret exit, allowing Aidan Gillen's Ariel to dive into the pond and vanish from sight.

as tools of coercion and as the means to ensure his return home through a carefully rehearsed dynastic marriage for his daughter Miranda. This play of magic, marriage, return and revenge was a powerful influence on Shakespeare's contemporaries and successors. It has had a near-unbroken history on the stage since those very first performances, a history striking for its spectacle, its music and its ability to amaze audiences, offering a rich case study in the changes and continuities in Shakespearean performance across the centuries.

Interior of the Sam Wanamaker Playhouse at Shakespeare's Globe, based on seventeenth-century designs of an indoor London theatre. The intimate auditorium is lit by candles, just as Shakespeare's Blackfriars Playhouse would have been.

The Tempest is usually understood as Shakespeare's final play, a document of retirement. Shakespeare, one with his protagonist, abjures the 'rough magic' of his playwriting, breaks his staff and drowns his book (Act 5, scene 1). 'Our revels now are ended,' he says of the abrupt halt to the masque of spirits he has conjured up for Miranda and Ferdinand's engagement (Act 4, scene 1), an agitated acknowledgement of failure that has been insistently smoothed over by actors and critics alike and converted into the play's motto. Theatre professionals typically come to this play with a point to make late in life – Sir John Gielgud, for instance, playing Prospero at 87 in Peter Greenaway's film *Prospero's Books* – or late in the cycle of a career or a building – Mark Rylance playing Prospero in his final production as Artistic Director of Shakespeare's Globe, or Jonathan Kent's choice of *The Tempest* as the last play to be performed, with a memorably aquatic Ariel, at London's Almeida Theatre before its closure for refurbishment in 2001. Yet this was not always the case – Gielgud had first played Prospero at the age of 26 – and the

assumption of the play's 'lateness' has likewise not always been there: though it has lasted, it is a story built on shaky foundations.

     Shakespeare in fact wrote several plays after *The Tempest*: three in collaboration with John Fletcher, plus arguably *Cymbeline* and *The Winter's Tale,* depending on the chosen chronology. Biographers invariably place *The Tempest* at the end of the short set of tragicomedies that begins in 1607 with *Pericles,* but we do not know for certain the order in which the other three were composed. It could be that *Cymbeline* is the last solo play – though few have ever wanted that to be the case, *The Tempest* fitting so much more easily into the retirement narrative. *The Tempest* has in fact repeatedly come *first,* not *last,* in Shakespearean sequences. It is the first play in the 1623 First Folio, and it was almost certainly the first of his plays to be written especially with the new playhouse in mind. And it is in the theatre that the play has repeatedly proven its worth.

John Gielgud as Prospero in Peter Greenaway's film *Prospero's Books* (1991).

Blackfriars and Theatre

When, in 1611, Ben Jonson's comedy *The Alchemist* was first staged at the Blackfriars, the audience would instantly have understood it as a satire both of the immediate neighbourhood and of *The Tempest* itself – and they would have been hugely amused. The title character is a *faux* alchemist who deploys an intricate vocabulary of spurious scientific terms to fool the gullible into parting with their money to acquire the Philosopher's Stone. This talisman was believed – though

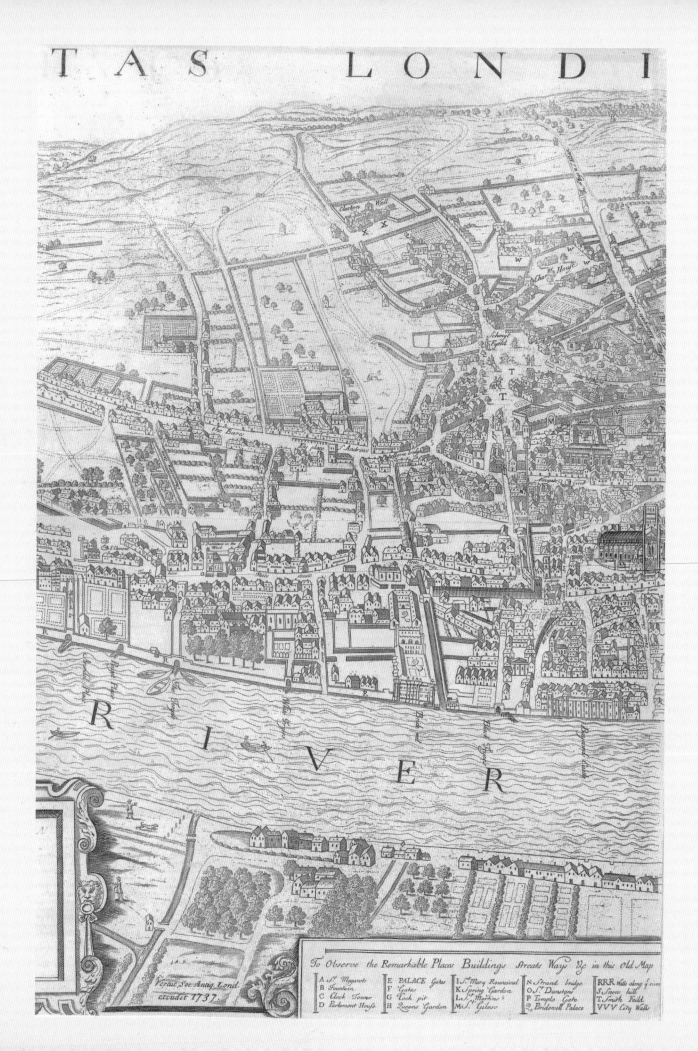

TAS LONDI

RIVER

Charterhouse Wall

Char. House

Charect Fyeld

Smithfield

the Bars

Virtue Soc. Antiq. Lond.
excudit 1737.

To Observe the Remarkable Places Buildings Streats Ways &c in this Old Map

A St. Margaret	E PALACE Gates	I St. Mary Rouncival	N Strand bridge	RRR Walls along ye river
B Fountain	F Gates	K Spring Garden	O St. Dunstans	S Snow hill
C Clock Tower	G Cock pit	L St. Martins	P Temple Gate	T Smith Feild
D Parlament House	H Queens Garden	M St. Giles	Q Bridewell Palace	VVV City Walls

in truth by very few in Shakespeare's lifetime – to have the ability to transform base metal to gold. It was the slightly tired lottery fantasy of its day, retaining its ability to entertain if not its efficacy as plausible physics. What Jonson shows is the particular culture – affluent, edgy – of this claustrophobic London precinct, a 'liberty' (an area not subject to the control of the city authorities) situated within the grounds of a former Dominican monastery, with the Royal Wardrobe (a building, destroyed in the Great Fire of 1666, which housed not only clothing but also other royal possessions, including arms) to the east and the former Bridewell Palace to the west. It is within this confined, bustling residential area that *The Tempest* was first performed.

We can get a glimpse of the attitudes of some of the inhabitants of Blackfriars from the continuing struggle between the actors and the enclave's residents over the question of performance. Shakespeare's company had long had in mind the possibility of

LEFT
Copy of the petition against the Blackfriars Playhouse, which was signed by thirty-one residents of the Blackfriars precinct and submitted to the Privy Council in 1596. Surprisingly, the petitioners included Shakespeare's patron, Lord Hunsdon, and the publisher of *Venus and Adonis*, Richard Field.

National Archives

OPPOSITE
The Latin title of this map translates as 'A View of London about the Year 1560'. This engraving, published in 1737, shows the Blackfriars area south-west of St Paul's Cathedral. The playhouse was very close to the Royal Wardrobe, which supplied costumes to the company of boy players who were based at the Blackfriars between 1576 and 1584 and may also have lent clothing to Shakespeare's company.

British Library Maps Crace Port. 1.8

acquiring an indoor theatre space. In 1596 – three years before the company disassembled their original playhouse, the Theatre, and transported the timbers across the Thames to create the Globe – James Burbage, father to Shakespeare's friend and colleague Richard Burbage, had, for the substantial sum of £600, acquired from Sir William More seven rooms in the monastery's Upper Frater (the erstwhile refectory) with a view to converting them into a playing space. He knocked down the internal walls and spent over £400 more creating a playhouse in this potentially lucrative location. Thirty-one of Burbage's new neighbours, however, had a different sense of what was appropriate to the precinct, and they came together in a classic case of what we would now call 'nimbyism' to petition the Privy Council against the opening of the playhouse. They objected to the 'great resort and gathering' of theatregoers and their 'pestering and filling up of the … precinct' which would, they claimed, increase the joint threats of plague and irreligion: 'the noise of the drums and trumpets', they argued, 'will greatly disturb and hinder both the ministers and parishioners in time of divine service and sermons'. Thus the petitioners wrecked Burbage's plans. What those plans actually were is not clear. Maybe the company aimed from the start to run two spaces concurrently, one indoors and one outdoors, with a view to acquiring a stability lacking in a theatrical scene that submerged new companies as fast as it threw them up. Or maybe, as Andrew Gurr has suggested, if the Blackfriars residents had not blocked the plan the Globe would never have been built. There was, in any case, irony in the identity of the second signatory to the petition: the company's own patron, the Lord Chamberlain, Lord Hunsdon, who, it seems, wanted to keep his players at a safe distance. Perhaps this is not surprising, given that he lived directly underneath the playing space.

The petition succeeded in its main aim – it kept the Lord Chamberlain's Men away for a sustained period – but it did not stop performances taking place at the Blackfriars. For the next few years, the space became home to performances by boy actors, first as the Children of the Chapel, then on James I's accession as the Children of the Queen's Revels. In its Jacobean form, this company was responsible for a rich and innovative repertoire with a remarkable range of tones from solemn to uproarious, and some of their plays were in due course acquired (not always with due process) by the King's Men when they reclaimed the space in 1608 after the Queen's Revels company was dissolved. For whatever reason, these boys' company performances seem not to have caused the disturbance the petitioning residents feared – or, if they did, nothing seems to have been done about it. Perhaps this was because there had been performances by boy actors in the Blackfriars as far back as the 1570s, and perhaps because the boys did not provoke the same status anxiety as the adult 'common players'. It took the Lord Chamberlain's Men – now elevated to the status of the King's Men company – twelve years to reclaim the Blackfriars, and it was a turning-point in their history (though, owing to lengthy enforced plague closure in 1608–10, it was a further two years before they could actually play

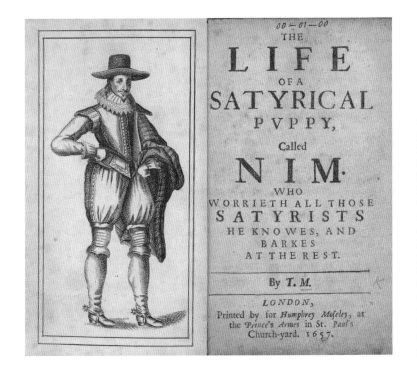

Title-page and frontispiece of *The Life of a Satirical Puppy Called Nim* (1657) by Thomas May. Blackfriars playgoers were frequently derided for their vanity and love of luxury. Here the dandyish protagonist, Nim, is depicted in a suit of clothes purchased especially to attract the attention of ladies in the Blackfriars audience.

there). Shakespeare may by this time have begun to contemplate letting go of London and the theatrical life, but *The Tempest* marked new beginnings for the King's Men.

The theatre clearly remained a mixed blessing for some, nonetheless: for the upmarket coterie that flocked to its plays, it was a source of amusement; to others it was a danger. Thomas May's *Life of a Satirical Puppy Called Nim* recalls the heyday of the Blackfriars and shows its fashion-victim protagonist attending the theatre to display himself and chat up long-suffering women. The account of his actions gives a flavour of the social event that was a show at the Blackfriars. It makes clear that many in the audience – typically paying six times more than they would to see a play at the Globe – were there for reasons quite other than earnest playgoing, and not least because playgoing was much more socially acceptable for women at the indoor theatre than at the Globe. Nim decides that he 'should go to see a Play in *Black-Fryars*: and there ... some rich Lady would cast her Eie on me, and same might me on her'. So he spends much money on clothes and 'like a true *English-man* ... enter'd the *Theatre,* and sat upon the Stage: making low Congies [bows] to divers Gentlemen' in order to make 'the Spectators suppose us of very olde, and familiar acquaintance'. His primary interest, however, is in the women:

> About the beginning of the Fourth Act, my Face withstood a fresh encounter, given me by a Ladies Eie, whose Seate opposed mine. She look'd stedfast on me, till the Play ended; seeming to survey my Limbs with amorous curiosity: whilst I advanced them all, to encounter her approbation.

Nim is taken aback to discover that the woman is unattractive, but reassures himself of her evident wealth: 'Yet she wore *Jewells,* for the which I could willingly have kiss'd her in the *dark'*. He approaches her:

> [F]ollowing her down the Staires[, I] resolved to discover a good-will to her, either by a wanton gesture of my Body, or whispering in her Ear just as she came forth into the Street, ... proffer'd my service to attend her home, if she missed any of her Friends.

Unfortunately for Nim, the woman understands him all too well:

> She suspecting that I thought her to be a Whore, told me aloud I was much mistaken. Her Brother (unknown to me) stood behind us, and asked her; what the matter was? M'arry, (quoth she) this Gentleman takes me for some common Creature. He with all violent dexterity strucke me on the Face; and afterwards went about to draw his Sword. But I slunk through the presse of people, and very tamely conveied my selfe home.

The upshot is that the pathetic Nim 'durst not visit *Theaters* any more, lest [he] should meete with him, or Women elsewhere, as fearfull of the like entertainment'.

Lecherous gallants were the least of the worries for some residents. There is a poignant entry in the register of St Anne's Church, Blackfriars, recording the burial of 'William Jordan a Beggar kild wᵗ a coach coming from the Play'. It seems that the 1596 petitioners, predicting an influx of theatregoers from other parts of London, with resultant traffic chaos, had had considerable foresight. Moreover, the death of William Jordan is not the only event to suggest that the presence of players in the Blackfriars precinct might bring destruction upon its inhabitants. In 1623, the year Shakespeare's First Folio was published, a disaster took place in the Blackfriars that became known as the 'fatal vespers', reminding Londoners powerfully of the precinct's Catholic past and its present dangers. The French ambassador, living at that time in the Blackfriars gatehouse, had invited a famous Jesuit preacher, Robert Drury, to give a sermon, and hundreds of locals, curious to hear proscribed opinions, were present. Too many, in fact: while Drury was speaking, the floor gave way, and nearly 100 people, including the preacher, fell two storeys and died. The telling of this tale is both vindictive and a little puzzled: naturally, God would bring judgement upon recusants who refused to renounce the Catholic faith, but why not also upon actors? 'Observe,' wrote one commentator, 'the Play-House stands in that place unshaken, though too often laden with sin-full multitudes of all sort, sexes, and sects.'

A resonant place, the Blackfriars, then: sex, death, social struggle, religious conflict, all embraced by a tiny quarter of a rapidly growing city, one that seems to have held a lasting fascination for Shakespeare. When Prospero speaks of 'the great globe itself' in the

Title-page of Richard Hord's *Black-Fryers* (1625) depicting the collapse of part of the former monastery complex in 1623; nearly 100 people who had gathered to hear a sermon were killed. This is the best surviving depiction of part of the Blackfriars precinct.

British Library C.123.d.1

famous 'revels' speech in *The Tempest* (Act 4, scene 1), he may well have been referring to the Globe Theatre, and it is possible that there are also local references for Blackfriars *habitués*: the 'solemn temples' perhaps indicating the monastery itself and the 'gorgeous palaces' the adjacent Bridewell Palace:

> These our actors,
> As I foretold you, were all spirits, and
> Are melted into air, into thin air,
> And, like the baseless fabric of this vision,
> The cloud-capped towers, the gorgeous palaces,
> The solemn temples, the great globe itself,
> Yea, all which it inherit, shall dissolve,
> And, like this insubstantial pageant faded,
> Leave not a rack behind.

In March 1613, just as he might be thought to be planning his return to Stratford-upon-Avon, Shakespeare signed a mortgage deed for an apartment in the Blackfriars gatehouse – within the very building where, a decade later, the 'fatal vespers' would take place. This may have been merely an investment property for Shakespeare, yet it suggests both that rumours of his retirement might be considered premature and that it was Blackfriars, more than Bankside, that endured as the London precinct for which Shakespeare felt the strongest tie.

The Tempest at the Blackfriars Playhouse

The Tempest is the first of Shakespeare's Jacobean plays designed not only for performance at the Globe and at court – where it was first performed in November 1611– but also at the Blackfriars. What would the new performance space have been like, and how different would it have been from the Globe? Structurally, the stage was not so very different: the playing space remained a thrust platform with galleries on three sides, a wall (the *frons scenae*) with doors at the rear and a musicians' gallery above the tiring house (area behind the stage). Yet it was half the size of the Globe stage, and the effective playing space was even smaller, given that one of the privileges for which fashion-conscious men – 'gallants' like Nim – would pay handsomely was to be able to sit on stools on the sides of the stage and be visible to the rest of the audience. Certainly it would take an actor less time than in the Globe to move from his entry through a door in the *frons scenae* to a position at the front of the stage, and Shakespeare responded accordingly, writing fewer lines between a character entering and that character either speaking or moving within earshot of those already on stage. With no need for stage posts to hold the roof up, and with seated gallants occupying the sides of the performance space, the standard theatrical activity of eavesdropping, which in the Globe could be performed by a character literally stepping 'aside' – that is, to the sides of the wide stage – or hiding

behind the stage posts, in the Blackfriars typically involved ascending to the musicians' gallery, something that substantially altered the dramatic topography.

As the intrusion of gallants on to the stage itself suggests, theatregoing at the Blackfriars took on a social and sartorial quality quite different from that at the Globe. Nim, on his first visit, notes that in order to

> appear no Novice, I observ'd all fashionable Customes; As delivering my Sute to a more apparent view, by hanging the Cloak upon one Shoulder: or letting it fall (as it were) by chance. I stood up also at the end of every Act, to salute those, whom I never saw before.

The indoor theatre offered fashion opportunities unavailable to audiences at the Globe, who needed to wrap up warm for most of the year; at the Blackfriars, by contrast, they could arrive in their finest clothes, wearing colours and jewellery selected to gleam particularly brightly in the candlelit theatre. The most immediately obvious difference between the Globe and the Blackfriars was light. The Globe is famous for its openness to the elements; the Blackfriars, by contrast, was an enclosed indoor space with candles as its primary light source. It seems probable that there were windows high up, but these may well have been shuttered for daytime performances, placing the focus firmly on the candles, housed in six or more chandeliers ('branches') over the stage and also probably in wall sconces. Francis Bacon in his essay 'Of Masques and Triumphs' notes that '[t]he *Colours*, that shew best by Candle-light, are; White, Carnation, and a Kinde of Sea-Water-Greene; And *Oes*, or *Spangs* [sequins], as they are of no great Cost, so they are of most Glory', making it clear how conscious members of an audience could be of their theatregoing attire. Shakespeare could not resist mocking Blackfriars fashion culture: in Act 4 of *The Tempest*, Stephano and Trinculo, en route to a reckoning with Prospero, are distracted by Ariel through the use of '*glistering apparel*' ('glistering' was a word particularly associated with meretricious clothing effects): 'O King Stephano! O peer! O worthy Stephano!' cries Trinculo, 'look what a wardrobe is here for thee!' – lines which not only poke fun at the audience but also remind that audience of the proximity of the Royal Wardrobe.

It was not only in respect of light that the move indoors provoked changes in company style. One of the major differences between the Blackfriars and the Globe was the aural environment: things would have sounded very different in the indoor theatre from the way they did in the large, open soundbox of the outdoor amphitheatre. And it is clear that music featured regularly in Blackfriars plays in a way it had not in the amphitheatres, as a direct result of the changes in lighting. At the indoor theatre, the five-act structure of Jacobean plays became fully established, facilitating four intervals with *entr'acte* music. These breaks were essential because of the quality of early modern beeswax candles, which needed trimming every half hour or so. Shakespeare's plays, to this

OPPOSITE
Title-page of *The Wits* (1673), a collection of 'drolls' or comic scenes from popular plays. The engraved frontispiece depicts the candlelit interior of an indoor playhouse.
British Library C.71.h.23

point written for the Globe, had had no need for such breaks in the action, but the practicalities of indoor playing required this change in the shape of the drama, and they explain in part the musicality of *The Tempest* and the other 'late plays'. Act breaks may also have contributed to the visuals, enabling the changing of stage hangings to depict shifts of setting from act to act. The aural context was very different: in the Blackfriars, a whisper on stage would be audible in the galleries, and plays written for the indoor theatre would tend to feature *sotto voce* scenes far more than those written for the amphitheatres. This also meant changes in the musical world of the Blackfriars.

For one thing, the instruments would have differed: lutes would have been more audible than in the Globe, and trumpets, too loud for the acoustically intense spaces of the Blackfriars, were replaced by hautboys and cornetts – not the modern valved cornet but a form of woodwind, loud enough for fanfares but quiet when accompanying voices. At the Blackfriars, the consort of musicians occupied the gallery above the stage and so were visibly involved in the performance in a way they had not been when, as in the early days at the Globe, they had played behind the *frons scenae*. This seems to have heralded a new level of integration of music into the action. The music of *The Tempest* is by no means restricted to the intervals or pre-show playing (the consort at the Blackfriars would play for up to an hour before the drama began): the play is famously crammed with both instruments and voices, from Ariel's haunting 'Full fathom five' (Act 1, scene 2) to the 'thousand twangling instruments' that 'hum about' Caliban's ears (Act 3, scene 2). Music drives the plot at times, as Ferdinand is led by Ariel – *'invisible, playing and singing'* – to his first meeting with Miranda (Act 1, scene 2), and it converts easily to cacophony: *'to a strange hollow and confused noise, they heavily vanish'* (Act 4, scene 1). Songs are intrinsic to the play, specially created with plot, action and company in mind. The songs of Shakespeare's late plays were written by Robert Johnson, former servant to Lord Hunsdon, lutenist to James I and Blackfriars resident. The survival of his settings means that we have original music for *The Tempest*, or something very close to it, the extant versions dating from the latter part of the century by way of John Playford's *Select Ayres and Dialogues* (1659) and John Wilson's *Cheerful Ayres* (1660).

Sound produces harmony in the play – 'sweet airs, that give delight and hurt not' – and also chaos – the roar of thunder created by rolling a cannonball down a lead pipe, the 'several noises / Of roaring, shrieking, howling, jingling chains, / And more diversity of sounds' that awakes the sailors from their entranced sleep in Act 5, or the 'noise of hunters' and their dogs – *'divers spirits in shape of dogs and hounds'* – that drive Stephano, Trinculo and Caliban from the stage in Act 4. All of which reminds us of the sheer spectacle of the Blackfriars performance of the play, perhaps above all when the king and his courtiers are about to dine on a magnificent banquet only to have it whipped away before their eyes as lightning strikes (Act 3, scene 3). The spirit Ariel, *'like a harpy'* – costumed perhaps like Inigo Jones's winged fiery spirits in Campion's *Lord's Masque*, performed

Early seventeenth-century lute by Matheus Buchenberg.

Musical Instrument Museums Edinburgh, University of Edinburgh

alongside *The Tempest* at court in 1613 – *'claps his wings upon the table, and with a quaint device the banquet vanishes'*. We are not clear how the *'quaint device'* worked, but we can imagine the sudden snuffing of candles and the table's rapid descent into the stage trap, or perhaps a revolving table-top of the kind used by magicians. The trap, with its hellish connotations, would be familiar to audiences from the Globe, but it probably had a heavenly counterpart at the Blackfriars – a chair descending from the roof above the stage that would enable the descent of Juno to bless the marriage of Miranda and Ferdinand in Act 4. Shakespeare clearly drew on these mechanisms for the dramaturgy of his Blackfriars plays, reminding us of the marked influence of the court masque on Shakespeare's late plays and foreshadowing the tradition of spectacular staging that lay in *The Tempest*'s future.

The Tempest after Shakespeare: Spectacle, Imagination, Resistance

The history of *The Tempest* in performance since Shakespeare's day is one of a continuing embrace of the play's theatricalism combined with a developing recognition that it is not only spectacular but also in certain ways uncomfortable. The late twentieth century demonstrated these sides of the play in a burst of energetic, contradictory engagement, yet in order to understand these expressions it helps to look back at three landmark productions: that of Davenant, Dryden and Shadwell in the mid-seventeenth century; that of Kean in the mid-nineteenth; and that of Beerbohm Tree at the beginning of the twentieth.

The story begins in November 1667, seven years after the reopening of the theatres in the wake of the restoration of the monarchy. This was an adaptation of the play by William Davenant with additions by John Dryden, entitled *The Tempest, or The Enchanted Island*. Davenant felt no need to be faithful to the Shakespearean original, and it was not until 1757 that audiences were again able to see Shakespeare's play unadapted (if heavily cut) in Garrick's production at Drury Lane. The Davenant–Dryden *Tempest* substantially reduces Prospero's role and provides sisters for Miranda (Dorinda) and Caliban (Sycorax, the name repurposed from his dead witch-mother of Shakespeare's original); there is also a youth named Hippolito who has never seen a woman, thus providing a parallel for Miranda. To modern eyes, this adaptation appears parodic, and it certainly absorbs many elements of burlesque and wilfully overplays a range of the spectacular and farcical elements of the original. Yet its recognition of some of the sexual tensions implicit in Shakespeare's play – Prospero's prurient, controlling attitude to Miranda's virginity, for instance – suggests that it is more than this, and it was an unquestioned success for a century and more. Its most successful avatar was Thomas Shadwell's 'operatic' version with music by Matthew Locke, which was crammed with visual effects, as recalled by John Downes, former prompter to the Duke's company:

> Scenes, Machines; particularly, one Scene Painted with Myriads of Ariel Spirits; and another flying away, with a Table Furnisht put with Fruits, Sweetmeats, and all sorts of Viands. ... all was things perform'd in it so Admirably well, that not any succeeding Opera got more Money.

The visual impact of this production, revived multiple times well into the eighteenth century, can be gauged through François Boitard's frontispiece to *The Tempest* in Nicholas Rowe's 1709 edition, which probably represents the kind of theatrical backcloth that would have been used in the eighteenth and early nineteenth centuries: in the foreground, a ship founders, its crew frantic, lightning zags across the sky and above the scene fire-breathing dragons and devilish spirits fly gleefully about, while, in the background, Prospero, magic staff raised, controls the action.

François Boitard's engraving illustrating the storm scene at the beginning of *The Tempest* from *The Works of Mr. William Shakespear* (1709), edited by Nicholas Rowe.

British Library C.123.fff.2 volume 1

Two centuries later, Shakespeare's text had returned, but spectacle remained integral to productions of *The Tempest*. As the set designs make clear, Charles Kean's *Tempest* of 1857 was a highly mechanised affair, with complex scenery that required over 140 stage hands to move; this necessitated heavy cutting to the text, but the show still ran for five hours. Kean created a more sentimental spirit world for the play, replacing Davenant's harpies and dragons with naiads and wood-nymphs, and he created a series of tableaux to establish key moments in the audience's memory:

> Clouds rise and fall. Night descends. The Spirits, released by Prospero, take their flight from the island into the air. ... The epilogue is spoken by Prospero from the deck of the vessel. The ship gradually sails off. The island recedes from sight and Ariel remains alone in mid-air, hovering over the sea, watching the departure of his late master.

Commentators continued to claim that spectacle was essential to a successful production of the play: reviewing Kean's production, one critic asserted that '[n]o objections can possibly be raised to the employment of the utmost extent of scenic effects or artistic accompaniments in the representation of those fairy productions of the genius of Shakespeare'. Yet not everyone felt the same way. Hans Christian Andersen saw Kean's production and found its excesses debilitating: 'Everything was afforded that machinery and stage direction can provide,' he reported, 'and yet after seeing it, one felt overwhelmed, tired and empty. Shakespeare was lost in visual pleasure: the exciting poetry was petrified by illustrations; the living word had evaporated', adding: 'A work of Shakespeare performed between three simple screens is for me a greater enjoyment than here where it disappears beneath the gorgeous trappings.'

Nonetheless, productions of Shakespeare's plays continued to be lavish – not least that of Herbert Beerbohm Tree in 1904, who argued that 'of all Shakespeare's works "The Tempest" was probably the one which most demanded the aids of modern stage-craft'. Yet Tree's *Tempest* developed other trends that had emerged in the course of the nineteenth century, notably in its handling of Caliban – played by Tree himself as primitive but soulful. This role, which had been played by comedians in the eighteenth century, began to appear in a very different light with the developing resistance to the slave trade and with its Darwinian association with the 'missing link', a hypothetical extinct creature half-way in the evolutionary line between apes and humans. Tree's production made the most of lighting effects – it was the first to use electric light – not purely for spectacle but to underline the sensitivity of Tree's performance as the play's 'monster'. 'We feel', wrote Tree, 'that from the conception of sorrow in solitude may spring the birth of a higher civilization.' It was from these beginnings, combined with the emerging understanding of *The Tempest* – its recognised sources including a narrative of a journey to the Virginia colony, new at the time Shakespeare wrote the play – as being in certain ways 'American',

that readings of the play began to emerge which ran counter to the received tradition.

The twentieth century thus inherited a history of spectacle; at the same time political readings of the play – embodying quite different politics from the conservatism associated with the influence of the masque – began to emerge, which uncovered significant tensions in the play, not least in Prospero's oppression of Caliban. An understanding of Caliban as the victim of Prospero's urge for power had been apparent since Robert and William Brough's 1848 parody *The Enchanted Isle* and certainly since Ernst Renan's *Caliban: Suite de 'La Tempête'* of 1878, in which Caliban rises to become a figure akin to Prospero himself. But it was in 1950, with the publication of Octave Mannoni's *Prospero and Caliban: The Psychology of Colonization* (in which *The Tempest* becomes a myth through which to understand the psychologies of colonialism and racism) that the colonial reading of the oppression of Caliban by Prospero and the mutual dependence of the two ('This thing of darkness I / Acknowledge mine', Act 5) emerged. This reading was to have a profound impact both on adaptations (notably, Aimé Césaire's *Une Tempête* of 1969) and on productions of the play. In Britain the production that broke the mould was that by Jonathan Miller at the Mermaid in 1970, reworked for his Old Vic production of 1988. In both productions Prospero was a white colonist, and Miller cast black actors as Ariel and Caliban, the former a 'subaltern' figure working in the service of empire but impatiently awaiting independence, the latter a slave resentfully doing Prospero's bidding. In both productions Miller created endings that left the audience recognising that post-colonial life was likely to be undermined by

OPPOSITE
Charles A. Buchel's painting of Caliban from the 1904 souvenir edition of *The Tempest* 'as arranged for the stage by Herbert Beerbohm Tree' in the first production to use electric light. Tree played Caliban, the first leading actor-manager to choose this role over Prospero.
British Library X958/23912

LEFT
Rudolph Walker as Caliban and Max von Sydow as Prospero in Jonathan Miller's 1988 revival of *The Tempest* at the Old Vic.

the reproduction of colonial relations, as Ariel is last seen trying on Prospero's discarded cloak of power. Hilary Spurling, reviewing the 1970 production, observed that '[i]t will be hard … ever again to see *The Tempest* as a fairytale'. The play's politics had begun to resurface in unsettling ways.

A different kind of unsettling is performed by Derek Jarman in his 1979 film of *The Tempest*, in which he set out 'to remould the play into a film unlike past Shakespearian productions' – an intention which he achieved in part (not least for budgetary reasons) by paring down the action and understanding the play as taking place in Prospero's unconscious. He sought to create

> a twilight never-never land, … a film of the night – one night, any night, Gothic, isolated, suspended within its own space, illuminated by quirky aspects and flickering candles, conjured lightning playing on faces, walls, storm clouds, reflecting, distending: mirrors of the mind – Prospero's mind.

Thus the island is a shadow-filled crumbling stately pile on the Northumbrian coast, Miranda (played by pop star Toyah Willcox) a knowing, lisping ingénue, Ariel a sardonic trickster disappearing by way of consciously awkward jumpcuts, Caliban (played by dancer and mime artist Jack Birkett) grotesquely physical. Jarman differentiates his film above all by exploring the play's complex sexual/familial pathology, giving us flashbacks to scenes of unnatural intimacy between Caliban and his mother and making it clear that once Miranda has achieved sexual maturity there will be nothing left for Prospero to live for, leaving a substantive question mark over the dynastic plot: for Jarman, '[t]he world doesn't see heterosexual union as a solution any more'. For all of its paring down, the film nonetheless ends with a distinct reminder of the spectacular tradition as veteran jazz singer Elisabeth Welch, combining the three goddesses of the masque, belts out 'Stormy Weather' with a conga line of camp dancing sailors in the background, generic models from operetta and Hollywood musical countering the expected styles of Shakespearean production. The film was described as 'Jarman's most visually accomplished, and audacious, film up to that time', though not everyone appreciated his distinctive style: the film 'would be funny', noted one discomfited reviewer, 'if it weren't very nearly unbearable. Watching it is like driving a car whose windshield has shattered but not broken. You can barely see through the production to Shakespeare, so you must rely on memory.' Curiously, despite Jarman's radical credentials and intentions, his intellectual engagement with the play emerged largely from mainstream criticism that pre-dated, for instance, post-colonial readings of the play. His interest lay primarily in its potential for visual expression: he saw this visual excess as an expression of the politics of the Thatcher era.

Spectacle, never wholly banished, returned with a vengeance at the end of the twentieth century with Peter Greenaway's *Prospero's Books*, first shown at the Venice Film Festival of 1991. It is a visually

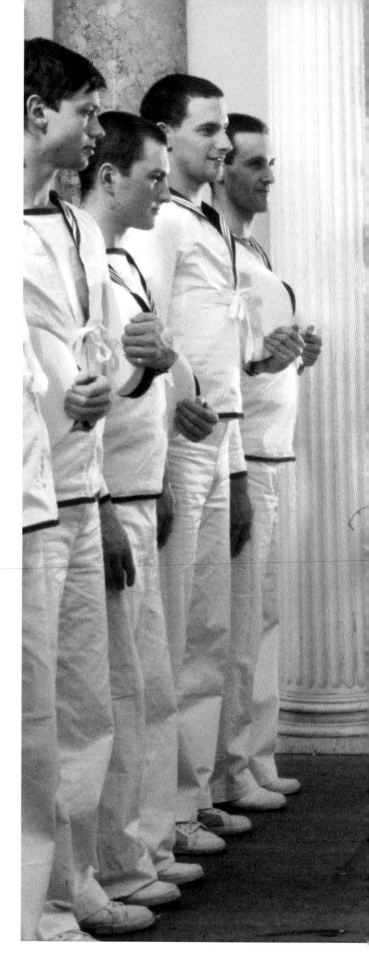

stunning, technologically cutting-edge film that, paradoxically, could be said to have set back developments in *Tempest* production by nearly a century. As visual spectacle, it is memorable, magical; as a reading of the play, it is conventional, even conservative, treating Prospero – played by the octogenarian Sir John Gielgud, who had turned down the same role in Jarman's film – as an avatar of Shakespeare, speaking nearly all the voices in the film (including that of Ferdinand, played by the young Mark Rylance, atypically silent); aestheticising Caliban (the dancer Michael Clark, elegantly menacing); and cutting all the lines on which post-colonial readings depend. Greenaway's relish at his deployment of 'Paint Box' technology to create a visual aesthetic of baroque richness informs his emphasis on Prospero's benign creative imagination: he effectively associates Prospero not only with Shakespeare but also with himself as filmmaker, thus bridging the gap between the technologies of early modern theatre and postmodern film. In this sense, for all of the political gulf between the two films, Jarman's and Greenaway's works are not as far apart as they might seem – and both are a long distance from the sociological readings of Miller and the colonial-*Tempest* approach.

The tradition of *Tempest* spectacle has thus retained its hold, in one way or another, to the present. This became most visibly apparent during the opening ceremonies of the 2012 Olympic and Paralympic Games. The Olympic ceremony began with the ringing of a bell inscribed with Caliban's line from Act 3, scene 2, 'Be not afeard; the isle is full of noises' and, a little later, Kenneth Branagh spoke this line twice before intoning the rest of Caliban's speech, giving the words full emotional weight, with the evocative 'Nimrod' from Elgar's 'Enigma' Variations swelling behind him. *The Tempest* was also woven through the Paralympic opening ceremony, co-directed by Jenny Sealey, artistic director of disability theatre company Graeae, this time with a disabled actress in a wheelchair, Nicola Miles-Wildin, playing Miranda. She was seen off on her 'journey of discovery' by Sir Ian McKellen as a benign Prospero, and provided 'the eyes through which the 65,000-strong audience in the stadium and millions more on television saw the show'. Later in the sequence, as Paralympian athletes flew over the audience's heads, Miles-Wildin spoke Miranda's speech from Act 5:

> O wonder!
> How many goodly creatures are there here!
> How beauteous mankind is! O brave new world
> That has such people in't!

For all the renegotiations of the play over the last century – political, sexual, colonial – the spectacular *Tempest* would seem to be alive and well.

PREVIOUS PAGE
Derek Jarman's 1979 film of *The Tempest* featured a sailors' hornpipe and an appearance by Elisabeth Welch singing 'Stormy Weather' as a spectacular alternative to the traditional masque scene.

OPPOSITE
Ian McKellen as Prospero in the Paralympic opening ceremony, London 2012.

Chapter 3

'The wide world': Shakespeare across the Globe

Sonia Massai

Hamlet at Sea

Shakespeare's formidable rise from early modern London playwright to global cultural icon makes for a compelling narrative, if not one that is altogether straightforward. Accounts of Shakespeare's global reach often begin with reports of English sailors performing *Hamlet* off the coast of West Africa a mere few years after the play was first staged at the newly built Globe Theatre in London. Evidence supporting these reports comes from independent transcriptions of three entries in the journal of Captain William Keeling, who headed the Third Voyage to India commissioned by the East India Company (1607–10). These entries, transcribed by one Ambrose Gunthio in 1825 and by East India Company archivist Thomas Rundell in 1849, offer tantalising records of two productions of *Hamlet* and one production of *Richard II* mounted by members of Captain Keeling's crew between September 1607 and March 1608.

The first entry, dated 5 September 1607, mentions a production of *Hamlet* on board Keeling's flagship, the *Red Dragon*, while it was anchored off the coast of Sierra Leone. Keeling reports that *Hamlet* was presented to an eminent guest, Lucas Fernandez, the local king's brother-in-law and interpreter, apparently 'a man of marvellous, ready wit' who spoke 'eloquent Portuguese'. After the play, Keeling 'went ashore' with a hunting party 'to see if we could shoot an elephant'. This colourful entry is followed by a further, shorter entry, dated 29/30 September. This time *Richard II* was 'acted' by Keeling's 'company', or 'companions', at a dinner party attended by Captain Hawkins, who was in charge of the *Hector*, the second

of the three ships that took part in the Third Voyage. Finally, a third entry dated 31 March 1608 records a second performance of *Hamlet*, which Keeling 'permitted' in order to keep his people 'from idleness and unlawful games, or sleep'. This performance reportedly occurred when the *Red Dragon* was becalmed just below the equator, off the coast of East Africa, and food and water supplies were running low.

Keeling's entries are corroborated by at least one other early seventeenth-century reference to theatrical entertainment in a journal compiled by Thomas Love during the Sixth Voyage, in which he mentions 'a great feast and a play playd' on board the *Trade Increase* on 18 June 1610. What Keeling's reference to 'acting' a play or Love's reference to 'playing' a play may have meant in strictly theatrical terms remains open to speculation. How many members of the crew took part in these productions? Did they memorise their parts or were these productions closer to what we would now call 'staged readings'? Such questions remain unanswered. Theatre historians have pointed out that the thrust stage in early modern London open-air amphitheatres, such as Shakespeare's Globe, and the upper decks on large merchant ships, such as the *Red Dragon*, shared several structural features. Both stage and upper deck were backed by the outside wall of the tiring house/officers' cabin, with two lateral doors leading in and out of it, and a trapdoor that connected the stage/upper deck to the cellarage under the stage/lower decks. We can therefore assume that Keeling's and Love's crews lacked neither the time nor suitable facilities to re-create a full theatrical performance on board, if they so wished.

Some scholars have questioned whether on board merchant ships such as the *Red Dragon* there would be playbooks that the sailors could use as scripts, or as the basis for the production of scripts, for the sort of amateur productions mentioned in Keeling's journal. It is certainly an interesting coincidence that Nicholas Ling, one of the original investors and founding members of the East India Company, who supplied 'bread', 'meal', 'beans', 'peas', 'oatmeal' and 'Steal Wheat' for the 280 men travelling on the Third Voyage, was also a member of the Stationers' Company and the publisher of the first and second quarto editions of *Hamlet*. It is therefore at least possible that he may have supplied books, including a few copies of those editions, along with his share of the victuals for the Third Voyage. Books were routinely sent out to, and then left in the care of, those who set up the first 'factories', or trading outposts, on the Indian subcontinent. These books were almost invariably of a religious, moral or theological nature and were specifically meant to be used on board ship, where morning and evening prayers were to be strictly observed, and at the factories, where early settlers were required by the Company to 'sanctify the Sabbath day, & to read upon … divine books'. However, recreational books, including playbooks, must also at some stage have found their way on to merchant ships and to the first English factories in India, because an elegantly penned manuscript catalogue listing all books held at Fort St George in Madras in 1729 includes 'Shakespeare's plays' among other English volumes.

OPPOSITE
Only surviving fragment of the journal of William Keeling, captain of the *Red Dragon* on the Third Voyage for the East India Company. The journal reputedly contained three references to performances of Shakespeare on board ship in 1607 and 1608.
British Library IOL/L/MAR/A/III

ABOVE
Model of an English warship *c.* 1580–1600 made for the Great Exhibition in 1851. It is based on a similar ship to the *Red Dragon*, which was built in 1595 and has been estimated as carrying a crew of around 200 men.
National Maritime Museum Greenwich

Unfortunately, Captain Keeling's journal is no longer extant and some scholars have questioned whether the two independent transcriptions recording productions of *Hamlet* and *Richard II* on board the *Red Dragon* are genuine, or whether they are later forgeries prompted by the growing desire in the eighteenth and nineteenth centuries for more archival evidence about Shakespeare's life and early responses to his works. Some have linked the pen-name 'Ambrose Gunthio' to the notorious scholar John Payne Collier (1789–1883), who forged other documents related to Shakespeare in the mid-nineteenth century. However, whether they are a nineteenth-century hoax or genuine records of the first productions of Shakespeare plays outside Europe, Keeling's journal entries have become a powerful 'performance' in their own right, and show how invested Shakespeare scholars have become in finding a memorable point of origin for the phenomenon now known as 'global Shakespeare'.

Continental European Shakespeare

Northern and Eastern Europe were other important (and much better-documented) settings for the early dissemination of Shakespeare's plays outside England. In Shakespeare's lifetime acting was even more precarious a profession than it is today, and many actors left England as a result of the protracted closures of London theatres due to plague, or other events that left them temporarily unemployed. By moving to mainland Europe, English players were able to take advantage of the absence of a professional theatre industry on much of the Continent and the relatively slow development there of vernacular drama. These English companies, also known as 'Die Englischen Komödianten' (English Comedians), became extremely popular during Shakespeare's lifetime, particularly in Germany. They enjoyed aristocratic patronage and regularly toured to major cities at times of public holidays or major events such as the Frankfurt Book Fair. A German friendship (or autograph) album (1597–1617) belonging to Franz Hartmann includes a watercolour of travelling players – possibly English – who criss-crossed Northern and Eastern Europe, and occasionally travelled as far south as Switzerland and Austria. English actors performed shortened versions of plays by Thomas Kyd, Christopher Marlowe, Thomas Dekker and of course Shakespeare, among others. Initially performing in English and later in translation, English troupes flourished on the Continent from the late sixteenth century up to and beyond the Thirty Years' War (1618–48), though the war dramatically reduced the number of companies and their ability to move freely across Europe.

Especially popular among the English travelling players were actors who specialised in comic routines, dumb-shows and slapstick, because their tumbling, miming and physical comedy helped the company overcome language barriers. Comic roles were added even to plays where there was little, if any, room for clowning. Shakespeare must have been aware of the popularity of English

actors on the Continent, because the famous Elizabethan clown
Will Kemp, who played Dogberry in *Much Ado about Nothing*, Peter
in *Romeo and Juliet*, Bottom in *A Midsummer Night's Dream*, Lancelot
Gobbo in *The Merchant of Venice* and possibly Falstaff in the two
parts of *Henry IV* and in *Henry V*, was among the first English actors
to cross the English Channel, when he accompanied the Earl of
Leicester on his campaign against Philip of Spain in the Netherlands
in 1585–6. While Kemp returned to England, other English actors who
left in the early 1590s were greeted with such popular acclaim that
they decided to settle on the Continent. One particularly successful
in this was Thomas Sackville, who, along with Robert Browne, John
Bradstreet and Richard Jones, travelled to Germany via Zeeland and
Holland in February 1592. Sackville's name features frequently in the
archives of the civic authorities and of the aristocratic patrons who
hosted him and his fellow actors, and also in much more personal
types of text, including a friendship album belonging to Johannes
Cellarius of Nuremberg, which Sackville signed on 1 February 1604.
Sackville signs his name after inscribing the Roman poet Horace's
famous injunction to 'mix profit with delight' ('omne tulit punctum
/ qui miscuit vtile dulci') in a section of the album tellingly devoted
to pleasure ('Voluptas'). The placing of Sackville's signature in this
section of the album is in keeping with his reputation for scurrilous
entertainments, clowning, improvisation and physical comedy, and

Travelling players
(possibly English) from
the friendship album
of Franz Hartmann,
a student in Marburg,
Germany in 1605–6,
around the time this
watercolour was painted.
British Library Egerton MS 1222

for devising a comic character who became widely known as 'John Bouset' or 'Posset', frequently represented as carrying the quack medicines that gave the character his name.

The popularity of Sackville's stock character suggests that Continental audiences were drawn more to clowning, music, dance and acrobatics, especially when performances were still in English, than to the plays, including Shakespeare's, which the English actors adapted to suit the expectations of their local audiences. An English traveller, Fynes Moryson, wrote disapprovingly about a company of English players who performed at the Frankfurt Book Fair in 1592, noting that they had 'neither a complete number of Actors, nor any good Apparel, nor any ornament of the Stage' and that local audiences 'flocked wonderfully to see their gesture and Action, rather than hear them speaking English which they understand not'.

When the English actors started to perform Shakespeare's plays in German, the dialogue, though still drastically simplified, played a more central role and often preserved some of its original features and phrasing. The increasing importance of the dialogue is demonstrated by the shortened German prose version of *Titus Andronicus* included in a small octavo volume entitled *Engelische Comedien und Tragedien*, first published in 1620. As recent editors of the play have pointed out, this early translation also seems to preserve some details of the original stage action that did not survive in the early English editions printed in London, starting with the first quarto of 1594. One example is the stage direction that prompts Lavinia to kiss her brothers' severed heads instead of her father Titus or her brother Lucius, as suggested by all major English editions since the eighteenth century. The stage direction in the German prose version of the play makes better sense of a remark made by Marcus, Titus's brother, according to which Lavinia's kiss is 'comfortless / As frozen water to a starved snake' (Act 3, scene 1). Since earlier in the same scene Titus attempts to kiss the violated Lavinia precisely in order to comfort her, it makes better sense for Lavinia to kiss the dead, who can derive no comfort from her kiss, than any of the surviving family members, who share this scene with her. Texts that record travelling players' performance decisions thus at times provide access to what we can tentatively regard as original practices.

Another German version of a Shakespeare play, *Der bestrafte Brudermord* (or, *Fratricide Punished*), has also attracted a great deal of scholarly attention since it was first published in Germany (partially in 1779 and in full in 1781) from a now lost manuscript dated 1710. *Brudermord* shares some of its language, plot and characters with all three early extant English versions of *Hamlet*, generally known as the first quarto of 1603, the second quarto of 1604, and the First Folio of 1623. Hidden Room Theatre's recent revival of *Brudermord* as a puppet show has tested (and largely confirmed) the theory that English players on the Continent often interspersed (or at times replaced) play-acting with puppetry in order to compensate for the small size of their companies and for the lack of permanent performance spaces equipped with the technology to create the special effects demanded by the plays.

Title-page of German translation of *Titus Andronicus*, published in *Engelische Comedien und Tragedien* (1620), three years before publication of Shakespeare's First Folio.
British Library C.95.b.36

Seen in the UK in the spring of 2015, Hidden Room's production proved not only interesting to scholars but also highly enjoyable for adult and younger audiences alike. The puppets used in this production were roughly half human size. They were beautifully manufactured and masterfully ventriloquised by two actors who delivered their lines standing in front of the puppet theatre, in full view of the audience. This revival was also particularly interesting for audiences who were already familiar with *Hamlet*, because it showed how this German play feels both intimately familiar and utterly alien: the ghost of Old Hamlet still spurs Hamlet to revenge him, by crying out 'swear' offstage, but the graveyard scene and the 'Alas, poor Yorick!' moment within it are replaced by an exchange between Courtier Phantasmo and a peasant, who is worried about not having paid his taxes.

The long afterlife of *Brudermord* and the inclusion of a German prose version of *Titus Andronicus* in the first collection of the

A scene from Hidden Room Theatre's production of *Der bestrafte Brudermord* (or, *Fratricide Punished*), based on the German version of *Hamlet* discovered in 1710.

Engelische Comedien und Tragedien are a testimony to the influence of Shakespeare on the rise of a local dramatic tradition in Germany. This collection of play texts also marks the beginning of one of the greatest traditions of scholarly and artistic engagement with Shakespeare outside England. This tradition found in the German writer Johann Wolfgang von Goethe one of its most passionate supporters, as attested by the famous speech he gave at a gathering at his parents' house on the first German 'Shakespeare Day' on 14 October 1772. The country also saw the foundation of the German Shakespeare Society in 1864, the first of its kind.

It is, however, important to stress that Shakespeare's popularity in Europe (like his popularity worldwide) is a far more complex, erratic and discontinuous phenomenon than is generally assumed. Shakespeare beyond England and the English-speaking world has not always been experienced as universally appealing or relevant. The French philosopher Voltaire (1694–1778), for example, was much maligned by his English contemporaries because he dared to claim that Shakespeare had a 'strong and fruitful genius … [but] not … a single spark of good taste'. Similarly, the Russian novelist Leo Tolstoy (1828–1910), who, 'in direct opposition to the [opinion] established in the whole European world', found most of Shakespeare's language 'trivial' and his lack of realism 'positively bad', and attacked the cult of Shakespeare as a 'great evil, as is every untruth'. Dissenting voices continued to be heard throughout the twentieth century: the Irish playwright George Bernard Shaw (1856–1950) referred to Shakespeare's style of playwriting as 'platitudinous fudge'. Such opinions are still heard today, especially among artists, who are more aware than readers or critics of the need to adapt Shakespeare to suit the changing tastes and expectations of their audiences. When asked why his version of *Hamlet* for the stage of the Schaubühne theatre in Berlin was so different from the Shakespearean source text, the German director Thomas Ostermeier candidly replied: 'Dramaturgically, [the play]'s a complete mess. It's much too long, too many plots. It's not a well-made play.' Ironically, one could of course argue that Ostermeier's *Hamlet*, which has become one of the longest-running productions in our time, has increased, rather than detracted from, the popularity of Shakespeare and of his best-known play.

The People's Shakespeare Goes Global

English-speaking communities living overseas have often elected to use Shakespeare for recreational reasons, well before the re-presentation of Shakespeare to international readers and audiences took a professional, institutional or colonialist turn. In fact, by the time Shakespeare became instrumental in the consolidation of England's leading role in colonial economies and cultures in the late eighteenth and nineteenth centuries, his plays and poems had already been read, collected and annotated for non-professional performance by English travellers and settlers, who seem to have

responded to the same popular drive that was turning Shakespeare into England's national poet back home.

Shakespeare's presence was probably most prominent among early settlers in the North American continent. The first recorded copy of Shakespeare's complete works reached North America as early as 1696. The practice of reading, collecting and discussing Shakespeare's texts as the focus of social events soon became a 'national pastime' and Shakespeare Clubs, modelled to a certain extent on the Shakespeares Ladies' Club, which championed the revival of Shakespeare on the London stage in the mid-1730s, numbered around 500 by the end of the nineteenth and the early twentieth century. One of these societies, which was founded in Philadelphia in 1850 and whose activities centred on group readings and close analysis of Shakespeare's texts, eventually led to the foundation of the *Variorum Shakespeare*, one of the most influential scholarly editions to date. A further testimony to the fertile ground that the amateur study, reading and collecting of Shakespeare's texts found in the New World is the fact that 150 out of the 233 extant copies of the First Folio of 1623, the most valuable and collectable of the earliest editions of Shakespeare's works, are now held in public libraries and private collections in North America.

Also extremely significant is the role played by Shakespeare in the rise of local North American theatrical traditions in the period following the American Revolution (1775–83), which ended British rule of the colonies. The increasing competition between English and American actors over ownership of Shakespeare as a cultural commodity culminated in the notorious rivalry between two leading Shakespearean actors, one English, William Charles Macready, and one American, Edwin Forrest. Their rivalry escalated into a full-

Great riot at the Astor Place Theatre, New York, on the evening of Thursday 10 May 1849. Hand-coloured lithograph published by Nathaniel Currier c. 1849.

blown street riot when Macready played the title role in *Macbeth* at the Astor Place Theatre in New York on 10 May 1849. The Astor Place Riot catalysed a continuing class struggle between the New York Anglophile elite, who supported Macready, and working-class immigrants, who supported Forrest, but it also showed how central Shakespeare was to the establishment of American (theatrical) culture more generally. Recent scholars interested in the place of Shakespeare in American culture, including Michael Bristol, James Shapiro, and Alden and Virginia Mason Vaughan, have gone as far as to claim that 'the history of Shakespeare in America is the history of America itself'.

Early printed editions of Shakespeare's works also continued to travel east long after the much-debated presence of Shakespearean playbooks on board the *Red Dragon*. A large stock of playbooks was, for example, sent to English settlers in Kolkata (then called Calcutta by the British) when the Playhouse Theatre, first built in 1753 and destroyed in 1756, reopened as the New Playhouse, or the Calcutta Theatre, in 1775. David Garrick, the English actor and theatre manager who had turned *Hamlet* into a star vehicle on the London stage, generating a genuine sensation also known as 'Garrick fever', played a key role in setting up the Calcutta Theatre. A notice published in the *London Chronicle* on 10–13 December 1774 credits Garrick for sending 'the best dramatic works in our language, together with complete sets of scenery, under the care of an ingenious young Mechanist from Drury Lane [Bernard Massink]'. In a letter to the Member of Parliament Grey Cooper, dated 2 June [1775], Garrick recounts how 'the Gentlemen of Calcutta' sent him the finest Indian textiles as a token of their gratitude but laments, in mock-heroic overtones, his wife's reaction to the loss of the 'unfortunate Chintz'. The chintz was seized by customs officers, to the bitter dismay of Mrs Garrick, whose re-upholstering plans had to be put on hold.

Reviews in the first English newspapers published in Calcutta in the early 1780s show that all-male groups of amateur actors staged Shakespeare for the exclusive benefit and entertainment of the English settlers. These reviews often refer to theatrical entertainment in Calcutta, and to Shakespeare's central place within it, as evidence that settlers could enjoy as high a standard of living as their friends and relatives back in England. In a letter written in verse by 'a Lady in Calcutta, to her Friend in England', published in the *Calcutta Gazette* on 12 August 1784, the said lady, after lamenting 'the plagues [she] bore / To reach this so much talk'd of shore', goes on to describe a typical day in the city. After a morning visit to the 'Europe shops', where customers scrambled for 'a share of caps and gauze', ladies would indulge in a 'sultry hour' of rest after lunch, followed by 'an hour of dressing' and flirting with 'men of worth' at 'the [race] Course'. Finally, ladies would flock to an evening concert or 'theatric shows' to admire the actors' 'dext'rous art'. Symptomatic of Shakespeare's popularity on the Calcutta stage is the fact that a letter praising such 'polite and refined entertainments, which have so strong a tendency to humanise the mind, and render life [as] pleasing and agreeable [as] in most of cities in Europe', is followed in the

Bengali translation of
Shakespeare's tragedies,
published in Kolkata, 1940.
British Library 14128.e.98

same issue of the *Gazette* on 21 October 1784 by a glowing review of a production of *The Merchant of Venice*, which is reported to have been performed 'to a very full theatre'.

The arrival of professional actors from London coincided with the opening in 1816 of the first Hindu College, for the training of selected groups of the local population, who needed to be well versed in English in order to support the expansion of British trade and British colonial rule in India. The professionalisation and institutionalisation of Shakespeare therefore fulfilled immediate political, economic and colonial ends. But the rise of amateur Shakespeare in the first English theatres in India, such as the Calcutta Theatre, was also responsible for sparking the development of a local Bengali theatrical tradition. A production of *Julius Caesar*, for example, inaugurated Prasanna Kumar Tagore's Hindu Theatre in Calcutta in 1831. The growing demand for Bengali plays started to drive Shakespeare and other English dramatists off the Bengali stage, until a Bengali repertory replaced English plays altogether during the struggle for independence in the 1920s. When Shakespeare plays returned to the Indian stage after independence, they did so in highly hybridised versions, thus reflecting a mode of radical and often politicised appropriation which turned Shakespeare into the world's most famous 'local' playwright, speaking to world audiences and readers in their own languages and through local theatrical traditions and conventions.

Two popular films influenced by *Romeo and Juliet* best illustrate how distinctive and independent from the source play local adaptations of Shakespeare have become in North America and in the Indian subcontinent. The 1961 film *West Side Story*, a cinematic adaptation of the musical that first opened on Broadway in 1957, and Raj Kapoor's *Bobby*, first released in 1973, fused Shakespearean motifs and plotlines with songs and dance routines drawn from popular culture. They also kick-started two important traditions in their respective countries. In North America, a series of teen movies were inspired by Shakespeare; Julia Stiles is most readily associated with this group of films for starring in both *10 Things I Hate about You* (*The Taming of the Shrew*; 1999) and *O* (*Othello*; 2001). In India, Shakespeare has been adapted to suit the conventions of contemporary Hindi cinema: director Vishal Bhardwaj has most notably risen to international prominence for his stunning and original adaptations of *Macbeth* (*Maqbool*, 2003), *Othello* (*Omkara*, 2006) and *Hamlet* (*Haider*, 2014).

Across the Wide World:
Shakespeare, Performance, Globalisation

The global dissemination of Shakespeare beyond English settlers' communities and English colonies coincided with the increasing globalisation of world economies and cultures in the nineteenth century. Since then, Shakespeare has been translated into all major world languages by great writers, poets and influential political leaders. Worth mentioning, among many others, are the German translators August Wilhelm Schlegel (1767–1845) and Ludwig Tieck (1773–1853), who authored one of the earliest and most literarily accomplished translations of the complete works (1834); the Italian poet and critic Giuseppe Ungaretti (1888–1970), who is best known by English readers for his lifelong engagement with the sonnets; and the first president of Tanzania, Julius Nyerere (1922–1999), who translated *Julius Caesar* into Swahili, because he, like many other African leaders including Nelson Mandela, had found in the play a source of inspiration for his country's struggle towards independence. Translation, as much as adaptation, has proved crucial to the dissemination of Shakespeare worldwide, thus questioning the assumption that Shakespeare is not Shakespeare without his language. In fact, the best translations seem to reproduce the rich, evocative and expansive quality of Shakespeare's language.

Similarly instructive is the realisation that many readers and theatregoers worldwide have encountered Shakespeare not only without his language but also without some of his sub-plots and characters, owing to the vastly influential impact of a literary adaptation called *Tales From Shakespeare*, written by Charles and Mary Lamb and first published in 1807. Initially aimed at younger readers, the *Tales* were translated and often adapted for the stage into a great variety of languages, including Mongolian and Buryat, Ga, Burmese and Mauritian Creole. The *Tales* offer short and morally straightforward prose versions of the tragedies and comedies and omit Shakespeare's English and Roman history plays altogether. A representative example is the tale drawn from *The Tempest*, where Caliban is described as an 'ugly monster', a 'strange … thing, far less human in shape than an ape' and does not speak for himself, while Ferdinand and Miranda are paragons of innocence and virtue, thus making Prospero's original monitoring of the young couple largely redundant. Also telling are the omission of Stephano and Trinculo and their drunken debauchery, and the addition of Antonio's repentance: while in the original, having betrayed his brother Prospero, Antonio refuses to speak or to show any sign of remorse, in the *Tales* he implores forgiveness 'with tears, and sad words of sorrow and true repentance'.

Other important developments in the history of Shakespeare's global dissemination were triggered by the advent of new media (film, radio and television) in the twentieth century and of new digital technologies in the late twentieth and early twenty-first centuries. Along with the increased speed and ease of travel, communication and access to information, these new media and technologies have had a very significant impact on the production and reception of Shakespeare in performance. It is, therefore, hardly surprising that the last 100 years have witnessed many 'firsts' in the field of 'global Shakespeare': the first and only feature-length film of *The Two Gentlemen of Verona* is a silent 1931 Chinese adaptation, called *Yi jian mei* (*A Spray of Plum Blossoms*); the first film entirely performed in Maori is a cinematic version of *The Merchant of Venice*, directed by Don Selwyn in 2002; the first Shona translation of a Shakespeare

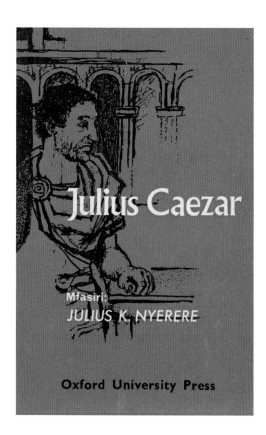

Swahili *Julius Caesar* (1963), translated by Julius Nyerere, who became the first president of Tanzania in 1964.
British Library 11768.aaa.60

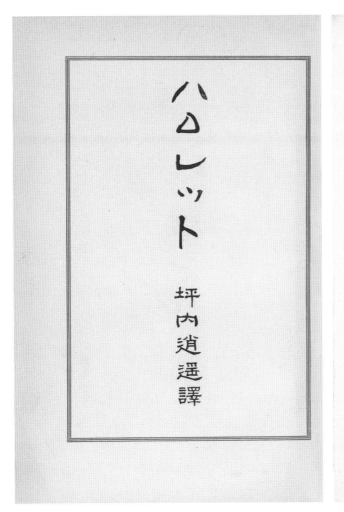

Japanese edition of *Hamlet*, translated by Tsubouchi Yuzō (Tokyo, 1909).

British Library 16104.a.34

play was used by the London-based company Two Gents when they performed *Vakomana Vaviri ve Zimbabwe* (*The Two Gentlemen of Verona*) at the Globe to Globe Festival in 2012. Internet searches that use 'Shakespeare' as a keyword produce on average 123 million results, covering productions, films, mash-ups and digital images of the texts, ranging from the earliest printed playbooks to new digital editions, scholarly resources and open-access databases entirely devoted to Shakespeare.

The sheer ubiquity of Shakespeare, not only in world theatrical traditions but also across art forms, would therefore seem to suggest that 'Shakespeare' is no longer an Anglocentric field mostly aimed at English-speakers but a complex network of practices and practitioners, within which the very notion of 'centre' and 'periphery' has become radically unsettled, if not altogether insignificant. This understanding of 'global Shakespeare' in performance is supported by the fact that the longest-running productions in our time are in languages other than English, and these have toured internationally as widely as, if not more so than, English productions mounted by the RSC or sponsored by the British Council. Two notable examples are the Brazilian *Romeu & Julieta* by the theatre company Grupo Galpão (1992–2013) and Eimuntas Nekrošius's Lithuanian *Hamlet* (1997

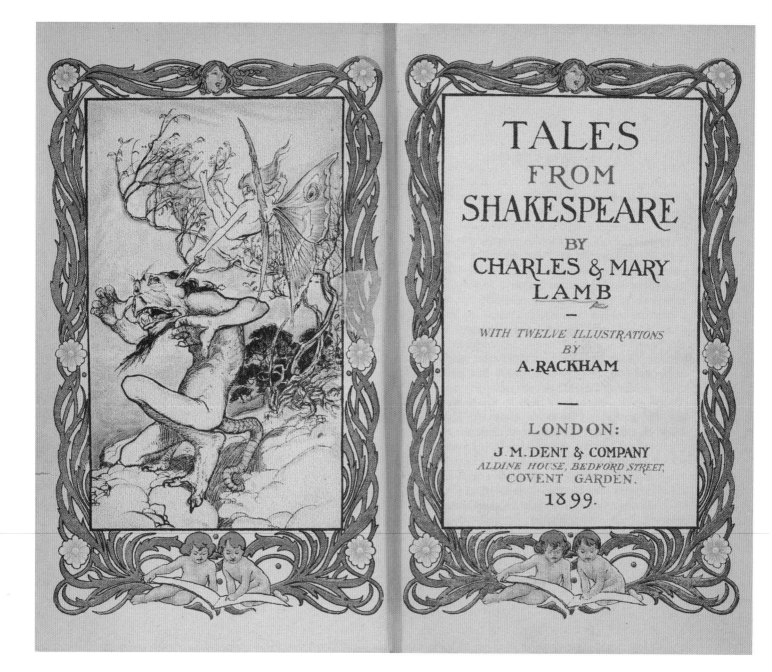

TALES
FROM
SHAKESPEARE
BY
CHARLES & MARY
LAMB
—
WITH TWELVE ILLUSTRATIONS
BY
A. RACKHAM

—

LONDON:
J. M. DENT & COMPANY
ALDINE HOUSE, BEDFORD STREET,
COVENT GARDEN.
1899.

to date). Also worth mentioning is the fact that leading international directors, including, most notably, Yukio Ninagawa from Japan and the Flemish Ivo van Hove, regularly tour their Shakespeare productions to the most prestigious venues in Europe, North America and Australasia. As a result, their productions are better known among international audiences than productions by leading English directors who work for national companies such as the RSC or the National Theatre (though recent digital initiatives such as NT Live, Digital Theatre and Globe Player are starting to redress the balance). The 'state of play' in the field of 'global Shakespeare' is in such flux that one would be justified in wondering 'whose Shakespeare is global Shakespeare anyway'.

Title-page and frontispiece of *Tales from Shakespeare* (1899) by Charles and Mary Lamb, illustrated by Arthur Rackham.
British Library O.12200.e.8/2

Coda: 'Out of Africa'

Since this essay opened with Keeling's journal as the source of one of the most powerful narratives to have informed our understanding of the origins of 'global Shakespeare', it seems appropriate to conclude by focusing on 'Shakespeare' and 'Africa' as one of the most interesting contexts for 'global Shakespeare' in contemporary performance. I would therefore like to end by considering some recent productions staged by companies based in Africa, or belonging to the African diaspora, to explain how their work is contributing to overcoming the colonial legacy of English rule in Africa and to consolidating the role of African artists within Anglophone communities.

One of these companies, the Theatre Company of Kenya, presented a radical, funny and fast-paced production of *The Merry Wives of Windsor* in collaboration with another London-based theatre company, Bitter Pill, at the Globe to Globe Festival. The look, the sound and the overall feel of this production surprised and entertained its audience at Shakespeare's Globe, while also prompting important questions about current misconceptions of the role of Shakespeare in Africa. The actors performed in Swahili, they wore modern dress, and they made full and confident use of the performance spaces at the Globe. Some reviewers were struck by how un-African this production seemed, because of the lack of music, dance, props, make-up and costumes conventionally used to represent 'Africa' to Western audiences as uniformly and reductively tribal. In fact, by refusing to be categorised as straightforwardly 'African', this production made a bold statement as to how 'Shakespeare' and 'Africa' can be made to signify together in a radically intercultural mode of theatrical production and reception that exceeds colonial and postcolonial legacies in regions of the world like Kenya.

This production also challenged the way in which Shakespeare has been used in the past in order to idealise or to denounce Kenya's colonial past. For example, in her memoir *Out of Africa*, the Danish writer Karen Blixen (1885–1962) described the 'great beauty' of the factory on her coffee farm in Kenya by paraphrasing *Romeo and Juliet* (Act 1, scene 5): 'the factory, you felt, hung in the great African night like a bright jewel in an Ethiop's ear'. She also recalled how her friend and lover, the English adventurer Denys Finch Hatton, quoted Jaques's song in *As You Like It* (Act 2, scene 5) to describe the East Africa of his voluntary exile as an idealised Forest of Arden, the setting of Shakespeare's play ('If it do come to pass / That any man turn ass, / Leaving his wealth and ease, / A stubborn will to please …'). Similar allusions to Shakespeare occur in the work of prominent post-independence Kenyan artists. Among them, Ngũgĩ wa Thiong'o (b. 1938), like Blixen, alludes to the setting of *As You Like It* in his memoir, *In the House of the Interpreter*. Most poignant is the moment when Ngũgĩ recalls that, on being unfairly arrested during the Mau Mau uprising that eventually led to Kenyan independence in 1963, he dreamt of being banished to Marsabit. In his dream,

Marsabit turned into a 'forest of green cacti … , where the exile finds a home and … leaflets, pinned on tree trunks, carry messages of love'. Allusion is here used not as homage but as a satirical weapon to show how Shakespeare had been deployed to hide or to justify the nefarious consequences of colonialism in Kenya. Waking from his dream, as Kenya woke up from its colonial nightmare, Ngũgĩ refused to forget his 'prison's night dream', thus ironically alluding to the ending of another Shakespearean play, *A Midsummer Night's Dream*. Despite acknowledging Shakespeare's influence on his literary upbringing and the relevance of the plays as political metaphors to aid understanding of the struggles for power in Kenya, Ngũgĩ went on to reject Shakespeare because he felt that Shakespeare and the English language were inextricably bound up with Kenya's colonial past.

Departing both from Blixen's colonial Shakespearean dream and from Ngũgĩ's rejection of Shakespeare as part and parcel of Kenya's colonial nightmare, the Theatre Company of Kenya and Bitter Pill presented a thoroughly intercultural, collaborative production within which Shakespeare became a globally recognisable, mobile and versatile resource or meeting point. While not unproblematic, this use of Shakespeare reflects the intercultural approach also championed by artists belonging to the African diaspora, who have started to present a new exciting brand of 'English' Shakespeare that foregrounds and celebrates cultural difference. The London-based Two Gents company, mentioned above, have been producing Shakespeare by using the conventions of South African township theatre since 2008. Their repertory so far includes productions of *The Two Gentlemen of Verona*, *The Taming of the Shrew*, *2 Henry VI* and *Hamlet* (the first quarto version). Their work is a testimony to the fact that Shakespeare is no longer anchored to ideals of Englishness understood as a combination of blood, land and language. After travelling 'the wide world', global Shakespeare is not only 'foreign Shakespeare', but is now thriving on the English stage, where Shakespeare's own journey first began.

OPPOSITE
The Merry Wives of Windsor by the Theatre Company of Kenya in collaboration with Bitter Pill, Globe to Globe Festival, 2012.

Chapter 4

'Do you not know I am a woman?': The Legacy of the First Female Desdemona, 1660

Hannah Manktelow

On 8 December 1660, in a hastily converted tennis court, London's newest playhouse opened with a revelatory production that would change the course of theatrical history. The role of Desdemona in Shakespeare's *Othello* was played not by an adolescent boy, as had been customary to this point, but by a woman: the first professional actress of the English stage. To the predominantly genteel members of the audience she was viewed as an entertaining novelty rather than a credible artiste, her identity so insignificant that it went entirely unrecorded. But her performance as Desdemona, one of Shakespeare's most compelling tragic heroines, captivated many of the spectators and helped to establish a permanent place for female players in British theatre. Presence did not, however, guarantee respect, and generation after generation of the first actress's successors struggled against institutional sexism. It would take thousands of performances and hundreds of determined and resourceful women to fight against a theatrical system that privileged men as a matter of course, and to prove that female voices were not just desirable but necessary for the survival and continuing popularity of Shakespeare's works.

Women and Shakespeare Performance, 1580s–1660

Throughout Shakespeare's lifetime and until 1660, women were largely absent from the playhouse stage; the female roles that Shakespeare and his contemporaries created were typically written

OPPOSITE
Charlotte and Susan Cushman as Romeo and Juliet. Coloured lithograph of a painting by Margaret Gillies, nineteenth century.
Folger Shakespeare Library

for boy players to perform. These acting-company apprentices underwent special training in order to impersonate the opposite sex. Most were aged between 13 and 21, and often played young male characters as well as females of all ages. In the early modern theatre, a physical resemblance between actor and character was not considered as important as it is today, but those portraying women still needed to reflect some feminine qualities in their figure and, most importantly, their voice. Upon reaching puberty and becoming unable to reach higher vocal registers, boy players were retired from female roles. Those unable to make the switch from playing heroines to heroes found their careers cut short just as they reached adulthood.

While it might be difficult for us to believe that children and adolescents were capable of portraying adult women convincingly, evidence suggests that sixteenth- and seventeenth-century audiences were untroubled by such casting practices. Shakespeare certainly showed no qualms about the ability of teenage boys to portray complex, challenging and stately women onstage, and he routinely introduced into his plays female characters who hold considerable power and sexual allure. Cleopatra, Gertrude and Lady Macbeth, for example, are by no means one-dimensional or insignificant figures, but characters with rich inner lives that demand as much skill in performance as their male counterparts.

A letter from a playhouse spectator in 1610 testifies to the success of all-male productions of Shakespeare's works. Writing in Latin, the author recounts his experience of witnessing *Othello* performed by Shakespeare's company, the King's Men:

> They also had their tragedies, well and effectively acted. In these they drew tears not only by their speech, but also by their action. Indeed Desdemona, killed by her husband, in death moved us especially when, as she lay in her bed, her face alone implored the pity of the audience.

Although he would have been well aware that 'she' was really 'he', the writer's evident reaction of empathy to Desdemona's plight makes it clear that the sex of the actor was no barrier to an effective, and emotionally moving, performance.

So popular were the boy players with seventeenth-century audiences that the tradition even survived the advent of women onstage, albeit very briefly. Edward Kynaston (?1643–?1712) began his acting career in 1660, the year in which public theatre performances again became legal (after the restoration of Charles II to the throne) and the first English actress made her debut. Along with a handful of other youths, Kynaston played both male and female roles in his first season onstage and he was an instant hit with London theatregoers. According to the actor Colley Cibber, Kynaston's female impersonations were of such high repute that 'Ladies of Quality prided themselves on taking him with them in their Coaches to Hyde-Park in his Theatrical Habit, after the play'. His feminine allure was said to rival that of his female colleagues, as John Downes

Portrait of Edward Kynaston, one of the last boy players to perform female roles when English theatres were reopened in 1660.
British Library 10854.i.1

recorded in his history of the English stage, the *Roscius anglicanus* (1708): '[Kynaston] being then very Young made a Compleat Female Stage Beauty, performing his Parts so well … that it has since been Disputable among the Judicious, whether any Woman that succeeded him so Sensibly touch'd the Audience as he.'

It was Kynaston's ability to convincingly portray hero and heroine with equal merit that most impressed his audience. In January 1661 he played Epicoene in Ben Jonson's *The Silent Woman* – a character who appears as a woman throughout the piece, only to be revealed as a man in the dénouement. Kynaston made a considerable impression on Samuel Pepys, who recorded that he 'was clearly the prettiest woman in the whole house … and then likewise did appear the handsomest man'. After actresses came to monopolise female roles, Kynaston's versatility and skill allowed him to make the transition into leading male roles for the remainder of his acting career.

London's all-male playhouses, however, should not be considered representative of wider early modern performance culture. Certainly England was 'out of sync' with custom in much of continental Europe: in France and Italy it was perfectly acceptable for women to work as actresses and singers, and on occasion foreign troupes or individuals – women among them – travelled across the Channel to give private performances at the homes of the English nobility.

Moreover, although they were excluded from the public stage in England, women from all social strata had in fact been involved in various forms of performance before 1660. At the Stuart court, aristocratic women often participated in a form of amateur dramatics: the court masques. These were extravagant allegorical shows that were intended both to entertain the court and to reinforce the social hierarchy. James I's wife, Anna of Denmark, was especially fond of masques and personally commissioned several works, including *The Masque of Queens* by Ben Jonson and Inigo Jones, which followed the established conventions of the genre. Professional actors were brought in to take speaking roles and represent base and malevolent characters – in this case witches – before the queen and her ladies appeared, as goddesses and monarchs, to restore order. Jonson, a renowned poet and playwright, composed the text, while Jones, a trained architect, designed the elaborate and risqué costumes and technologically advanced stage machinery. Although each masque was performed only once, thousands of pounds would be spent on lavish dresses and sets.

It was not only in aristocratic circles that women participated in amateur performance. Dancing, singing and playing were all traditional pastimes in the sixteenth and seventeenth centuries. There were long-standing customs of parish performance in which both sexes appeared, from religious processions and pageants to civic guild celebrations and plays, although successive waves of church reformation had slowly eroded such practices. Women from the lower orders also performed professionally in a number

of roles: as circus acts; as mountebanks or peddlers, selling various entertainments to lure in punters for their dubious 'medicines'; and even, according to one German visitor to the capital in 1584, as a kind of dancing-and-fighting human spectacle in the Southwark Bear Garden.

Occasionally, women on the margins of society crossed into the territory of the playhouses, as in the case of Mary Frith, aka 'Moll Cutpurse'. A notorious thief and drunkard who was known to play the lute in the streets and adopt men's clothing, Frith fascinated the London public and inspired numerous tales of her misadventures, notably Thomas Middleton and Thomas Dekker's play *The Roaring Girl, or, Moll Cutpurse*. On its opening night at the Fortune Theatre in April 1611, Frith appeared onstage 'in mans apparell & in her boots & with a sworde by her syde' and performed a jig to draw publicity for the piece. Such transgressive behaviour, however, did not go unnoticed by the authorities, and in January 1612 Frith was sent to Bridewell prison for indecency. With such harsh consequences in place for women who dared to step into the public arena, it was little wonder that Frith's story failed to inspire others to tread in her footsteps.

The Restoration Actress and Shakespeare

Following the outbreak of the Civil War in 1642, Parliament issued the 'Order for Stage Plays to Cease'. Although originally intended to be a temporary measure until peace was restored, the order remained in place under Oliver Cromwell's Protectorate, and public playing largely disappeared for the duration. After the fall of the Commonwealth in 1660 the theatres were re-opened, which Royalists saw as symbolic of their cultural triumph over Parliamentarians. As a consequence, Restoration theatre was closely associated with court culture. During the Civil War, Charles II and his supporters had spent time in exile at the court of Louis XIV, cultivating a love of theatre and an appreciation of the French professional actresses. Initially, however, this influence was not apparent: some pre-war theatres resumed playing as soon as the Commonwealth was dissolved, but their productions followed Jacobean and Caroline traditions, taking place in open-air venues with all-male casts.

The first Restoration theatre did not open until December 1660. Warrants were issued by royal decree to two courtiers, Thomas Killigrew and William Davenant, in July of that year. These granted them exclusive rights to form acting companies, establish new theatres and produce new works, creating a theatrical duopoly that was to remain in place until 1843. The theatrical drought of the previous eighteen years meant that it was necessary for both companies to rely initially on repertoire created before the Civil War. The works of established dramatists such as Ben Jonson, John Fletcher and Shakespeare were divided between the two, but not equally: Killigrew, in possession of a more experienced cast and the favourite of the king, was issued with the lion's share, while

OPPOSITE
Inigo Jones's design for a costume to be worn by an aristocratic lady performing at court, c. 1610.

Devonshire Collection, Chatsworth

ABOVE
Thomas Dekker's play *The Roaring Girl, or, Moll Cut-purse* (1611).

British Library 162.d.35

Davenant was left with only eleven established plays. Most of these were penned by the playwright considered – at that time – the most old-fashioned and thus the least desirable, namely, Shakespeare.

With their warrants in place, each entrepreneur set about converting former sporting venues into theatres suitable for a Restoration audience. Davenant opted to replicate the standards of court masques, installing moving scenery and a lavish interior; Killigrew chose to make fewer alterations, seeking to trounce his competitor by being the first to bring onstage the newest in continental fashion: women. It was on 8 December 1660, seven months before Davenant's opening, that the first professional English actresses made their debut, in a production of Shakespeare's *Othello* at Killigrew's Vere Street Theatre.

The identity of the first Desdemona is unknown, her name unrecorded in theatrical accounts. However, research undertaken by Elizabeth Howe suggests that Anne Marshall, who was active on the stage between 1660 and 1682, is the most likely candidate. A talented actress, Marshall often took leading roles in Killigrew's acting company, playing tragic and comic parts with equal merit. In 1664 she caught the eye of Samuel Pepys when he noted that she played 'most excellently well as ever I heard woman in my life'. As with so many Restoration actresses, there is little documentary evidence of Marshall's life, and her name only appears in association with the theatre. It is likely that she came from a respectable family fallen on hard times, as this would have equipped her with the manners and decorum required to play a lady onstage convincingly, as well as the financial motivation to enter such a disreputable profession. Anne often acted alongside her sister Rebecca; her stage career lasted over twenty years, but there are no surviving images of her. Several portraits have, however, been misattributed, partly because of confusion surrounding the similarity of her married name, Quin, to that of another, more famous Restoration actress: Nell Gwyn (1650–1687).

Gwyn's notorious rise from lowly orange-seller to celebrated actress and acknowledged mistress of Charles II may not have been the typical trajectory of the Restoration actress, but it was certainly a model to which many women aspired, given their limited options. From the moment the unidentified first actresses appeared in the theatres they were viewed primarily as sexual objects, placed in the public arena to titillate the audience. Thomas Jordan's prologue and epilogue for the Vere Street production of *Othello,* composed to mark the entrance of female performers, focuses almost exclusively on the sexual accessibility of the anonymous Desdemona. In the prologue, the speaker assures the audience that he 'saw the Lady drest' and can confirm that she is 'No Man in Gown, or Page in Petty-Coat'. Despite lines protesting the virtue of the women onstage, the audience would have understood well the numerous insinuations about the availability of the actresses that were littered throughout Jordan's text. Such suggestions were not unfounded: Elizabeth Howe has estimated that between 1660 and 1689 only one-quarter of professional actresses led conventionally 'respectable' lives.

Ironically, the introduction of professional actresses had initially been framed as a social reform, intended to raise the moral tone of the theatres rather than lower it. In 1662, Davenant and Killigrew received individual patents from the king that confirmed and expanded the rights awarded to them in their 1660 warrants. These were notable for their confirmation that 'women's parts … may be performed by women'. The patents presented this as a remedy for those who had 'taken offence' when women's parts were 'acted by men in the habit of women'. Before the theatres had closed in 1642 there had indeed been some in society who considered cross-dressing to be dangerous and sinful, but it was somewhat disingenuous for theatre managers to claim that this was their motivation in bringing women to the stage. In truth, the actresses served as financial assets to their companies, and morality was, in fact, rather bad for business.

Managers made sure that remaining chaste was logistically difficult for their female players. Actresses were used as sexual bait, and men were permitted to visit them backstage, as Pepys

Thomas Killigrew's theatre patent, granted by Charles II in 1662. This document confirmed that 'women's parts… may be performed by women'.
Really Useful Group/ Victoria & Albert Museum

himself experienced. On 5 October 1667, he recorded visiting Killigrew's theatre, now located on Drury Lane, and meeting the actress Elizabeth Knepp, who 'took us up into the tireing-rooms: and to the women's shift, where Nell [Gwyn] was dressing herself, and was all unready, and is very pretty, prettier than I thought'. Observing actresses in a state of undress became so popular that it could be enjoyed as a diversion in itself, divorced from the onstage entertainments entirely. In 1709, Mrs Crackenthorpe of the *Female Tatler* recalled that 'Men of Figure and Estates … would frequently pay four Shillings a night to sit in the Green-Room, and never trouble their Heads about the Play in Action'. Although attempts were made to legislate against such behaviour in 1664 and again in 1675, there is no evidence that these were effective deterrents.

Sexual exploitation was as much a part of an actress's experience onstage as it was behind the scenes. With many in doubt about the ability of women to perform to as high a standard as men, actresses were initially treated as mere stage decoration. As a result, productions in the late seventeenth century tended to employ a variety of techniques to expose the body of the actress as much as possible, to ensure maximum entertainment value. The illustrations from Nicholas Rowe's *The Works of Mr. William Shakespear*, published in 1709, demonstrate how much flesh could have been revealed in daring costumes that followed the fashions of the day. While in most cases there is no evidence that the images were based on actual performances, many are presented as theatrical scenes, suggesting that they were at least reasonable representations of onstage practice. Rowe's Shakespearean heroines are typically depicted in modern dress, with heaving bosoms and in some cases, as with Desdemona from *Othello* and Imogen from *Cymbeline*, a bared breast.

Even more appealing to Restoration audiences was the close-fitting attire worn by actresses playing breeches roles, which originally emerged as a consequence of the early Restoration theatre's reliance on Elizabethan plays in their repertory. Disguise was a common device in early modern theatre, and when female characters took on men's clothing in the original context the result would have been a comedic double cross-dress, with boys-playing-women-playing-men. However, when female performers played such parts, donning tight men's breeches that revealed their calves and thighs, the effect was decidedly more erotic.

Shakespeare's *Twelfth Night,* in which the central character, Viola, masquerades as a male page for much of the play, was a Restoration favourite, but the majority of the Shakespearean canon offered insufficient opportunities for the new actresses. The solution reached by both William Davenant and Thomas Killigrew was to stage adaptations in which female roles were expanded or inserted and adjustments made to the plot in order to appeal to contemporary tastes. One of the most enduringly successful Shakespearean adaptations was Davenant and Dryden's version of *The Tempest*, subtitled *The Enchanted Island.* This featured several new roles for women, including one – Hippolito – which was a travesty role, designed to be played by a woman in male dress throughout. These

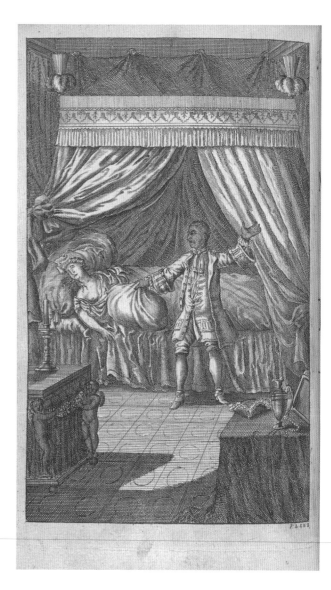

Othello and Desdemona in the first illustrated edition of Shakespeare, edited by Nicholas Rowe (1709).
British Library 81.g.21

were less common than breeches roles, but allowed for even greater attention to be drawn to the actress's sexual identity. The prologue to *The Tempest* warned the audience that they should not

> expect in the last Act to find, / Her Sex transform'd from man to Woman-kind. / What e're she was before the Play began, / All you should see of her is perfect man, / Or if your fancy will be farther led, / To find her Woman, it must be abed.

Despite their exploitation on and off the stage, the most celebrated actresses were not entirely powerless. Playwrights often created roles in order to showcase the talents of certain performers: Hippolito was written for Jane Long, who was known for her acting talent as well as her shapely legs, while Mrs Barry inspired Colley Cibber to develop the role of Queen Elizabeth in his adaptation of *Richard III*. Although they were still chiefly under the control of their male managers, playwrights and patrons, the first English actresses had breathed new life into Shakespeare's female roles. By facilitating fresh interpretations of his works and performing with skill, grace and wit, these women secured a permanent place in English theatre for both female players and the works of Shakespeare.

Shakespeare and the Actress in the Eighteenth and Nineteenth Centuries

In the mid-eighteenth century, the Prime Minister, Robert Walpole, introduced an extraordinarily restrictive piece of legislation that would transform British theatrical culture: the 1737 Licensing Act. The act stipulated that performance of spoken drama was to be restricted to theatres with a royal patent: Covent Garden and Drury Lane were now the only legal performance venues in the entire country. With severe penalties in place for those found flouting the law, the act marked the end for groups of itinerant players, some of which had offered a great deal of autonomy to their female members. William Hogarth captured what was soon to be lost in his 1738 painting *Strolling Actresses Dressing in a Barn*. Hogarth's work depicts an all-female troupe preparing for one of their last performances together as a result of the act, which can be seen resting on top of a crown in the bottom left corner.

In order to continue performing, women were forced to operate within the firmly patriarchal world of the patent theatres. Men held all positions of authority and power: they owned the buildings, sat on the boards, managed the productions and designed the sets. Yet, as public interest in performers grew steadily throughout the 1700s, a select number of actresses had a powerful new commodity at their disposal – fame. The first celebrity actress to attract national veneration was Sarah Siddons (1755–1831). After training for years in provincial theatres, Siddons joined Drury Lane in 1782 and was a resounding success. Audiences found her naturalistic acting style refreshing and engaging, and she quickly

gained popular favour. Despite a reputation for professional ruthlessness, Siddons was careful to exert control over her public image and presented herself as a devoted wife and mother. By her thirties she was considered a national treasure and was adored by high society. Aristocratic ladies borrowed her stage costumes for masquerade balls, and at Queen Charlotte's command she was engaged as a reader to the royal princesses.

Tragedy was Siddons's forte, and she was renowned for her portrayal of Shakespearean heroines such as Portia in *The Merchant of Venice*, Volumnia in *Coriolanus*, Queen Katharine in *Henry VIII*, Constance in *King John* and Hermione in *The Winter's Tale*. Her most iconic role, however, was Lady Macbeth, which was memorialised by the theatrical painter George Henry Harlow. Siddons brought a new interpretation to the part, choosing to play her as a devoted wife warped by ambition for her husband rather than the manipulative fiend of tradition. Hers became the definitive Lady Macbeth against

ABOVE
William Hogarth,
Strolling Actresses Dressing in a Barn
(1738).
British Museum

OPPOSITE
Sarah Siddons as Lady Macbeth, by George Henry Harlow (1814).
Garrick Club

Enamel miniature of
George Anne Bellamy
and David Garrick in
Romeo and Juliet,
c. 1765.
Folger Shakespeare Library

which all others were measured. Though she was forced to hide personal difficulties, including a philandering husband, from the public, Siddons's commitment to upholding her morally impeccable persona helped to rehabilitate the popular image of the actress and improved the respectability of the profession as a whole.

 While she worked hard for her achievements, Siddons undoubtedly benefited from the progress made by those before her, many of whom suffered considerably for their art. George Anne Bellamy (1727–1788), a star of the mid-eighteenth century, was plagued by financial problems throughout her career. Onstage she specialised in pathetic roles requiring displays of love and tenderness, playing Juliet to David Garrick's Romeo, but in person she was strong-willed and ambitious. When the role of Cordelia, which Bellamy had previously played, was given to another actress, she retaliated by distributing handbills to the audience that informed them of the switch and stated that Bellamy would 'be ready in case I should, that evening, be honoured with the preference'. The crowd cried in her favour, and she was waiting in the wings to replace her humiliated rival. Despite commanding the largest salary of any female performer at Covent Garden, Bellamy ran up ruinous levels of debt as a result of her lavish lifestyle and gambling habit. Towards the end of her life she wrote increasingly desperate begging letters to friends and acquaintances, including Robert Clive (of India). Although many did send funds, it was ultimately not enough to save her from her fate. Bellamy died penniless, aged 55, in the King's Bench debtor's prison.

For women with a more secure hold on their finances, the unconventional world of the theatre offered greater freedom than mainstream society. Anne Barry (?1733–1801), who took up acting against her family's wishes, was considered one of the finest actresses of her generation. Beautiful and talented, she had a wide repertoire, playing Lady Macbeth, Ophelia and Constance, as well as Rosalind in *As You Like It* and Jessica in *The Merchant of Venice*. Though she married three times, the wealth that Barry accumulated was the product of her own endeavours. She out-earned her first and third husbands, and provided financial support to the latter when his business ventures failed. Elizabeth Younge (d. 1797), who was initially hired by David Garrick to give him leverage over Barry, also supported her spouse. A leading actress who played comedy and tragedy with equal merit, Younge knew her value to Garrick and negotiated hard for her salary. When she was in her forties she married a struggling artist twenty years her junior, but by mutual agreement retained control over her property and finances. This was a remarkable act of independence at a time when women were legally considered the property of their husbands.

The comic actress Jane Lessingham (1739–1783) went even further in rejecting social norms. While her naval commander husband was away at sea she bore her lover, the poet Samuel Derrick, a daughter, and was consequently divorced for adultery. She and Derrick lived together outside wedlock for a time, during which he introduced her to the stage. She began working with Thomas Harris, the manager of Covent Garden, and they embarked on a lengthy affair that resulted in three children. Far from feeling beholden to Harris, Lessingham was an outspoken character who fought for her right to a private dressing room. Like George Anne Bellamy, she also sought ownership over specific roles, including Imogen in *Cymbeline*. In addition to her acting, Lessingham pursued a secondary career as an author and was known to frequent coffee houses in men's clothing. Her unorthodox lifestyle appeared not to affect her professional success, and she frequently took major Shakespearean roles until her retirement from the stage in 1782.

Perhaps the most defiant of all the eighteenth-century actresses was Dora Jordan (1761–1816), Sarah Siddons's greatest rival. She began acting in Dublin aged 18, but was forced to flee to England three years later after the father of her illegitimate child threatened to send her to debtor's prison for failing to repay a substantial loan. At Drury Lane she specialised in comedy parts in order to differentiate herself from Siddons. Said to sport 'the best leg ever seen on the stage', Jordan was particularly popular in cross-dressed roles. Her talent and beauty drew the attentions of Prince William Henry, Duke of Clarence, who later took the throne as King William IV, and in 1790 they embarked on a love affair that lasted over twenty years. Even though she lived openly with the duke in Bushy House, Jordan maintained a fierce work ethic and toured the provinces

Decorative title featuring Jane Lessingham as Ophelia, *c.* 1777–80.
Folger Shakespeare Library

endlessly in addition to her commitments in London. This was necessary to support both her constantly expanding family – she had ten children with Clarence – and the couple's extravagant lifestyle. While her status as royal mistress was public knowledge, Jordan was no less controlling of her image than Siddons, founding her appeal on the appearance of authenticity rather than virtue. Her warm and energetic stage presence was so popular that she inspired 'Jordan-mania' in the capital, and when Clarence left her in 1811 to seek a rich wife, the public was outraged on her behalf. In her final year of performing Jordan earned an astronomical £7,000, but in retirement her spending habits caught up with her. She chose to live the rest of her life abroad in self-imposed exile to escape her creditors, and was buried in Paris in 1816.

Following the success of Jordan and Siddons, mastering Shakespeare's heroines became ever more important to nineteenth-century actresses. Some even began to take on male roles in order to expand their repertoire and showcase the full extent of their abilities. While Siddons had experimented with playing Hamlet on tour in the provinces, it was not until Charlotte Cushman (1816–1876) and her sister Susan played Romeo and Juliet together at the Haymarket in 1845 that this type of cross-gendered casting reached a wider audience. Charlotte, an established tragedienne in her native America, took London by storm with her performance as the romantic lead. Audiences and actors alike had struggled to engage with Romeo throughout the early 1800s, finding his fervent desire incompatible with contemporary masculine ideals. The stocky Cushman, who cultivated a masculine appearance offstage as well as on, allowed spectators to overcome their aversion to feminine masculinity and emotionally connect with the character. Considered unattractive by the conventions of the day, Cushman broke new ground for female performers. Although the trend for romantic friendships allowed her to keep her lesbian relationships private, her obvious lack of interest in men freed her from the financial and sexual exploitation that had troubled so many before her and ushered in a new era of independence for those who were willing to disregard tradition.

Cushman's innovations opened the door – if half a century later – for one of the most influential Shakespearean actresses of all time. Sarah Bernhardt (1844–1923) was born and raised in Paris, and trained for a time at the prestigious Comédie-Française. A canny self-promoter, Bernhardt cultivated her image as a mysterious, exotic outsider. She claimed to sleep in a coffin and encouraged the circulation of outlandish rumours about her eccentric behaviour. In 1899, when Bernhardt was an established theatrical coach, manager and performer, she took the controversial decision to play Hamlet. Her production was an immediate success, touring extensively across Europe and America. In stark contrast to the melancholic interpretation of English tradition, Bernhardt's Hamlet was youthful, energetic and volatile. She claimed to be more suited to the role than any man, arguing that 'a boy of twenty cannot understand the philosophy of Hamlet', while the older actor 'does not look the boy,

OPPOSITE
Playbill advertising the Cushman sisters in *Romeo and Juliet* at the Theatre Royal, Haymarket, 1846.
British Library Playbills 142

Theatre Royal, Hay-Market,

Mr. B. WEBSTER, Sole Lessee and Manager, Old Brompton.

††† Unrivalled Combination of Talent & Novelty!

FOR THE BENEFIT

AND

LAST APPEARANCE

OF THE EMINENT TRAGIC ACTRESS,

Miss C U S H M A N,

AND HER SISTER,

Miss SUSAN CUSHMAN.

Who will appear THIS EVENING, for the 25th & **Last Time,**

in the Tragedy of

ROMEO and JULIET

FROM THE TEXT OF SHAKSPERE.

Being their Last Appearance in London,
for some considerable time.

The OLD SCHOOL

Having met with decided approbation by Fashionable Audiences, it
will be repeated TO-NIGHT.

Louis, · · Mr. W. FARREN.

The NEW FARCE, called

LEND ME FIVE SHILLINGS?

Having been received with shouts of laughter & applause, will be repeated

EVERY EVENING.

Mrs. G L O V E R,

Mrs. W. CLIFFORD,

Mrs. EDWIN YARNOLD, Miss TELBIN,

AND

Miss P. H O R T O N,

Mr. W. F A R R E N,

Mr. H. HOLL,

Mr. J. BLAND, Mr. HOWE,

Mr. STUART,

Mr. TILBURY, Mr. BRINDAL,

AND

Mr. B U C K S T O N E,

Will have the honour of appearing.

THE FREE LIST IS SUSPENDED, THE PUBLIC PRESS EXCEPTED.

This Evening, FRIDAY, Feb. 27th, 1846,

Will be presented,

(Twenty-fifth and **LAST TIME**)

the Tragedy of

ROMEO

AND

JULIET.

FROM THE TEXT OF SHAKSPERE.

Prince Escalus,	Mr. CAULFIELD,	Paris,	Mr. CARLE,
Montague,	Mr. GOUGH,	Capulet,	Mr. JAMES BLAND,
Romeo,	-	Miss	C U S H M A N,

(Her LAST APPEARANCE in London for a considerable period)

Mercutio,	-	Mr. H. HOLL,
Benvolio,	-	Mr. BRINDAL,
Tybalt,	-	Mr. HOWE,
Friar Lawrance,		Mr. STUART,
Friar John, Mr. SANTER, Balthazar, Mr. ENNIS,	Samson, Mr. H. WIDDICOMB,
Peter,	-	Mr. BUCKSTONE,
Gregory, Mr. T. F. MATHEWS,	Abram,	Mr. W. SANTER,
Apothecary, Mr. CLARK,	Page to Paris,	Miss WOULDS,
Juliet,	Miss	S U S A N C U S H M A N,

(Her LAST APPEARANCE in London for a considerable period)

Lady Capulet,	Mrs. STANLEY,	Lady Montague,	Mrs. POWELL,
Nurse,			Mrs. G L O V E R.

OVERTURE,	"LA GAZZA LADRA,"	ROSSINI.
	AND	
WALTZ,	"LOVE'S SERENADE,"	C. COOTE.

(Chappell, Bond Street.)

Lafayette – Photo – London.
SARAH-BERNHARDT (HAMLET.)

Sarah Bernhardt as
Hamlet in 1899.

nor has he the ready adaptability of the woman, who can combine
the light carriage of youth with … mature thought'.

The critics, however, were not so sure. Many felt that
Bernhardt and the actresses she inspired were fundamentally
incapable of understanding male drives and emotions. Max
Beerbohm wrote that

> [c]reative power, the power to conceive ideas and execute
> them, is an attribute of virility: women are denied it. In so
> far as they practise art at all, they are aping virility, exceeding
> their natural sphere. Never does one understand so well the
> failure of women in art as when one sees them deliberately
> impersonating men upon the stage.

Attitudes such as these would persist into the twentieth and
twenty-first centuries, presenting yet further challenges to women
determined to enjoy the same opportunities as their
male equivalents.

Twentieth- and Twenty-First-Century Gender Roles

Despite the achievements of Cushman and Bernhardt, Ellen Terry (1847–1928), the biggest star of the twentieth century, chose to present a socially respectable and traditionally feminine public image. A former child star, Terry's tender, soft and decorous Shakespearean heroines had secured her a committed fan base. As the Lyceum Theatre's leading lady she excelled in Shakespeare's most virtuous roles: Ophelia, Cordelia, Desdemona, Portia, Beatrice and Imogen. By the age of 36 she was the highest-paid woman in Britain and a confirmed national treasure.

In order to reach such heights, Terry was obliged to exert considerable control over her public profile. Late Victorian and Edwardian audiences demanded authenticity from their actresses, seeking similarities between the characters they played and their comportment offstage. Terry accordingly presented herself as a paragon of feminine tenderness and virtue, successfully concealing the illegitimacy of her two children by the interior designer Edward Godwin and avoiding charges of greed by playing consort to her professional partner Henry Irving, allowing him to choose her roles and set her salary. In her autobiography, however, Terry revealed feelings of compromise and regret at some of the opportunities she missed. Her portrayal of Lady Macbeth, immortalised by the painter John Singer Sargent, fell somewhat short of her ambitions. While Sargent depicted her as an armoured Machiavelli in her glittering beetle-wing dress, onstage Terry was fragile and passive. In later life she became more outspoken, touring her 'Shakespeare's Women' monologues, sometimes performing especially for women's suffrage societies. In 'Shakespeare's Women' Terry praised heroines for their bravery and urged her listeners not to 'believe the anti-feminists if they tell you, as I was once told, that Shakespeare had to endow his women with virile qualities because they were always impersonated by men!' Whatever tension Terry felt between her private and public selves, she was unwilling or unable to shed her image of perfect womanhood and remained 'the charming Mrs Terry' for the entirety of her career.

As the century progressed, more experimental productions of Shakespeare's works arose alongside the traditional. The Danish actress Asta Nielsen (1881–1972) offered one of the first gender-bending performances in her 1921 silent film *Hamlet*. Following a theory put forward by Edward Vining in his 1881 book *The Mystery of Hamlet*, Nielsen played the prince as a girl who had been raised as a boy in order to preserve her family's lineage. However, while Vining's rationale was born of Victorian incredulity that a character displaying so many unmasculine traits could truly be male, Nielsen's performance took a contrary approach, drawing attention to the artificial nature of gender roles. Her Hamlet excelled in male disciplines such as fencing, but exhibited feminine wistfulness in the presence of Horatio, her secret love. Despite its controversial premise, *Hamlet* was a phenomenal box-office success, which allowed Nielsen's interpretation to go on to reach a global audience.

Programme for Ellen Terry's recital *The Triumphant Heroines of Shakespeare with Illustrative Acting* (1911).
National Trust, British Library Loan MS 125/23a/8

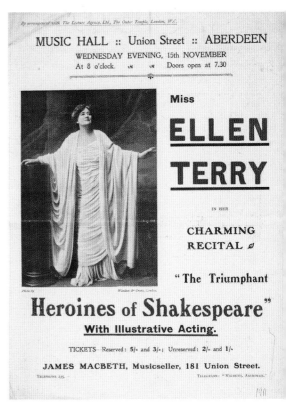

In the years that followed, however, it was Nielsen's androgynous look rather than her disregard for gender delineations that became widely imitated. The possibilities that her *Hamlet* had awoken remained largely unexplored for decades, and only with Neil Bartlett's production of *Twelfth Night* did such interpretations begin to receive serious critical attention. Originally staged in 1991 at the Goodman Theatre, Chicago, and revived in 2007 by the RSC, this production of *Twelfth Night* featured a number of cross-gendered characters, including Viola, Sir Toby Belch and Sir Andrew Aguecheek. In his rationale, Bartlett wrote that his decision to play with gender came from a desire to evoke the 'bizarre beauty' of the original performance, which would of course have featured boys in the roles of Viola, Olivia and Maria. By creating a production in which identity was treated as 'a joke', Bartlett intended to make 'the poetic part of the play, that part which deals with sexual confusion and possibility, become potent and troubling again'.

While Bartlett sought to recapture what post-Restoration casting has lost, Sarah Frankcom's 2014 production of *Hamlet* at the Manchester Royal Exchange used gender re-casting to bring a fresh perspective to the most popular Shakespeare play of all. The Player King became the Queen; Polonius Polonia; the First Gravedigger was a woman; and Rosencrantz a distinctly unfeminine, but discernibly female, biker. Maxine Peake's androgynous Hamlet was slightly more difficult to pin down, and seemed to defy gender conventions. In interviews, Peake identified her portrayal of the prince as one who was 'born a woman and decided to take on the mantle of a man', explaining that the court's reaction to her transition served 'as a backdrop for the production'. This approach allowed judgement of Hamlet's masculinity to be excluded altogether, and created a reading of the play in which, as the critic Michael Billington observed, 'character … matter[ed] more than gender', rendering the piece particularly relevant to twenty-first-century audiences grappling with gender equality in wider society.

The second-wave feminism of the 1960s and 1970s had a limited impact on Shakespearean performance as a direct result of the absence of women in positions of power within the profession. The movement's impact was still felt, however, in the form of criticism directed at both exploitative productions and the play texts themselves. Roman Polanski faced considerable censure over the appearance of a naked Lady Macbeth and the depiction of brutal violence against Macduff's wife and children in his 1971 film adaptation of *Macbeth*. The director, a vehement opponent of 'women's libbers', rejected all suggestions of provocation and flatly denied that he was deliberately evoking the recent murder of his pregnant wife, Sharon Tate, by the Manson family.

The Sphinx theatre company was one of the first to take a determinedly feminist approach to Shakespeare. Originally formed as the Women's Theatre Group, the company sought to challenge male dominance and create new works that reflected the female experience. They staged *Lear's Daughters*, an exploration of the childhoods of Regan, Goneril and Cordelia in 1987, and in 1992

Asta Nielsen as Hamlet in the 1921 silent film.

produced *The Roaring Girl's Hamlet*, which told the story of Hamlet through the eyes of Moll Cutpurse. While Sphinx remained relatively fringe, in more recent years there have been a number of female-dominated productions in prestigious theatres. Phyllida Lloyd's all-female productions of *Julius Caesar* and *Henry IV* at the Donmar Warehouse in London have also drawn praise for challenging power dynamics and subverting gender roles. Lloyd's cast – composed of women representing a variety of ethnic backgrounds, regional accents and body types – did not attempt to imitate men, but instead looked to secure legitimacy for the female voice in these highly masculine plays.

Such productions, however, still receive criticism from those who, like Max Beerbohm, believe women are incapable of playing kings and heroes and accuse directors who dare to play with gender of tainting Shakespeare's works in order to make cheap political points. In spite of the persistence of nineteenth-century views imposed on twenty-first-century performers, the Shakespearean canon remains as enticing to the modern actress as it did to her Restoration counterpart. The most popular roles continue to be those which best fit contemporary notions of ideal femininity: Desdemona, once adored as the very model of womanhood, has been replaced by the more stimulating Cleopatra and Lady Macbeth. And while, as Sphinx point out, men still hold the majority of senior roles in the theatre, greater representation will surely usher in a new era of possibility for female Shakespeareans.

Dearest Anna

As thou haste allwaye fownde mee toe mye worde
moste trewe soe thou shalt see I have stryctlye
kepte mye promyse I praye you perfume thys mye poore Locke
withe thye balmye Kysses forre thenne indeede shalle
Kynges themmeselves bowe ande paye homage toe itte I doe assure thee
no rude hande hathe knottedde itte thye Willys alone hathe done the worke
Neytherre the gyldedde bawble thatte
envyronnes the heade of Majestye noe
norre honoures moste weyghtye wulde give mee
halfe the joye as didde thys mye lyttle worke forre thee
The feelinge thatte dydde neareste approache untoe the
whiche commoundes all mee worke thee thenne
publique honneste praye doe untoe all mee and
give toe Anna thye faire Anna thysse
love toe alle I doe thenke thys mee doe thee
ffare thee welle alwaye love thys bee
lyttle lovynge tokenne and toe the ende ande truste
mee Anna toe mee love alwaye I remaine

Thyne everre

Wm Shakspeare

Anna Hathevrewaye

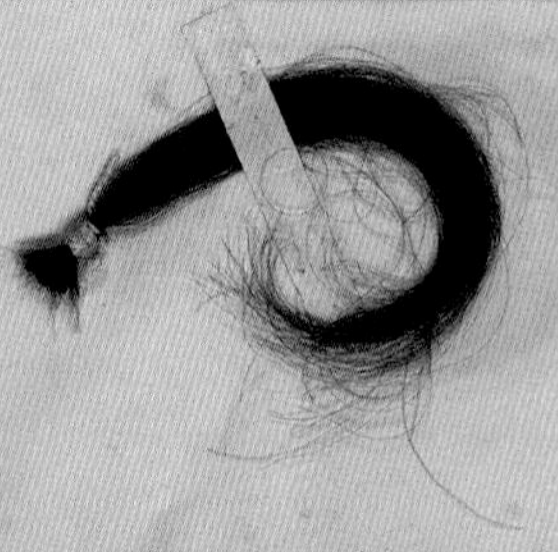

Chapter 5

''Tis mad idolatry': *Vortigern*, the Ireland Forgeries and the Birth of Bardolatry

Kathryn Johnson with Greg Buzwell

L ondon, 2 April 1796. The streets surrounding the Theatre Royal in Drury Lane are much noisier than usual. Hysterical excitement at the prospect of the evening's entertainment is in the air – not because of the cast, although renowned actors John Philip Kemble and Dora Jordan are to appear, but because tonight's play is Vortigern, *claimed to be a recently discovered work by Shakespeare – though there are many who say it is nothing of the sort. The only tickets left unsold are in the two-shilling gallery. When the doors open, the crowd overwhelms the ushers and doorkeepers and fills all available seats without paying a penny. The performance begins promisingly, but poor acting and clumsy stagecraft – encouraged by the leading actor Kemble, who delivers his lines with lingering scorn – turn the performance into a disaster. An attempt to announce a second performance is howled down by the audience, leading to fights in the auditorium between those who believe in the merits of the play and those who consider it a fraud – as it is, in due course, demonstrated to be. For more than 200 years, the play disappears from the stage, its claims to be by Shakespeare completely destroyed.*

So ended, as far as the public was concerned, the scandal of *Vortigern* and the Shakespeare forgeries, a story that had absorbed the nation for eighteen months and continued long afterwards to infuriate those who had believed the claims of the young lawyer's clerk, William Henry Ireland, and his father, Samuel, who keenly promoted his son's 'discoveries'. Twenty-five years after the chaotic first and only performance of the forged play, James Boaden – then an eminent man of letters but formerly a leading Believer (as they were known) in the Ireland papers – happened to meet William

OPPOSITE
William Henry
Ireland's forgery
of a letter from
Shakespeare to his wife
'Anna Hatherrewaye',
with a lock of hair
which he passed off
as Shakespeare's.
Folger Shakespeare Library

The Spirit of Shakespeare Appearing to His Detractors (1796), hand-coloured etching by Silvester Harding. One of many satirical prints and pamphlets on the subject of the Ireland forgeries.

Victoria & Albert Museum

Henry in Bond Street, and they fell to talking of the events of 1795. Boaden could not help bursting out: 'You must be aware, Sir, of the enormous crime you committed against the divinity of Shakespeare. Why the act, Sir, was nothing short of sacrilege; it was precisely the same thing as taking the holy Chalice from the altar and p*****g therein.'

   'The divinity of Shakespeare': the degree of outrage at the fraud could not have been sustained without the idea – still relatively new at this moment in history – that Shakespeare was a kind of god with a unique place in literature that it was akin to blasphemy to insult or question. To understand the emergence of what has become known as 'bardolatry' – and thus to make sense of the extraordinary circumstances of the Drury Lane *Vortigern* performance – it is necessary to go back thirty or so years to the emergence of what we now know as the 'Shakespeare industry', so neatly parodied in the Oscar-winning 1998 film *Shakespeare in Love*. In one scene Joseph Fiennes, playing the young Shakespeare, is practising his signature, a different spelling each time, finally trying 'Will Shagsbeard' – at which point he screws up the offending sheet of paper and hurls it across the room, where it lands in a pottery mug labelled 'A Present from Stratford-upon-Avon'.

Garrick and the 1769 Jubilee

The germ of Shakespeare worship appeared early in the eighteenth century. Stratford-upon-Avon had remained a quiet country town for a century after Shakespeare's death, and the habit of seeking souvenirs of the town's most famous son began very slowly. By the late 1730s, however, visitors were regularly asking to have plaster

OPPOSITE
Portrait of David Garrick as Richard III by Henry Robert Morland (after Nathaniel Dance), late eighteenth century.
Garrick Club

copies made of the memorial bust in Holy Trinity Church, and sufficient of them were asking to see the interior of Shakespeare's last house, New Place, along with the venerable mulberry tree in its garden (allegedly planted by the poet himself) as to constitute a nuisance to the house's owners. From 1753 the owner of New Place was Francis Gastrell, a wealthy clergyman who came to loathe the visitors who disturbed the peace of his summer residence and the boys who climbed over his garden walls to obtain fragments of mulberry wood. One night in the summer of 1756 he had the tree chopped down and sawn into logs, provoking a small riot the next day during which a mob broke his windows. The logs were sold to Thomas Sharp, a local tradesman, who began a trade in Shakespeare souvenirs by making all kinds of goods, from small ornaments to substantial pieces of furniture, from the stock of wood. One of his most eminent customers was David Garrick, the actor, playwright and theatre manager, who had visited Stratford to see the living tree back in 1742 and who later bought several pieces from Sharp, including a substantial armchair which became one of his most treasured possessions.

After the flurry of activity occasioned by the restoration of the memorial to Shakespeare in Holy Trinity Church in the 1740s, enthusiasm seems to have ebbed again, and the bicentenary of Shakespeare's birth in 1764 passed without celebration. In 1767, however, the town council decided to rebuild their town hall, and in an effort to secure external funding, they approached Garrick, offering to make him an honorary burgess of the town. Garrick agreed and suggested to the council that the opening of the town hall should be marked by a grand public gathering in the summer of 1769. If the burgesses expressed alarm at the prospect of more expenditure, Garrick's personal magnetism soon convinced them they had nothing to worry about: he, Garrick, would bring the fashionable world to Stratford to celebrate William Shakespeare, and all the council had to do was bask in the reflected glory. Garrick announced his plans for the celebration in a notice sent to the *St James's Gazette* on 9 May 1769:

> A jubile [*sic*] in honour of and to the memory of Shakespeare will be appointed at Stratford the beginning of September next, to be kept up every seventh year. Mr. Garrick, at the particular request of the Corporation and gentlemen of the neighbourhood, has accepted the stewardship. At the first jubile, a large handsome edifice, lately erected in Stratford by subscription, will be named Shakespeare's Hall, and dedicated to his memory.

None of those involved seems to have had a sense of what organising and mounting a large-scale public event would involve. Moreover, the September date, chosen to allow the maximum amount of time for the necessary preparations, was not only perilously late in relation to the English summer but also fell at a time when provincial actors would be in short supply because of the benefit performances they relied on for income out of season. Even more worryingly, complicated new features were still being added to the programme in late July. The main indoor venue for the celebration, the Rotunda, a huge octagonal pavilion made entirely of wood, was still not finished in late August, despite the best efforts of the architect John Latimore. Only the arrival of Joseph Cradock, a determined friend sent from London by Garrick himself with a large number of trained carpenters, set the project back on course.

From a quiet beginning, the press created a frenzy of interest in the Jubilee. By the evening of the first day, Wednesday 6 September, the town was full to bursting with visitors, many of them already complaining about the discomforts and expense of accommodation and refreshments. Souvenirs were also much in evidence. Visitors could buy a Jubilee ribbon, a favour devised by Garrick himself, or a Jubilee medal, carved, inevitably, from mulberry wood, or join those

Scene at the High Cross during the Garrick Jubilee at Stratford-upon-Avon in 1769, British School.
Shakespeare Birthplace Trust

visiting the masquerade warehouse of Mr Jackson from Tavistock
Street in Covent Garden, who had set up in business in Chapel Street
with at least 150 trunks of costumes, for which he charged twice
or more the normal hire prices.

Wednesday opened to a cloudy sky and the occasional
light shower. At 6am there was a cannonade on the banks of the
Avon, followed by bells ringing from every bell tower for miles.
A grand breakfast was served in the new town hall, followed by a
performance of an oratorio in the parish church. Lunch followed
in the Rotunda, delayed until 4pm by the crush of people and an
insufficient number of waiters. At 5pm, there was singing led by
the beautiful Mrs Baddeley and a concert that many visitors would
later recall as the finest moment of the whole event. At 9pm came
the ball, in a Rotunda swept clean and garnished anew by an army
of workmen. The streets and meadows were illuminated by bonfires
and torches while the Rotunda itself was lit by thousands of candles.
The ball began with stately minuets to specially composed tunes
by Charles Dibdin; at midnight the orchestra switched to playing
country dances, which continued until 3am. The day had been a great
success, so much so that Garrick and his pyrotechnician Domenico
Angelo decided to wait for even better weather and stage their grand
firework display on the second day.

This was a mistake. Thursday morning began with persistent
rain. Visitors had to keep their shutters closed lest the crowded
rooms became as wet inside as the streets rapidly became outside.

Shakespeare's Jubilee.

Wednesday, SEPTEMBER 6th.

FIRST DAY.

Began at 6 o'Clock in the Morning, with a grand Difcharge of Cannon, ringing of Bells, &c. At Seven, o'Clock a Grand Seranade confifting of Guittars, German Flutes, &c. accompanied with feveral good Voices. At Nine o'CLOCK, was a PUBLIC BREAKFAST at the TOWN-HALL; During which, the Drums of the *Warwickfhire Militia,* beat feveral fine Marches, accompanied by the Fifes.

From thence they proceeded to the CHURCH to hear

The ORATORIO of *JUDITH,*

Which began exactly at ELEVEN.

From Church there was a full CHORUS of VOCAL and INSTRUMENTAL MUSIC to the AMPHITHEATRE; where, at Three o'Clock, was

An ORDINARY for Gentlemen and Ladies.

About Five o'Clock, a Collection of NEW SONGS, BALLADS, ROUNDELAYS, CATCHES, GLEES, &c. was performed in the AMPHITHEATRE; after which was a BALL, which began at Nine, with NEW MINUETS, (compofed for the Occafion) and played by the whole Band.

SECOND DAY

Was a PUBLIC BREAKFAST, at Nine o'Clock, accompanied as before, from thence they proceeded to the Amphitheatre, where

AN ODE

(Upon Dedicating a BUILDING and Erecting a STATUE to the Memory of *SHAKESPEARE*) was performed.

This Day was to have been a PAGEANT of the principal Characters in the inimitable Plays wrote by the Immortal *Shakefpeare,* but the Weather being bad was obliged to be omitted.

At Four An Ordinary for Ladies and Gentlemen.

At Eight, The following FIREWORKS:

FIRST FIRING.

No.
1 Twelve Half-pound Sky Rockets.
2 Fuor Tourbillons.
3 Two Vertical Wheels, illuminated.
4 Two Cafcades, with Reports; one Fir Tree, in Chinefe Fire.
5 Two regulating Pieces of three Mutations each; viz. Sun and Stars; Porcupine's Quills; and, large double Stars of eight Points.
6 Two Pidgeon Wheels, with feven Pidgeons each.
7 Two Horizontal Tables, with fix Vertical Wheels and Globes illuminated,

SECOND FIRING.

8 Twelve Pound Sky Rockets.
9 Four Tourbillons.
10 Two regulating Pieces of three Mutations: 1ft, Brilliant Wheels with yellow and blue Lights. 2d, A brilliant Sun. 3d, A brilliant Star with eight Points.
11 Two Diamond Pieces of Stars and Fountains, to finifh with Mines.

No.
12 Two Pyramids of twenty-one Chinefe Fires and Boxes, each.
13 Two new Pieces of changeable Fires, interfecting each other.

THIRD FIRING.

14 Twelve Pound Sky Rockets, with Flames, Tails, Stars, &c.
15 Four Tourbillons.
16 Two large horizontal Wheels, changing into a vertical Sun illuminated.
17 Two Figure Pieces, containing fixteen Furilonies of brilliant Fires, and vertical Wheels in the Centre, with yellow Fires.
18 Two regulating Pieces of three Mutations each; viz. A large Wheel, illuminated, two brilliant Suns; fix Branches of new Fires, reprefenting Ears of Corn.
19 Two Pieces called the Fort, confifting of brilliant Fountains, Roman Candles, and Chinefe Jurbs, with Reports.

And at Eleven the MASQUERADE, the moft brilliant ever feen.

THIRD DAY.

At Twelve o'Clock, a Race for a *Jubilee Cup,* of 50l. Value, for which the following Horfes ftarted:

Mr. *Pratt's* Brown Colt, *Whirligig, J. Pratt,* Blue - - - - 4 1 1
Hon. Mr. *King's* Bay Colt, Name unknown, *T. Camel,* White 1 4 4
Lord *Grofvenor's* Colt, *Scholes* - - - - - - - - - - 2 3 3
Mr. *Fettiplace's* Bay Colt, *Pompillion, E. Freeman,* Green - - 3 2 5
Mr. *Watfon's* Grey Colt, *Lofty. John Rider,* Red. - - - - 5 5 2

At Nine o'Clock the following Fireworks, which, thro' the badnefs of the Weather, could not be let off the Night before, viz.

1 Four Balloons.
2 Four Air Balloons.
3 Four Tourbillons.
4 Two Figure Pieces, confifting of five vertical Wheels and fpiral Wheels, illuminated.
5 One Figure Piece, confifting of five vertical Wheels, &c. four Spiral Wheels, illuminated.

7 Twelve large Chinefe Jurbs.
8 Four Dozen of Water-Rockets.
9 Twelve Mortars with Air Balloons, illuminated.
10 One large Sun on the Top of a tranfparent and illuminated Building, with fix Pots d'Airgrefs, &c. and a Flight of fix Dozen Half-Pound Sky Rockets.

And, at Eleven, by the Requeft of the LADIES, was a BALL, at the HALL, now call'd SHAKESPEARE's-HALL.

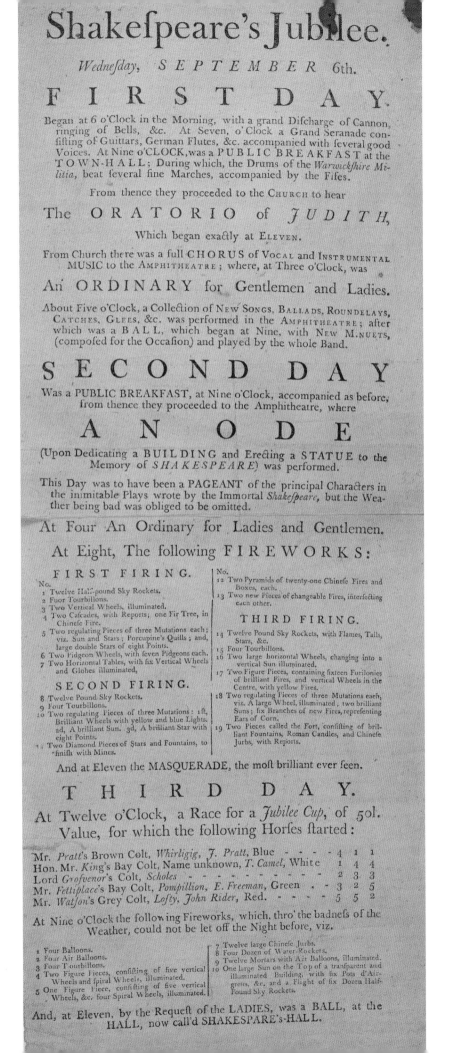

Handbill advertising David Garrick's Shakespeare Jubilee celebrations of September 1769. Not a single scene from Shakespeare's plays was performed in the entire three-day programme.

Mr Garrick reciting the Ode, in honor of Shakespeare, at the Jubilee at Stratford; with the Musical Performers, &c.

Flags and bunting hung dull in the relentless downpour and Bridge Street was partly flooded by midday. The programme for the day was nonetheless printed: it listed a great outdoor pageant to begin at 11 am, leading up to the intended climax of the entire event, the performance of the *Jubilee Ode* in the Rotunda, while in the evening the firework display would be succeeded by a costume ball. The day began badly for Garrick when his barber, hungover from the night's celebrations, managed to cut him from nose to chin. After breakfast, still bleeding, Garrick called an emergency meeting. The final decision was made for him by his business partner, James Lacy, who was responsible for the finances of Drury Lane. He was horrified at the prospect of costumes worth as much as £5,000 being ruined by mud and water ('None of the clothes shall walk!' he commanded) and persuaded Garrick to postpone the pageant to the third and last day in the hope of better weather.

Garrick knew that, despite the first day's success, if he did not perform the ode, his critics would say the Jubilee had failed. He therefore decreed that the Rotunda would open at 11am, with a performance of the ode to follow at noon. As many as 2,000 people crammed themselves into the pavilion, as desperate to escape the rain as to hear the ode, and it was this damp and resentful audience that Garrick had to win over. The ode began with Garrick declaiming the verse to quiet, sustained chords on strings, swelling into a rapturous version of the same words sung by the chorus, both solo

Engraving of David Garrick reciting the *Jubilee Ode* before the statue of Shakespeare by Louis François Roubiliac, *c.* 1769.

and chorus sections ending with the ecstatic cry of 'Shakespeare! Shakespeare! Shakespeare!' There were eight passages of recitative interspersed with seven airs and choruses, ending with the verse:

> The song will cease, the stone decay
> But his name
> And everlasting fame,
> Shall never pass away!

In the words of one listener, '[t]he effect was inexpressible. Insomuch that even Envy must have stood abash'd, and Detraction sunk in Silence', and Dibdin, even though he had fallen out with Garrick badly over the music, fell into raptures: 'There never was exhibited in England a Performance more pleasing, more grand, or more worthy the Memory of Shakespeare, and the Genius and Talents of Garrick.' Even while the audience watched puddles forming under their feet, they did not barrack but sat spellbound as Garrick had the side doors of the Rotunda flung open for a view of the River Avon while the soprano Mrs Baddeley hymned its beauties. At the close the audience erupted in wild acclamation, so many people jumping onto their seats to cheer that two benches and one of the doorframes collapsed.

During the early evening, the rain came back with a vengeance. At the costume ball, which began at 11pm, determined guests danced until first light, but at 6am they were urged to leave the Rotunda at once, as the Avon was rising so rapidly that there was a danger the entire structure would be swept away. By the following day, the Rotunda was not just uncomfortable but dangerous, and the pageant and a repeat performance of the ode were cancelled. Furthermore, the difficulties of getting to Stratford turned out to be nothing compared with the journey home. The visitors, wet, tired, cold and hungry, all wanted to leave at the same time, and even those who had their own coaches found it difficult to make progress on the muddy, congested streets. The remaining events petered out in damp embarrassment, the communal dinner abandoned since the floor of the Rotunda was now under water. The horse race for the Jubilee Cup was run at Shottery when the downpour briefly relented, but even so the horses ran up to their hocks in water. Back in Stratford itself, the event stuttered to a close with a rudimentary firework display and a small and apologetic ball on the upper floor of the new town hall.

The initial success of the event was thus washed away by the damp farce of the succeeding two days. Garrick was bitterly disappointed. He lost over £2,000 of his own money, mostly because of damage to properties belonging to Drury Lane, and he spent weeks in acrimonious dispute over the accounts. While Garrick and his colleagues bickered, his enemies rushed into print with such works as *Shakespeare's Jubilee* and *Garrick's Vagary, or England Run Mad*. Inside a fortnight, a comedy with the title *Scrub's Trip to the Jubilee* took to the stage at the Haymarket, while Garrick's main rival, George Colman, prepared to mount a Jubilee-inspired play

at Covent Garden before Garrick had even finished writing his own. Improvising rapidly, Garrick turned his *Jubilee Ode* into an afterpiece that followed a performance of *The Country Wife* at Drury Lane and scored a wild success. He presented scenes in dumb show from across the Shakespeare canon, with sets that included a realistic perspective view of a street in Stratford, with Holy Trinity Church at the far end, and a bigger cast – 320 individuals – than had ever been seen onstage before. Dibdin's music reappeared in its full splendour, with the addition of bells, drums, fifes, trumpets and even cannon. *The Jubilee* became so successful that for years Garrick used it as an afterpiece to be sure of filling the house when the main play of the night was a weak one. The initial successful run alone may have

Among the merchandise produced to commemorate the Shakespeare Jubilee of 1769 was this satirical printed handkerchief featuring a central panel titled 'STRATFORD upon AVON, or the JUBELITES taken in a STORM', lampooning the farcical nature of the rain-drenched celebrations.
Shakespeare Birthplace Trust

made Garrick as much as £8,000, four times the amount he had lost in the Stratford downpours.

Thus although Garrick did not himself initiate the cult of Shakespeare worship that became known as bardolatry, the Jubilee established a recognition of Shakespeare as, in the words of the Shakespeare scholar Jonathan Bate, '*the* National Poet, and for many people not merely a poet but a god', together with Stratford as a place of pilgrimage. Garrick was also by no means the first person to make the sale of souvenirs of Shakespeare a profitable business – Mr Sharp of Stratford and his everlasting supply of mulberry wood had seen to that – but he made Shakespeare into a cult figure, a process that itself generated relics. As scholars have pointed out, the interest in Shakespeareana was heightened by the fact that very little documentary evidence of the writer's life had come to light, let alone any literary manuscripts. The records that had been uncovered tended to show the romantic genius in a less than flattering light: shrewd, litigious and possibly not the most loving of husbands. What must he have thought of his wife, if he bequeathed her his second-best bed in his will? What did Shakespeare's mortgage deed for the Blackfriars gatehouse (discovered in 1768) reveal about the playwright, other than the fact that he had invested in property? The recent spate of literary forgeries – notably the fake medieval poetry of Thomas Chatterton – and the rapid growth of fascination with and study of Shakespeare made it almost inevitable that someone would embark upon Shakespearean forgeries and thereby provoke a crisis. There had already been small-scale forgeries, all of which had been quickly exposed, but the scanty verifiable facts of Shakespeare's life seemed to encourage a growing passion to discover and possess written relics of Shakespeare's life and work. What other treasures, then, might still be discovered?

The Ireland Forgeries and the 'Discovery' of *Vortigern*

The answer came in December 1794 when Samuel Ireland, a keen collector of prints, paintings and historical relics, made it known that he was in possession of a document bearing Shakespeare's signature. It had been found by his son, William Henry, a youth of 19 apprenticed to a conveyancer in Lincoln's Inn, who told his father that he had discovered the deed, with many others like it, at the house of a gentleman to whom he referred only as 'Mr H.' Despite the mystery of Mr H.'s identity, Samuel Ireland was delighted, and visitors began to arrive at his house near the Strand in order to view the document and its signature. Before the end of the year, these visitors could see another treasure from the document chest of the mysterious Mr H., a promissory note to Shakespeare signed by John Heminges, and in January and February 1795 a whole stream of papers emerged – a letter of thanks from the Earl of Southampton to Shakespeare, with the poet's reply, a letter from Shakespeare to Anne Hathaway, with verses and a lock of his hair, Shakespeare's profession of faith (the Protestant faith, of course – to put paid to suspicions that Shakespeare and his father had been secretly Catholic), a letter to Shakespeare from Elizabeth I and, most remarkably, the author's original manuscript of *King Lear*.

The great and the good of London hastened to see these remarkable finds, including the writer James Boswell, who was so overcome that he fell to his knees and kissed the edge of the papers, saying that having seen them he could now die in peace – which he did, just three months later. Despite a sceptical article in the *Morning Herald* in mid-February, Samuel Ireland announced to the press that he would be publishing the entire collection by subscription at the end of the year. He opened an exhibition of the documents in his house, for which tickets cost an exorbitant £4, although subscribers were generously admitted at half price. Those who had opinions about the documents began to take sides. Samuel Parr, a notable if eccentric scholar who had already sworn to the authenticity of Shakespeare's profession of faith, now drew up what he called the 'Certificate of Belief' and set about collecting signatures from the enthusiasts who became known as Believers. In March 1795, however, came the first serious whispers that Samuel Ireland's collection might not be all that he claimed. The *Gentleman's Magazine* published anonymous correspondence on both sides of the argument, the most serious charges of the non-Believers being that no recognised authority in the field had been permitted to study the papers and that the Irelands refused to reveal where the papers had come from. The stream of discoveries had not stopped, and the latest finds were extraordinary. The first was a deed of gift from Shakespeare to a friend who, some years before, had saved the poet from drowning and whose name, by stupendous coincidence, was 'William Henry Ireland'. The *Morning Herald* once more voiced its doubts – that Shakespeare should have had a friend with exactly the same name as the 'discoverer' of the document was beyond belief, and besides, it was exceptionally rare for anyone to be endowed with two Christian names in the Elizabethan and early Jacobean period. Then came another deed of gift, this time addressed to Shakespeare's friend John Heminges, dated 1611. It was in effect an earlier version of Shakespeare's will of 1616, the incontestably genuine version of which had been found at Somerset House in 1747. This new document had Shakespeare making an extremely generous settlement on his wife Anne (in contrast to the genuine will, with its famous bequest of the seemingly paltry second-best bed) and instructing Heminges to take manuscripts of his plays from a trunk at the Globe Theatre and share them out between a small group of actors. The most shocking provision, however, was that the bulk of Shakespeare's estate was to go to an unnamed illegitimate son.

Samuel Ireland was too busy drumming up subscribers to take much notice of non-Believers even when a rumour spread that a visitor to the exhibition, a scholar familiar with documents of the Elizabethan period, had said that the handwriting of the texts he had seen bore no resemblance to genuine Elizabethan scripts. Instead Samuel wrote yet again to the shadowy Mr H., begging for further details of the treasures that his son William Henry claimed to have

Ticket of admittance to view the 'Shakespeare Papers' at the home of Samuel and William Henry Ireland on the Strand, London.

British Library Add MS 30347

seen in the equally shadowy trunk. He was successfully distracted by the arrival of the greatest treasure yet, an original play by Shakespeare: *Vortigern*, based on the story of the ancient British king from Holinshed's *Chronicles* (which was known to be the source of some of Shakespeare's plots). Ignoring the absence of corroborating evidence, and even before he had seen the whole play for himself, Samuel started making arrangements for it to be produced at Drury Lane by Thomas Sheridan. He was anxious that the play should appear before the collected manuscripts were published in December and held out for a handsome payment to be made before production started.

The Drury Lane management, however, wanted to pay a percentage of takings over the whole run. Samuel Ireland refused to hand the full manuscript of the play either to the theatre's manager, Richard Brinsley Sheridan, or to his leading actor, John Philip Kemble, who was expected to play the title-role of Vortigern, unless he was promised the money he wanted; while Sheridan demanded the full manuscript before he would pay Ireland and certainly before he committed himself and the resources of Drury Lane to the production. It was late December before Samuel Ireland capitulated and Kemble and Sheridan got their play. The delay had done great damage to the cause of the Believers. The *Morning Herald* returned to the attack by serialising a mock version of *Vortigern*, which ran for weeks despite Samuel's frantic denials in another newspaper.

'The Oaken Chest, or the Gold Mines of Ireland, a Farce', print by John Nixon satirising the 'discovery' of what turned out to be forged Shakespeare manuscripts, 1796.
British Museum

Other non-Believing newspapers vied with each other to publish the most ludicrous mock-Shakespeare letter: one supposed to be from Shakespeare to Ben Jonson ran: 'To Missteeree Beenjaammiinnee Joohnssonn. Wille youe doee meee theee favvourree too dinnee wytthee meee onnn Friddaye nextee att two off thee clocke too eatee somme muttone choppes andd some pottaattooesse?'

Nevertheless, Samuel had the documents published on Christmas Eve 1795, with a preface in which he admitted not the slightest doubt. This stated that subscribers to the volume had been allowed to view the papers on request, though it was widely known that Samuel had refused access to any but friends and fervent Believers.

The tide of belief was turning steadily against the Irelands. James Boaden, formerly an enthusiastic supporter who had helped Samuel place supportive articles in journals such as the *Oracle*, now turned against them. Stung by Samuel's refusal to allow him to see an advance copy of the published documents, he managed to borrow a copy elsewhere and on Christmas Day began a savage campaign of mockery and accusation with a clear message that all the documents were forgeries. Meanwhile, rumours abounded that the two foremost textual critics of the day, Edmond Malone and George Steevens (once Malone's patron but now his rival), were about to publish pamphlets condemning the documents. Steevens had seen the papers at the Irelands' house but had kept his opinions to himself. Malone had had his suspicions from the start but had been prevented from seeing the papers by Samuel Ireland, who had declared that he would never expose the documents 'to any Commentator or Shakespeare-monger'. Malone was convinced that the whole collection was an imposture within hours of reading Ireland's publication, *Miscellaneous Papers*, and began to write a pamphlet to be published by mid-February 1796. February passed, and March too, but still Malone did not publish. The remaining Believers attacked him for the delay, driving him to publish the first outright announcement that the Shakespeare papers were spurious. *An Enquiry into the Authenticity of Certain Miscellaneous Papers ... Attributed to Shakespeare* appeared on 31 March, two days ahead of the first performance of *Vortigern*. It was not a slim pamphlet but a book of 424 pages, and it destroyed without hope of recovery the credibility of the documents and the reputation of the Irelands. Malone demonstrated that 'Mr H.' was a complete fiction, that every single aspect of the Queen Elizabeth letter – spelling, handwriting, vocabulary and place names – was wrong and that the spellings throughout the collection, with their manic abundance of doubled and trebled letters, were utterly bogus. Page by page, Malone took the documents apart, ending with his judgement that the perpetrator of the forgeries 'knew nothing of the history of Shakespeare, nothing of the history of the stage, nothing of the history of the English language'. The entire edition of 500 copies sold out in two days and the book was almost instantly reprinted.

Vortigern was due to receive its first performance on 2 April 1796 (despite John Philip Kemble's original attempt to schedule the opening on April Fool's Day). Samuel Ireland had hoped to the last

NEVER ACTED.

Theatre Royal, Drury-Lane.

This present SATURDAY APRIL 2 1796.

Their Majesties Servants will act a new Play in 5 acts called

VORTIGERN.

With new Scenes Dresses and Decorations.
The CHARACTERS by
Mr. BENSLEY, Mr. BARRYMORE,
Mr. CAULFIELD, Mr. KEMBLE,
Mr. WHITFIELD, Mr. TRUEMAN, Mr. C. KEMBLE,
Mr. BENSON, Mr. PHILLIMORE,
Mr. KING, Mr. DIGNUM,
Mr. PACKER, Mr. COOKE,
Mr. BANKS, Mr. EVANS, Mr. RUSSEL,
Mr. WENTWORTH, Mr. MADDOCKS, Mr. WEBB,
Master GREGSON, Master DE CAMP.

Mrs. POWELL,
Mrs. JORDAN,
Miss MILLER, Miss TIDSWELL,
Miss HEARD, Miss LEAK.
The Prologue to be spoken by Mr. WHITFIELD.
And the Epilogue by Mrs. JORDAN.
The Scenes designed and executed by
Mr. GREENWOOD, and Mr. CAPON.
The Dresses by Mr. JOHNSTON, Mr. GAY, and Miss REIN.
To which will be added a Musical Entertainment called

MY GRANDMOTHER.

Sir Matthew Medley, Mr. Maddocks, Vapour, Mr. Bannister, jun.
Woodly, Mr. Sedgwick, Gossip, Mr. Suett, Souffrance, Mr. Wewitzer.

Charlotte, Miss De Camp, Florella, Signora Storace.
The Publick are most respectfully informed, that this Evening, and during
rest of the Season. the Doors of this Theatre, will be Opened at Half past Five,
the Play to begin at Half past Six.
Printed by C. LOWNDES, Next the Stage-Door. *Vivant Rex et Regina*

The 36th. night, and last time this Season, of HARLEQUIN CAPTIVE.
Will be on Monday.
On Wednesday, (3rd time The Comedy of The PLAIN DEALER.
A new COMICK OPERA, in which Mr. BRAHAM will make his First
Appearance, will be produced as speedily as possible.
Due notice will be given of the next representation of The IRON CHEST.

VORTIGERN.

A *Malevolent* and *impotent* attack on the SHAKSPEARE MSS. having appeared, on the *Eve* of reprefentation of the Play of *Vortigern*, evidently intended to injure the intereft of the Proprietor of the MSS., Mr. Ireland feels it impoffible, within the fhort fpace of time that intervenes between the publifhing and the reprefentation, to produce an anfwer to the moft illiberal and unfounded affertions in Mr. Malone's enquiry. He is therefore induced to requeft that the Play of *Vortigern* may be heard with that *Candour* that has ever diftinguifhed a *Britifh Audience*.

*** *The Play is now at the Prefs, and will in a very few days be laid before the Public.*

that Shakespeare would be credited as author on the playbills, but Sheridan refused. On the day, crowds formed in Drury Lane long before the doors were due to be opened. There was noise on all sides, with hawkers selling the latest pamphlets on the scandal augmented by a squad of urchins hired by Samuel to give out handbills attacking Malone and pleading with the audience to judge the play on its own merits. When the theatre doors were finally opened, the crowd waiting for the few seats not already sold mobbed the doorkeepers, gaining access to the two-shilling gallery without paying and filling it to overflowing The pit and the lower tiers of boxes had been sold out for weeks. In this perfervid atmosphere, the first two acts went surprisingly well, despite the fact that the actor speaking the prologue dried completely and had to be roared on by the audience. The turning-point, however, came in Act 4, in which the role of a baron was taken by an actor who had a misplaced faith in his high tenor voice. With the mischievous encouragement of Kemble, he exaggerated his diction to such an extent that the audience roared with laughter every time he spoke. Even worse, when the act ended with the Saxon general Horsa lying dead on stage, the heavy curtain came down right across the actor's midriff, leaving his ample legs on show to the audience. Kemble played his leading role shamelessly for laughs, so much so that even Sheridan thought he had gone too far. The play staggered to a conclusion, the gallant Mrs Jordan speaking the epilogue, though prudently dropping the lines that claimed Shakespeare as author. A prominent Believer, the Member of Parliament Charles Sturt, who had been drinking throughout the play, scuffled with a theatre usher while, around him, fights broke out in the pit between other Believers and non-Believers.

That night Samuel conferred until dawn with some of his remaining supporters as to how they could force 'Mr H.' out into the open and vindicate their faith in the documents. After a month of inconclusive debate, the group agreed that someone should go and see Mr H. and hear the whole story. That 'someone' turned out to be Albany Wallis, friend, neighbour and discoverer of genuine Shakespeare documents, who volunteered on condition that he be allowed to undertake the task alone. Wallis – who must have guessed the truth – met privately with William Henry, who confessed that he was responsible for the forgeries. In May, William Henry told his sisters what he had done and then his mother. She simply refused to believe him. Samuel likewise professed not to believe his son and would not even allow William Henry into the same room to talk to him. Not long afterwards, William Henry left the family home, never to return. In December 1796 he made his confession public in the form of a pamphlet entitled *An Authentic Account of the Shakespearian Manuscripts*. The confession was less an admission of guilt than a calculated way to make money out of the scandal and brag about his skills as a forger (something which he continued to promote by making and selling albums of his Shakespeare forgeries). The other purpose of the *Account* was to clear his father's name: William Henry maintained that he alone had committed the forgeries in order to seek the love and the approval of his father. (Malone, the chief architect of the Irelands' downfall, refused to believe that Samuel Ireland was not involved, and so did many others.) Father and son met only twice more: while William Henry begged for forgiveness, Samuel simply would not believe him capable of the forgeries. In July 1800, Samuel, who had had to sell his house and his collections, died in poverty, never admitting that his son was a forger. William Henry wrote nearly 100 literary works, all forgotten, and died in 1835, like his father, in poverty.

It might seem incredible that so many intelligent people should have been deceived for so long when, from the beginning of William Henry's scheme, there were those who had not only reasonable grounds for doubt but also actual proof that William Henry was a forger. There were the stationers who supplied the young scrivener with dozens of leaves from old books and specially brewed ink; an office colleague who actually caught William Henry forging a Shakespeare signature; visitors to the Shakespeare exhibition documents in the Irelands' house who, when they heard about *Vortigern,* remarked how providential it was that there should be a large pencil drawing of Vortigern and Rowena above the fireplace in Samuel's study. To a large extent this passionate desire to believe in spite of the evidence was perhaps an inevitable result of the exaggerated respect for Shakespeare encouraged by Garrick and his 1769 Jubilee. People such as Samuel Ireland and the Believers were taken in by crudely forged manuscripts because they wanted so very badly to believe that tangible relics of Shakespeare were still in existence and – just possibly – within their own grasp.

Bardolatry Today: Parody and Pastiche

The seeds of bardolatry, sown by Garrick at the Stratford Jubilee and brought to a curious fruition by William Henry Ireland and his scandalous Shakespeare forgeries, have grown and flourished ever since. Today, Shakespeare's status as national icon is assured. Theatre producers, musicians, comedians, authors, video bloggers, academics, amateur enthusiasts and so on all take inspiration from his work, endlessly reinterpreting the plays and using and adapting Shakespeare's language and characters in ways that would have been, in many instances, unimaginable to previous generations. Of course we still have the 'Presents from Stratford-upon-Avon' – the expensive designer teapots made for collectors and the Starbucks Shakespeare mugs upon which Shakespeare's face is used to personify England – but this only touches the surface. In particular, during the twentieth and twenty-first centuries, bardolatry has found new outlets in the sphere of popular entertainment. James Boaden's comments to William Henry Ireland about 'the divinity of Shakespeare' have been cheerfully cast aside by many contemporary artists and, as a result, the Swan of Avon now provides a rich source of inspiration for pastiches, parodies, skits and songs. The results are often brilliant. 'Brush up Your Shakespeare' from Cole Porter's musical *Kiss Me, Kate* (1944), for example, has a dazzling bawdiness ('When your baby is pleading for pleasure / Let her sample your Measure for Measure') that would surely have met with Shakespeare's approval. Other examples are iconic: The Beatles playing *Pyramus and Thisbe* from *A Midsummer Night's Dream* as part of the 1964 celebrations for the 400th anniversary of Shakespeare's birth, for example, or Peter Sellers recording their song 'A Hard Day's Night' a year later in the manner of Laurence Olivier playing Richard III – a comedian lampooning a pop group by parodying an actor performing Shakespeare. The success of such parodies and pastiches is built entirely upon our existing knowledge of Shakespeare, while their widespread popularity only serves, in turn, to reinforce Shakespeare's iconic status.

Shakespeare provides a particularly rich source of material for comedians. Hamlet has been analysed on a psychiatrist's couch during a *Monty Python* sketch (his problems all come down to sex, inevitably); Morecambe and Wise discussed the possibility of making easy money by performing Shakespeare rather than writing their own material ('Olivier and Gielgud … they've been doing this rubbish for years and the theatres are packed'); Edmund Blackadder travelled back through time, met Shakespeare and made sure to obtain his autograph before knocking him to the floor as an act of revenge on behalf of every schoolchild who has had to wade laboriously through *A Midsummer Night's Dream* in the futile search for a single joke. The possibilities are infinite, but the comedy only and precisely works because Shakespeare and his plays are part of our cultural DNA, part of who we are. Someone walking on to a stage holding a skull automatically puts the audience in mind of Hamlet, regardless of the wider context. Even Shakespeare's language is all-pervasive. One only has to hear the words 'To be …', or, 'Once more unto the breach …' to begin automatically to complete the quotations.

Academia's modern fascination with Shakespeare has also provided rich material for satire. In the *Doctor Who* episode 'The Shakespeare Code' (2007), the Doctor, played by David Tennant (who himself would make front-page news playing Hamlet on stage just a few years later), finds himself back in Elizabethan London, where he meets Shakespeare. 'Always he chooses the best words! New,

Poster for *Shakespeare in Love* (1998) starring Joseph Fiennes as William Shakespeare and Gwyneth Paltrow as his fictional lover, Viola De Lesseps.
BFI

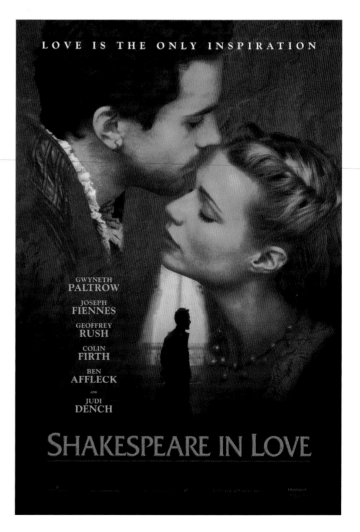

beautiful, brilliant words,' says the Doctor to his companion Martha, only to be somewhat crestfallen when Shakespeare addresses his audience with the less than immortal 'Oi, shut your big fat mouths'. Later, after battling the witch-like Carrionites – something that provides the budding playwright with the outlines for both *Macbeth* and *The Tempest* – Shakespeare turns his amorous thoughts away from Martha and instead briefly flirts with the Doctor. Rolling his eyes, the Doctor delivers a withering '[f]ifty-seven academics just punched the air' – a knowing nod towards contemporary academia's insatiable curiosity regarding Shakespeare's sexuality.

Bardolatry, it seems, persists in the face of – perhaps even hand-in-glove with – irreverence. In Angela Carter's *Wise Children* (1991), a novel imbued with a profound love for Shakespeare's comedies, the twins Dora and Nora Chance leave London for America, and the opportunity to star in a lavish Hollywood production of *A Midsummer Night's Dream*. With them they take a box of earth collected from Stratford-upon-Avon, sacred earth intended to be sprinkled upon the set of the film in an act of almost religious significance that symbolically bring the Immortal Bard to the New World and the modern stage of Hollywood. Sadly such noble intentions go awry and fate has other plans. The box of earth is temporarily mislaid en route and when Dora finds it again she discovers that the leading lady's cat has been using it as a litter tray. Dora, not oblivious to the irony of events, throws the tainted earth away and replaces it with the first handful of fresh soil she can find. With nobody but her any the wiser the ceremony goes ahead with great, if chaotic, fanfare – a situation that would, if they cared to admit it, have been familiar enough to Garrick and the Irelands.

Theatre Royal, Covent-Garden.

COMPLETE SUCCESS!!!

THE NEW SERIO-COMIC LEGENDARY FAIRY TALE, called

The ELFIN SPRITE,
AND
The Grim Grey Woman,

was received on its 2d representation with roars of laughter and applause.—The SPLENDID SCENERY and MACHINERY were honored throughout with enthusiastic approbation. This HIGHLY SUCCESSFUL NOVELTY will therefore be repeated

Every Evening until further notice.

This present WEDNESDAY, April 10, 1833,

Will be performed SHAKSPEARE's Tragedy of

OTHELLO.

The Duke of Venice, Mr. RANSFORD,
Brabantio, Mr. DIDDEAR,   Gratiano, Mr. TURNOUR,
Lodovico, Mr. PAYNE,   Montano, Mr. HAINES,
Othello   by   Mr. ALDRIDGE,

(A NATIVE OF SENEGAL,)

Known by the appellation of the AFRICAN ROSCIUS.

who has been received with great applause at the Theatres Royal, *Dublin,*
Edinburgh. Bath, and most of the principal provincial Theatres.

His First Appearance on this Stage.

Cassio,   Mr. ABBOTT,
Iago,   -   Mr. WARDE,
Roderigo, Mr. FORESTER,   Antonio, Mr. IRWIN,   Julio, Mr. Matthews
Giovanni, Mr. J. COOPER,   Luca, Mr. BRADY,   Lorenzo Mr. Bender
Messenger Mr MEARS, Marco Mr Collet, Cosmo Mr Heath, Paolo Mr Stanley
Desdemona,   -   Miss E. TREE,
Emilia, Mrs. LOVELL.

To which will be added, (3d time) a New SERIO-COMIC LEGENDARY FAIRY TALE, called The

Elfin Sprite;
AND THE
Grim Grey Woman.

The Scenery, Machinery, Dresses and Decorations are entirely new.
The Overture and Music composed and selected by Mr. G. STANSBURY
The Scenery painted by Mr. GRIEVE, Mr. T. GRIEVE, & Mr. W. GRIEVE.
Assisted by Messrs. PUGIN, THORN, MORRIS, &c.
The Tricks, Decorations, Changes & Transformations by Mr. W. BRADWELL
The Machinery by Mr. SLOMAN.——The Dresses by Mr. HEAD & Mrs. BALDING.
The whole arranged and produced by Mr. FARLEY.

The ELFIN GLEN,
In the DRACKENFIELDT.

Elfin Moth,   (the Elfin Sprite,)   Miss POOLE,
The Grim Grey Woman, Mr. W. H. PAYNE,   Principal Elfin, Master W. MITCHINSON
Elfins. Sprites, and Fairies, Masters Platt, Melvin, Mears, Norman, Daly, Stansbury, Waite, Addison, Burton,
Erwood, Flowers, Wells, W. Wells, Simpson, Bull, G. Matthews, Girnard, Packer, Cross, Clark, May, Alger.

A FERRY across the RHINE,
Sir Joddril's Chateau in the distance.

Julian of Hilldersheim,   Mrs. VINING,
Vintagers, Messrs. RANSFORD, HENRY, IRWIN, Butler, Guichard, May, Newcomb, Shegog,
S. Tett, C. Tett, Willing, &c.
Vintage Girls, Mesdames Davis, Ryalls, Blaire, Fairbrother, Jones, Hall, Hill, Payne, Vials, Wells, &c.

INTERIOR of JULIAN's COTTAGE.
Grand Tapestry Chamber,
In the CHATEAU of HILLDERSHEIM.

Sir Joddril, *of Hilldersheim,* Mr. KEELEY,
Glibbert,   (*his Steward*)   Mr. F. MATTHEWS,
Michael and Martin,   Mr. T. MATTHEWS and Mr. BENDER,
Tailor, Mr. ADDISON,   Hatter, Mr. STANLEY,   Bootmaker, Mr. LEG,
Agatha,   (*Confidant to Lady Blanch*)   Mrs. KEELEY.

Chapter 6

'Haply, for I am black': The Legacy of Ira Aldridge

Tony Howard and Zoë Wilcox

Praised by audiences but savaged by hostile critics, Ira Aldridge (1807–1867) was the first black actor to play a Shakespearean role in Britain. With his first performance as Othello in 1825, he began a long career that would see him travel all over Europe and become perhaps the most widely seen Shakespearean performer of the nineteenth century. In a life that ran parallel to the struggle for black emancipation, Aldridge garnered support from liberal Abolitionists, but equally he was a target for those – and there were many - who saw a man of colour playing Shakespeare as a transgressive act. This was never truer than when he appeared as Othello at the Theatre Royal, Covent Garden, in April 1833. Stepping out to perform on Britain's most fashionable stage at the height of the struggle to end slavery, he provoked a racist campaign in the press for daring to speak the words of the English national poet in one of England's national theatres. It was a historic night – an iconic moment in the relationship between Shakespeare and the politics of race – and one that resonates even now.

Aldridge in America

Ira Aldridge was born in New York City in 1807, the son of Daniel Aldridge, a lay preacher and straw vendor, and his wife Lurona. As a teenager Ira was educated at African Free School No. 2 in Lower Manhattan, where he won prizes for declamation and developed an interest in performing, despite his father's hope that he would

OPPOSITE
Playbill for Ira Aldridge's
first and only engagement
at the Theatre Royal,
Covent Garden,
10 April 1833.

British Library Playbills 105

become a clergyman. In the decades before the Civil War (1861–5), New York was a refuge for 'free blacks' like the Aldridge family, but, even so, opportunities there for African Americans were limited by prejudice: a career on stage, for example, was an impossibility. Ira Aldridge does at least seem to have had some experience of seeing plays, and though black people were generally barred from attending public theatres, the Park Theatre in New York was an exception, thanks to its manager Steven Price's eye for a commercial opportunity. It may have been here at the Park – in a segregated section of the uppermost balcony – that the young Aldridge had his first taste of professional theatre, perhaps even witnessing the Shakespearean performances of visiting actors from England.

Luckily for Aldridge an opportunity to act presented itself with the opening of the African Grove Pleasure Garden, a tea garden providing evening entertainment for the black community of Manhattan. It was founded by William Brown, became known as the African Theatre, and was so successful that within a few years Brown was able to build a playhouse on Mercer Street. Sadly, the story of this important venture is only scantily documented, but the acting company was certainly led by James Hewlett, a West Indian, who played Othello and Richard III and is consequently remembered as the first black American known to have performed Shakespeare. In the earliest biography of Aldridge, *Memoir and Theatrical Career of Ira Aldridge, the African Roscius* (c. 1848), Ira is said to have played Romeo at the African Theatre. In the words of the anonymous author, Shakespeare 'described what was universal', so why should 'there not be an Ethiopian Juliet to an Ethiopian Romeo?'

White American audiences were not always so accepting of or respectful towards black performers and this created trouble for the African Theatre. When Brown decided to allow whites into the audience, they caused so much disruption that he was forced, ironically, to segregate them, and his problems quickly worsened. In 1822, after his theatre was closed down by the police, Brown hired a hall close to the Park Theatre and presented *Richard III*. The Park had recently staged the same play and Steven Price saw the duplication as provocation. Newspapers reported that the African Theatre's performance was disrupted by thugs (allegedly hired by Price) and that the black actors were arrested. Tellingly, they were released only on the promise 'never to act Shakespeare again'. Not long afterwards the African Theatre was burned down, never to reopen.

It was in this tense atmosphere that the young Ira Aldridge met the visiting English actor Henry Wallack, who encouraged him to try his luck across the Atlantic. In 1824 they set sail together for Liverpool. As another black actor, Paul Robeson, would write in 1958, '[t]he right to travel has been a virtual necessity for the Negro artist. A century ago it was not possible for a Negro actor to appear on the American stage in any role – not even as a buffoon.'

1825: Aldridge in Britain

A few African American performers had preceded Aldridge to Britain after the American Revolutionary War (1775–83). They included the dancing fiddler Billy Waters, who played himself onstage in Pierce Egan's *Life in London* at the Adelphi Theatre (1822), but was more usually to be found busking outside the theatre or sweeping the streets to earn a living. Ira Aldridge's career was quite different from those of black street entertainers like Waters. In May 1825, at the age of 17, he appeared as Shakespeare's Othello at the Royalty Theatre near London's docklands. The *Public Ledger*'s 'agreeably surprised' reviewer praised his death scene as 'one of the finest physical representations of bodily anguish we ever witnessed'.

The critic's surprise at Aldridge's talent may have owed something to the popular English comedian Charles Mathews, who had visited New York in 1822–3. During his stay Mathews had seen a black actor playing Shakespeare, and on his return to Britain he cruelly parodied the man's performance in his hugely popular revue-style show *A Trip to America* (1824), which toured the country for years. *A Trip to America* mocked the very idea of a black tragedian and, in doing so, set a pattern for decades of racist minstrel shows. British theatregoers who went to see Aldridge – who was billed as

BILLY WATERS.

Billy Waters, the dancing fiddler, in *Costume of the Lower Orders of London* (1820).
British Library 7742.e.19

Mr. MATHEWS'S
Trip to
AMERICA.

Colonel Hiram Peglar

Agamemnon

Jonathan W. Doubikin

Mifs Mangelwurzel

J. Limbird 143 Strand.

hailing from the African Theatre of New York – mistakenly assumed they were watching the very actor Mathews had lampooned, though in reality it was James Hewlett whom Mathews had seen. Incensed when he learned of Mathews's new routine (not least because he had performed privately for him at the comedian's invitation), Hewlett sent an eloquent open letter to the press which was published in both New York and London:

> I was particularly chagrined at your sneers about the Negro Theatre. Why these reflections, my dear Matthews [sic], on our color, so unworthy [of] your genius and humanity, your justice and generosity? Our immortal bard … (and he is our bard, as well as yours) … makes sweet Desdemona say, 'I saw Othello's *visage* in his *mind*.' Now, when you were ridiculing the 'chief black tragedian' …, was it my 'mind' or my 'visage', which should have made an impression upon you?

Some historians have suggested that Ira Aldridge wrote this letter for Hewlett (certainly Aldridge went on to deliver forceful afterpieces and speeches in a similar style). We do know that he ingeniously and brilliantly turned Mathews's routine on its head by incorporating parts of it into his own repertoire. He was probably under pressure to adopt the kind of material seen in commercially successful blackface acts, but in fact Aldridge's appropriation of minstrelsy challenged racism throughout his career: night after night, he subverted audience expectations by proving his extraordinary ability to flip between charming clowns and complex tragic heroes.

That year Aldridge's two main roles were Othello and Oroonoko in *The Revolt of Surinam* – both Africans born into royalty but sold as slaves. Parliament had abolished the slave trade in 1807, but the fact that slavery itself remained legal throughout the British Empire prompted many theatrical protests. The Royal Coburg Theatre (today the Old Vic) billed the melodrama *Surinam* as a 'faithful portrait of the horrors of that dreadful traffic', featuring a new star from 'the very race whose wrongs it professes to record'. Aldridge's skills were quickly hailed by liberals as proof 'that blacks as well as whites may be equally fashioned by education' and that European superiority was a myth. At the time, 46,000 Britons had a financial interest in slavery. The Society of West India Planters and Merchants was one of a number of organisations founded to protect those interests and one of its tactics was to form a 'literary committee' to plant anti-Abolitionist propaganda in the press. *The Times* accepted funds from the society in 1826 and the paper now began a long and vicious campaign against Ira Aldridge: 'it is utterly impossible for him to pronounce English' properly, 'owing to the shape of his lips'.

Unable to secure an engagement anywhere for more than a few nights at a time, Aldridge embarked on a tour of the provinces. Despite a promising start, by August 1826 he was

OPPOSITE
Engravings by George Cruikshank from *Mr. Mathews's Trip to America* (1825). Mathews's one-man show cruelly parodied two black characters – Agamemnon, a slave (pictured), and the Shakespearean actor and associate of Ira Aldridge, James Hewlett.
British Library 12332.g.60

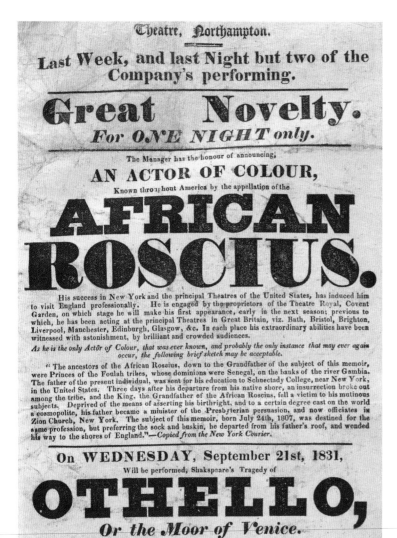

Theatre, Northampton.

Last Week, and last Night but two of the Company's performing.

Great Novelty.

For ONE NIGHT only.

The Manager has the honour of announcing,

AN ACTOR OF COLOUR,

Known throughout America by the appellation of the

AFRICAN ROSCIUS.

His success in New York and the principal Theatres of the United States, has induced him to visit England professionally. He is engaged by the proprietors of the Theatre Royal, Covent Garden, on which stage he will make his first appearance, early in the next season; previous to which, he has been acting at the principal Theatres in Great Britain, viz. Bath, Bristol, Brighton, Liverpool, Manchester, Edinburgh, Glasgow, &c. In each place his extraordinary abilities have been witnessed with astonishment, by brilliant and crowded audiences.

As he is the only Actor of Colour, that was ever known, and probably the only instance that may ever again occur, the following brief sketch may be acceptable.

" The ancestors of the African Roscius, down to the Grandfather of the subject of this memoir, were Princes of the Foulah tribes, whose dominions were Senegal, on the banks of the river Gambia. The father of the present individual, was sent for his education to Schnectady College, near New York, in the United States. Three days after his departure from his native shore, an insurrection broke out among the tribe, and the King, the Grandfather of the African Roscius, fell a victim to his mutinous subjects. Deprived of the means of asserting his birthright, and to a certain degree cast on the world a cosmopolite, his father became a minister of the Presbyterian persuasion, and now officiates in Zion Church, New York. The subject of this memoir, born July 24th, 1807, was destined for the same profession, but preferring the sock and buskin, he departed from his father's roof, and wended his way to the shores of England."—*Copied from the New York Courier.*

On **WEDNESDAY**, September 21st, **1831**,

Will be performed, Shakspeare's Tragedy of

OTHELLO,

Or the Moor of Venice.

Othello, the Moor of Venice, by the African Roscius.

Duke of Venice, Mr. YOUNG..Cassio, Mr. MASON..Brabantio, Mr. POWELL
Montano, Mr. MILLTON .. Lodovico, Mr. BECKWITH
Roderigo, Mr. BARRATT..Leonardo, Mr OWEN..Messenger, Mr. COOK
And Iago ....Mr. STUART
Desdemona, Miss PENLEY .. Emilia, Mrs GREEN

Playbill for Ira Aldridge's 1831 appearance at Northampton. He is billed as the 'African Roscius' after the greatest actor of ancient Rome.

British Library Playbills 296

destitute. The *Theatrical Observer* reported that his 'theatrical speculation' had 'completely failed'; and whether his talents were 'too original' or 'really below mediocrity' did not matter – 'he *is* in distress'. Supporters appealed for donations to assist him and his wife (a white Englishwoman whom he had married the previous year) in returning to America, but Aldridge proved resilient. His most recent biographer Bernth Lindfors's exhaustive research shows that in town after town Aldridge overcame distrust and established himself as a skilled, sensitive actor; his reputation grew, especially in northern towns with Abolitionist sympathies. In early 1827 he appeared in Manchester, the centre of the anti-slavery campaign, and later that year his portrait was put on display in the first exhibition of the Royal Manchester Institution. Though not identified as being of Aldridge at the time, James Northcote's painting was judged the 'best executed' work of the

A Moor by James
Northcote RA, 1826.
Portrait of nineteen-
year-old Ira Aldridge
in the character of
Othello, the first work
to be acquired by the
Royal Manchester
Institution in 1827.
Manchester Art Gallery

exhibition and was the first piece acquired for the institution's
permanent collection – the foundation for the Manchester
Art Gallery. The quiet dignity of this portrait makes it the
finest attempt by any contemporary artist to capture Ira
Aldridge's likeness.

That same year the Republic of Haiti, founded in 1804 after
a historic slave rebellion, conferred an honorary army captaincy
on Aldridge, 'the first man of colour in the theatre'. By 1828 he was
popular enough in the British Midlands to manage the Coventry
Theatre for a season, and as his celebrity grew his long absence from
the London stage (except for a few short turns at minor venues)
began to seem incongruous. Appearances at the two prestigious
patent theatres – Drury Lane and Covent Garden (whose companies
derived from those licensed by Charles II to present 'serious' spoken
drama, as opposed to comedy, melodrama or pantomime) – were
announced repeatedly on playbills in the late 1820s, but never
happened. Was Aldridge really promised work? Did he fail to appear
at Drury Lane because Steven Price – the African Theatre's old enemy
from New York – took over the management in 1826? Was Covent
Garden's manager Charles Kemble scared off by the insults Aldridge
had faced? In the end, it was a crisis at Covent Garden that brought
about the long-overdue appearance of the 'African Roscius', as
Aldridge was now known (after Roscius, the legendary Roman actor

who had once been a slave). Edmund Kean, the theatre's greatest star, collapsed on stage while playing Othello on 25 March 1833 and died days later, giving Aldridge the chance he had been waiting for. If Kean had known of Aldridge's appointment he would probably have approved, having seen him perform and praised his 'wondrous versatility'. Much of the London press, however, would not be so generous.

Title-page and frontispiece of John Pope's *Othello-Travestie* (1813), one of several racist parodies of Othello to appear in the decades before slavery was abolished.
British Library 2300.b.11.(1)

1833: Covent Garden

Racial tensions were high in the spring of 1833 as Abolitionary agitation gathered momentum and the pro-slavery lobby fought back in whatever way it could. This tension, which had been brewing ever since the 1807 Act to end the slave trade had made total abolition a realistic prospect, had a lasting effect on the way Shakespeare's *Othello* was perceived by foregrounding its racial elements. Several parodies of *Othello* appeared at this time and even John Pope's *Othello-Travestie* (1813), a mild satire on Shakespearean scholarship, ended as a tract against interracial marriage: 'Nor let the fair sex ever wed the black'. In 1834 in the slave-trade city of Liverpool, Maurice Dowling's own *Othello Travestie* turned Shakespeare into a minstrel show that targeted Aldridge and his recent honours, making Othello a Captain 'from the Republic of Hayti [*sic*]'. Sexual anxieties became explicit ('De piccaninnies may be white') and Othello's great speech to the senate was reduced to:

Massa, him neber do de ting dat wrong;
Him tell him all about it – in him song.
              AIR …
(*To the tune of 'Yankee Doodle'*)

When Aldridge came to play Othello, the fashion, begun by
Edmund Kean, was for the role to be played as a light-skinned
Arab, which avoided any uncomfortable associations with
slavery. The poet Samuel Taylor Coleridge claimed that to imagine
Desdemona, 'this beautiful Venetian girl[,] falling in love with
a veritable negro' was 'monstrous'. For Aldridge, however, his
ethnicity was his selling-point, and in reply to those who sneered
that he must be an escaped slave or an uppity footman, he
romanticised his African heritage. Reconstructing his identity on
Shakespearean lines, his playbills claimed that his grandfather
was a prince of the Foulah tribe who had been overthrown by his
subjects and that Ira himself had narrowly escaped from Senegal
with his life – a story that is later embellished further in the
Memoir.

The myth of Senegalese royalty did not go down well in
certain quarters of the press, which were primed to sabotage his first
prestigious London engagement; days in advance, *Figaro in London*
called for the so-called prince to be driven from the stage. Aldridge's
supporters at the Garrick Club responded by printing handbills
begging for him to be given a fair hearing. So when he stepped on
to the boards at Covent Garden on 10 April 1833, he knew he needed
to pull off the performance of his life. He launched into the part he
had, by then, been playing for eight years, finishing to resounding
applause and demands for a curtain-call. But then the anxious wait
for the morning papers began.

There was much that was positive. Aldridge's voice
received unanimous praise from the critics, some comparing him
favourably with the leading actors of the day, and the final scene
was 'played with extraordinary and heartrending effect' according
to the *Guardian and Public Ledger*. Yet the favourable reviews
were drowned out by an onslaught of bile, much of it focused
on Aldridge's ethnicity. The *Athenaeum* delivered one of the most
damning assessments:

> On Wednesday, this establishment … aimed another blow at
> its respectability, by the presentation of Mr. Henry Wallack's
> black servant in the character of *Othello* – *Othello* forsooth!!!
> *Othello*, almost the master-work of the master-mind – a part,
> the study of which occupied, perhaps, years of the life of the
> elegant and classical Kemble; a part, which the fire and genius
> of Kean have, of late years, made his exclusive property; a
> part, which it has been considered a sort of theatrical treason
> for anyone less distinguished than these two variously but
> highly gifted individuals to attempt; and this to be personated
> in an English national theatre, by one whose pretensions
> rest upon the two grounds of his face being a natural instead

Hand-coloured etching
of Edmund Kean as
Othello by Charles
Tomkins, 1824.
Victoria & Albert Museum

of an acquired tint, and of his having lived as a servant to a low-comedy actor. It is truly monstrous …. [and] sufficient to make [Shakespeare's] indignant bones kick the lid from his coffin.

It also raised the spectre of miscegenation, which was, for some, the heart of the matter:

> We protest against an interesting actress and lady-like girl, like Miss Ellen Tree, … being pawed about by Mr. Henry Wallack's black servant; and finally, in the name of consistency, if this exhibition is to be continued, we protest against acting being any longer dignified by the name of art.

The Times – which had been paid to print anti-Abolitionary propaganda in 1826 – called attention to his foreignness:

> His accent is unpleasantly, and we would say, vulgarly foreign; his manner, generally, drawling and unimpressive; and when by chance (for chance it is, and not judgment), he rises to a higher strain, we perceive in the transition the elevation of rant, not the fiery dignity of soul-felt passion.

However, even they had to grudgingly admit that Aldridge was 'extremely well received'. In fact the playbill for the next day, 12 April, announced that 'by the unanimous desire of the audience', Aldridge would repeat the part of Othello that night and then star in *The Revenge* and *The Padlock* the following Tuesday. However, it was not to be. Influenza had broken out in London and on 13 April the management decided to close Covent Garden as business dwindled. The theatre remained dark for five nights, yet the flu epidemic does not adequately explain why Aldridge was dismissed and never invited to return. The London establishment had had its say, and the elite theatres would not take such a risk again.

According to the *Memoir*, Aldridge was deeply hurt by the attacks and especially by the racist mockery. However, he swiftly crossed the Thames to the Surrey Theatre in Lambeth, where a more radical climate prevailed and he was welcomed as a hero. In retrospect Aldridge's appearance at Covent Garden blighted his career because of the timing: in July the Abolition of Slavery Act was passed and the hysteria of the preceding months began to dissipate; if Aldridge had appeared a few months later, his reception might not have been so hostile. As it was, the new act resulted in forty per cent of all government expenditure being paid to slave owners as compensation and, since the financial threat to them had passed, even Dowling's *Othello* parody could end with the cast (including Desdemona's ghost) happily singing, 'Let the past be all forgot!' Attitudes were changing and Aldridge's work helped change them.

For over the next three decades, Aldridge continued to perfect his skills and expand his repertoire. He donned whiteface to play Shylock, Macbeth, Richard III and Lear (plus Iago when a crowd in

Playbill advertising Ira Aldridge's appearance as Othello, Richard III and Shylock in Newcastle, 1845.
British Library Playbills 262

MR IRA ALDRIDGE AS AARON.

"He dies upon my scimetar's sharp point.
That touches this my first-born son and heir!"
TITUS ANDRONICUS.

Engraving of Ira
Aldridge as Aaron in
Titus Andronicus, from
*The Complete Works of
Shakspere* (J Tallis & Co,
1851–53).
British Library 2300.h.5

Newport wanted their local favourite to play the Moor). Few black
actors have played these roles even today. Challenging stereotypes
from another direction, Aldridge commissioned a new version of
Titus Andronicus ('Not acted for 200 years') that turned Shakespeare's
villain Aaron the Moor into the hero. In one sensational scene
described by the *Sunday Times*, his baby was thrown into the Tiber
'while Aaron is chained to a tree, from which he breaks free by main
strength, leaps into the river, and saves his child'. Othello, however,
remained Aldridge's signature role. Honed to perfection over a long
career, it came to be seen as a model of carefully modulated realism:
'No clap-trap, no rant' – simply 'truth to nature' was the *London
Telegraph*'s verdict. In 1848 Aldridge returned to the Surrey Theatre
for a season that was widely admired; the *Era* called it 'a great moral
lesson'. He had the *Memoir* printed following this success and the
biography closed with the hope that now, surely, Covent Garden
would invite him back. It never happened. Four years later *Reynold's*

Newspaper revealed his frustration: 'Mr Ira Aldridge, the African Roscius, is making up a company, with which he is about proceeding to Paris'. At this point, everything changed: it was the first of many European tours, and it took Aldridge's Shakespearean career in an unimagined direction.

Othello in the World

Aldridge was a sensation across the Continent, from Germany and France to Poland and Russia. After the first tour, he dismissed his English company and decided to play alongside local actors who delivered their lines in their own languages while he spoke English. In Sweden he wrote, '[t]he leading man is grumbling about the disadvantage he says he will bear not understanding English. He forgets that I am at a greater disadvantage, his language is understood by the entire audience.' In fact he became famous for the training he gave his casts. Aldridge's impact was extraordinary for several reasons. He was an ambassador for Shakespeare – some of the plays were hardly known locally – and for a new realism. Now that he no longer needed to support his classical roles with English melodramas, his subtler strengths shone out and influenced some of the directors and actors who laid the foundation for modern theatre in Berlin and Moscow. Crowned heads showered him with awards while, as an African American artist in the build-up to the Civil War, Aldridge became an icon for European liberals. His Shylock was seen as particular proof of his universal sympathies: he ended *The Merchant of Venice* after the Trial Scene, with Shylock 'martyred'. A theatre critic in Breslau (modern Wrocław), who knew Aldridge, said 'he understands like no other how to portray … the full bitterness the Jew feels. Aldridge himself comes from a mistreated race.'

Ever divisive, he was shadowed by the very regimes that honoured him. Modern biographers have discovered, for instance, that his friendships with Hungarian revolutionaries made him 'a suspicious person'. According to a report in the *Deutsche Theater-Zeitung* from 14 January 1854, 'all our security services have been instructed to watch the African Roscius'. He was banned from performing *Lear* and *Macbeth* in Russia when the Tsar decided they were attacks on monarchy. Yet at the same time his reputation was transforming, not least because of his regular appearances on international society pages. In 1858 the *Illustrated London News* praised the Lyceum Theatre for finally bringing Aldridge's Othello into the West End – it was his 'triumph'. *The Times* and the *Athenaeum*, always his fiercest critics, completely reversed their verdicts of 1833. He became a British citizen in 1863, and he was the first British actor to be knighted, becoming the Chevalier Ira Aldridge, Knight of Saxony. Moreover, at long last, his reputation had spread to America, and after slavery was abolished there in 1865 he began to plan a tour back home. 'Before the [civil] war', wrote an American *Times* correspondent, 'a white artist could not possibly have been persuaded to appear on the same stage with a man of colour'; now 'two actresses of distinction had consented'. Aldridge was honoured on the Continent and accepted in fashionable London at last, his return to his native land 'was anticipated with something like anxiety'. But it was too late. In 1867 he died suddenly in Poland, and it would be for another black American actor to continue Aldridge's legacy. That actor was Paul Robeson (1898–1976) and, as with Aldridge, his most famous role was Othello.

Paul Robeson

In some ways Paul Robeson's Shakespearean career retraced Aldridge's closely. His father – an escaped slave – was a preacher,

Paul Robeson as Othello and Peggy Ashcroft as Desdemona at the Savoy Theatre, London, 1930.

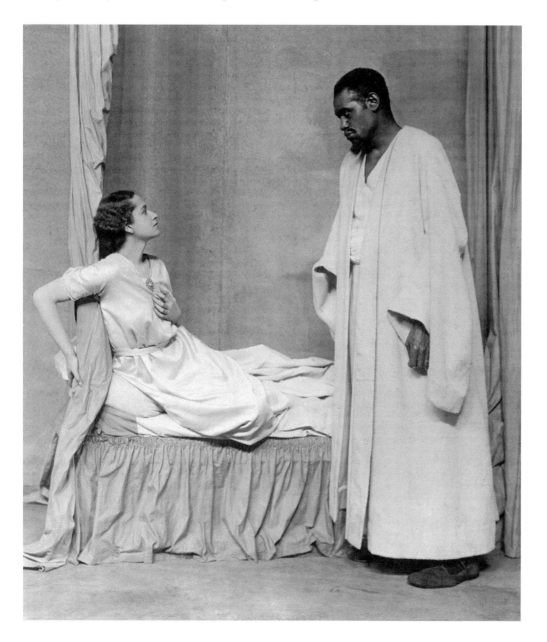

and even though a century had passed since Aldridge's emigration, Robeson too played Othello in London because he faced racism at home. He told the press in 1930: 'They certainly wouldn't stand in America for the kissing and for the scene in which I use Miss [Peggy] Ashcroft roughly ... The audience would get very rough: in fact might become very dangerous.' Robeson had become a star in London playing Joe in the musical *Show Boat* (1928): he was cast as a racial stereotype ('Tell me he's lazy, tell me he's slow ...') but stunned audiences with his majestic rendition of 'Ol' Man River', which he later turned into a protest anthem by adding the line 'I'll keep on fighting until I'm dying'. His Othello of 1930 was a West End success, but racist prejudices lived on in many reviews, while offstage, Peggy Ashcroft received threatening letters: miscegenation was still an obsession for some sections of the British public.

Robeson was aware of Aldridge's achievements and saw the continuity between his own work and that of his – by then almost forgotten – predecessor. He sought out and trained with Aldridge's daughter Amanda, and he celebrated Ira's memory with an exhibition at the Savoy Theatre. His politics, however, were far more vocal than Aldridge's: he used the new mass media to insist that the play was a challenge to the modern world. 'It is a tragedy of racial conflict,' he told transatlantic radio audiences. 'Othello in the Venice of that time was in practically the same position as a coloured man in America today.'

In 1937 Robeson rejected an offer to play the role again; instead he sang at the front in the Spanish Civil War. 'The Artist,' he said, 'must elect to fight for freedom or for slavery. I have made my choice.' But when he and his family returned to America he became convinced that *Othello* spoke to a racially divided nation at war. As he had predicted, commercial producers were nervous of this 'dangerous' play; nevertheless, Robeson's second *Othello* opened in New York in 1943 and ran for 296 performances. That is still the longest Shakespearean run in Broadway history. 'Robeson as Othello made my blood run cold,' wrote the young playwright Tennessee Williams, 'Christ, what majesty!' Robeson toured the play across America, but he avoided the South and refused to play in cities where, as in 1821, theatres were still segregated: 'If there are any seats for blacks, they are up in heaven somewhere.' '*Othello* was a weapon in racial relations,' he said later, 'showing that we could do things too.' FBI agents bugged his phone on the tour.

Every time Robeson revived *Othello*, its meaning evolved. In London in 1930, a young newcomer to Shakespeare, he explored insecurity. 'Here was a member of an alien race,' he said, 'in a precarious position ... facing a highly developed white civilization.' During World War II, Robeson – by then a global public figure himself – embodied Othello the General. 'We stand at the end of one period in human history and before the entrance of a new,' he said. 'Audiences from coast to coast found Shakespeare's *Othello* painfully immediate.' Paul Robeson's final Othello took another tack again, but for that there would be a very long wait.

OPPOSITE
Scene from *Othello* with Paul Robeson as Othello and Uta Hagen as Desdemona in the Theatre Guild production, Broadway, 1943–4

As a pioneering champion of civil rights and a suspected Communist, Robeson was hounded throughout the post-war McCarthy period. He was blacklisted in the United States and denied a passport to work abroad. As the best-known African American in the world, meanwhile, he won passionate support, and his Othello became an international symbol of resistance. In England, trade unions, politicians and eminent artists planned a production that would star Robeson, and they petitioned for his passport to be returned. Actors who would *not* campaign for Robeson's Othello included Donald Wolfit (on political grounds) and Laurence Olivier, who wrote, 'I am afraid that I don't feel inclined to make this gesture, either for Mr Robeson's sake or my own. ...There comes a time when one rather wants to have a bash oneself.'

Alone, Robeson worked ceaselessly on the play. His son described how he explored *Othello* in many languages so as to deepen his understanding of its poetry – French 'for its soft, almost caressing quality when Othello speaks about his love'; German for 'a special kind of harshness'; Russian for 'its extraordinary range of imagery' and 'subtle shadings of emotion'; and 'Yiddish for its light and sardonic humour and its bittersweet sadness'. 'I've worked on it,' he explained, 'and I feel I would give a better performance ... sprung from my political conviction that all people should be unified.'

In 1958 the travel ban was declared unconstitutional. Robeson's comeback concert at Carnegie Hall included – to cheers and whistles – 'the last speech of Othello'. Robeson made its significance clear to the audience:

> He [Othello] has killed Desdemona. From savage passion? No.
> Othello came from a culture as great as that of ancient Venice.
> He came from an Africa of equal stature, and he felt he was
> betrayed, his honor was betrayed, and his human dignity
> was betrayed.

In his concerts he changed the text: whereas Shakespeare's Othello 'loved not wisely, but too well', Paul Robeson's Othello 'loved *full* wisely': his love for Desdemona was his love of humanity. In 1959 at Stratford-upon-Avon, Robeson played Othello for the last time alongside the Iago of Sam Wanamaker, another victim of McCarthyism. Tony Richardson, the director of *Look Back in Anger*, surrounded Robeson with jazz drummers, spectacle and a young generation of actors – many of whom, like Vanessa Redgrave, regarded him as a legend. Ill after a decade of persecution, Robeson now stressed 'cultural' rather than simply racial differences as the core of this tragedy; in interviews he asked white English audiences to *identify with* Othello, comparing him to a lost British serviceman in Malaya. 'I am overwhelmed by the reception I have been given tonight,' he said after nine rapturous curtain-calls; 'It is the greatest moment of my life.' And just as he had addressed radio listeners in 1930, Robeson spoke to a mass television audience in 1959:

ABOVE
Paul Robeson as
Othello at the
RSC, 1959.

OPPOSITE
David Oyelowo as
Henry VI at the
RSC, 2006.

Shakespeare, the genius that he was, seemed to foreshadow and understand many of the problems that have since arisen in our world – perhaps were present then. Here is a part that has dignity for the Negro actor. Often we don't get those opportunities.

Yet Paul Robeson was the only non-white actor in the company, and opportunities for black actors to perform Shakespeare were still very rare.

In Robeson's Footsteps

During the 1960s, West Indian and South African actors played small parts at the RSC, and in the 1970s and 1980s British Shakespearean theatre slowly – step by step, inspirational 'first' by 'first' – began to reflect the growth of a multicultural society. In 1973 Oscar James (born in Trinidad) and Mona Hammond (from Jamaica) became the first black actors to play Macbeth and Lady Macbeth in Britain. The *Black Macbeth* at the Roundhouse, adapted by Peter Coe, made the tragedy both an 'exotic' picture of tribal superstition and a response to modern Africa's 'winds of change'. James and Hammond, who drew on their childhood memories of Caribbean legends and traditions in this production, each went on to co-found key black theatre companies – Temba and Talawa.

'Colourblind' or 'colour-neutral' casting, where an actor's ethnicity is overlooked, was slow to gain acceptance. In 1984 Josette Simon (born in Leicester) played Rosalind in *Love's Labour's Lost*, the first black woman to play a lead role at the RSC. Simon had graduated from playing smaller parts in the company, including a spirit in *The Tempest*, and she remembered the discussions that surrounded her casting as Rosalind:

> It caused a lot of head-scratching as to whether they should give me a lead role. Would the audience walk out, saying 'What's a black person doing in Elizabethan England?' That began something that followed my work for the next eight or nine years – newspapers printing articles commenting on whether I should be doing the role.

But at the same time as individual actors struggled to make their mark within established Shakespeare ensembles, new companies emerged with the agenda of encouraging diversity. Jatinder Verma founded the British Asian company Tara Arts in 1976 (its productions included *The Merchant of Venice*, *The Tempest* and *Macbeth*); then in 1985 Mona Hammond created Talawa with the director Yvonne Brewster. Doña Croll played the first black British Cleopatra in Brewster's 1991 production of *Antony and Cleopatra* (the role is still played almost exclusively by white actors today, despite Cleopatra's non-European heritage). Three years later, Ben Thomas scored another first when he played King Lear for Talawa, a role which had not been played by a black actor in Britain since Ira Aldridge.

From the turn of the new millennium onwards, key performances by black actors emerged more frequently. In the year 2000 Adrian Lester played Hamlet for Peter Brook and David Oyelowo became the first black British actor to play one of Shakespeare's English kings, Henry VI, at the RSC. There had been complaints in the 1980s when Hugh Quarshie played Banquo – an ancestor of Elizabeth II – in *Macbeth*, so when the RSC cast Oyelowo it was a press story. He responded by saying:

> Theatre by its very nature is make-believe. If I'm on stage and I say I'm in tears, you believe me. If I say I've got an army of 30,000 offstage, you believe me. I don't know why if I suddenly say that I'm the King of England that is so much more controversial.

If theatre is make-believe, television and film impose more 'realistic' expectations on to our perception of Shakespeare. In 1995 Josette Simon played Hotspur's wife Kate on television in a colourblind period production of *Henry IV*. In contrast, Parminder Nagra's Viola in a present-day *Twelfth Night* for Channel 4 in 2003 was culturally specific: she and her brother were Asian refugees in a version of modern London. All were accepted, but the old charges of 'anachronism' resurfaced when the BBC's high-profile history cycle *The Hollow Crown* cast Paterson Joseph as the Duke of York in *Henry V* (2012). It was therefore profoundly significant when, despite the controversy, Sophie Okonedo was chosen to play Queen Margaret in *The Hollow Crown*'s second series, to be broadcast in 2016. Fighting her way through four plays – from *Henry VI* to *Richard III* – Margaret is arguably the largest and most dominant role in Shakespeare.

Through individual commitment and institutional change, Shakespeare's plays have been inspirational for new communities and new generations finding a voice. What is clear from all these stories is that role models matter. Just as Robeson's work with Amanda Aldridge in the 1930s brought her father's achievements alive again, so Adrian Lester's performance as Aldridge in Lolita Chakrabarti's play *Red Velvet* (2012) brought his name to a new generation. The play was directed by Indhu Rubasingham, who spoke for many when she said: 'It shocked me that I'd never heard of Ira Aldridge.' Through the success of the play at the Tricycle Theatre, the struggles Aldridge faced and the contribution he made to Shakespearean acting were once again in the spotlight.

THEATRE ROYAL, COVENT-GARDEN.

This Evening, THURSDAY, January 25, 1838,
Will be performed the Tragedy of

KING LEAR.
FROM THE TEXT OF
SHAKSPEARE.

King Lear, ... Mr. MACREADY,
King of France, Mr. HOWE, Duke of Burgundy, Mr. BENDER,
Duke of Albany, Mr. DIDDEAR, Duke of Cornwall, Mr. SERLE,
Earl of Kent, Mr. BARTLEY, Earl of Glo'ster, Mr. G. BENNETT,
Edgar, Mr. ELTON, Edmund, Mr. ANDERSON,
Locrine, Mr. ROBERTS, Curan, Mr. PRITCHARD, Physician, Mr. YARNOLD,
Oswald, (the Steward,) Mr. VINING, Herald, Mr. HOLMES,
Old Man, Mr. AYLIFFE, Officer, Mr. COLLETT,
The Fool, Miss P. HORTON.

Lords—Messrs. Partridge, Boulanger, Morgan, Jenkins, Jackson, Wallis, &c.
Knights—Messrs. C.J. Smith, Herbert, Willis, Becket, Paulo, Thorne, Kirke, Brady, &c.
Duke of Cornwall's Attendants—Messrs. Payne, Butler, Gough, Jones.

Goneril, Mrs. W. CLIFFORD,
Regan, Mrs. WARNER, (late Miss HUDDART,)
Cordelia, Miss HELEN FAUCIT,
Ladies—Mesdames Corder, Payne, Mew, Vallanduke, Hunt, Mathews, &c.

To conclude with (Twenty-Seventh Time) an entirely new, TRAGICAL—COMICAL—HISTORICAL—PASTORAL "GRAND CHRISTMAS PANTOMINE, called

HARLEQUIN
AND
PEEPING TOM OF COVENTRY:
OR,
The Ladye Godiva and The Witch of Warwick.

Principal Characters and Order of the Scenery:
Fields of Fungi, in the Osier Island, and view of the Ancient City of Coventry, by Moonlight. Mother Holly, (the Witch of Warwick) Mr. YARNOLD, Edith, (the Mayor's Daughter, called the Rose of Coventry) Miss FAIRBROTHER, Nicolas Nimbletongue, (the Parish Orator) Mr. COLLET.——High Street, Coventry, in the year 1052, and Workshop of Tom the Cooper. Peeping Tom, (the Cooper of Coventry, in love with Edith) Mr. C.J. SMITH, Daggobert Donkeybrain, (the Mayor of Coventry) Mr. F. CLARKE, Sheriffs, Messrs. Thorne and Sharpe. Beadle, Mr. Paulo.——Ignorant Impatience of Taxation, and the awful ceremony of attempting to read the Riot Act.——Berkhamstead Castle, the domains of Leofric, Earl of Mercia. Return of the Earl from the Wars, attended by his Porcupine Guard, and Grand Procession. Leofric, (Sovereign Earl of Mercia, and Baron of Berkhamstead) Mr. W.H. PAYNE. The fair Godiva, (his lovely wife) Mademoiselle FREDERICA FATTY-MA FENTONI, Withreed Bugleblast, (warder of Berkhamstead Castle) Mr. BANNISTER, Wildwolf Quartercoat, (the Herald) Mr. BENDER.——Citizens of Coventry relieved by the imposition of a Window Tax.——The Silver Saloon leading to the Sleeping Chamber of Godiva.——The Old Cross and Market Place of Coventry, from which is seen the Steeple of St. Michael's Church, Herbert Bellenclapper, the Crier, (Proclamation, with bell obligato) Mr. PAUL BEDFORD.——Inside of Tom's House.——Window-bolt and Thunder-bolt.——The Transformation.——Harlequin, Mr. C.J. SMITH, Columbine, Miss FAIRBROTHER, Pantaloon, Mr. F. CLARKE, Clown, Mr. JEFFERINI.——Lodgings for Invalids in a quiet Neighbourhood.——Pursuit—getting into hot water—send for the Doctor—"throw physic to the dogs"—repose necessary—try again—confusion, worse confounded.——The Golden Gridiron.——Copper-plate Printers' and Office of the Mirror of Parliament.——Out of the frying-pan into the fire—fancy snuffs—bills to be presented—whigs and tories—a well known view of China—printers' devils nearly allied to the soot-bag.——World Inn, Booking-office of the Warwickshire Hunt, and station of the London Parcels Delivery Company.——Old King's Head on the road to Fulham.——Inn yard and Optician's shop.——"Reform your Tailors' bills."——How far that little candle throws its beams.

THE
DIORAMA
BY
STANFIELD,

Consisting of SCENES AT HOME AND ABROAD; comprising a series of views in the North of Italy, Savoy, the Alps, Germany, through French Flanders to the Sea,—commencing at MAZORBO and TREVISANO, in the Gulph of Venice.——LECCO and the ADDA MILANESE.——VALLEY of AOSTA, at Villeneuve, and Summit of the COL DE BON-HOMME by Moonlight, Piedmont.——HUY on the MEUSE.——The HUNDSRUCK MOUNTAINS and CHATEAU ELZ.——BRITISH CHANNEL Temple Bar.—Return of an Old Friend, and general reconciliation.—THE BANQUET AT GUILDHALL, And View of the Procession near St. Paul's.

BOXES—5s. Second Price—2s. 6d. PIT—2s. 6d. Second Price—1s. 6d.
LOWER GALLERY—1s 6d. Second Price 1s. UPPER GALLERY—1s. Second Price—6d.

PEEPING TOM OF COVENTRY;
OR,
The Ladye Godiva, and the Witch of Warwick, will be repeated EVERY EVENING until further Notice.

SHAKSPEARE'S HISTORICAL TRAGEDY OF
MACBETH
Will be repeated EVERY MONDAY NIGHT until further Notice.

AMILIE; or THE LOVE TEST,
Will be played twice a week, till further notice.

To-morrow, AMILIE; or, THE LOVE TEST, with PEEPING TOM OF COVENTRY.
On Saturday, will be revived, Mrs. Centlivre's Comedy of The

WONDER! A WOMAN KEEPS A SECRET.
Don Pedro, Mr. Strickland, (his first appearance at this Theatre) Don Lopez, Mr. Meadows, Don Felix, Mr. Macready, Col. Briton, Mr. Vining, Frederick, Mr. Diddear, Gibby, Mr. Bartley, Lissardo, Mr. W.J. Hammond, Alguazil, Mr. Bedford, Donna Violante, Miss Helen Faucit. Donna Isabella, Miss Ellen Clifford, Flora, Mrs. Glover, (her first appearance here this Season) Inis, Mrs. Humby, (her first appearance here these four years), With PEEPING TOM OF COVENTRY.

On Monday, Shakspeare's Historical Tragedy of MACBETH.
Duncan, Mr. Waldron, Malcolm, Mr. Anderson, Macbeth, Mr. Macready, Banquo, Mr. Elton, Macduff, Mr. Phelps, Rosse, Mr. Diddear, Hecate, Mr. Leffler, First Witch, Mr. G. Bennett, Second Witch, Mr. Meadows, Third Witch, Mr. W.H. Payne, Lady Macbeth, Mrs. Warner, (late Miss Huddart,) Spirits and Witches, Mr. Wilson, Mr. Manvers, Mr. Bedford, Mr. Stretton, Miss Shirreff, Miss Taylor, Miss P. Horton, Mrs. Serle, Mrs. East, Miss Garrick, &c. &c.
With PEEPING TOM OF COVENTRY.

On Tuesday, Jan 30th, THERE WILL BE NO PERFORMANCE.

A NEW PLAY, IN FIVE ACTS,
Is in preparation, and will be speedily produced.
The Principal Characters by Mr. ELTON, Mr. MEADOWS, Mr. BARTLEY, Mr. WALDRON, Mr. DIDDEAR, Mr. HOWE Mr. PRITCHARD, Mr. YARNOLD, Mr. ROBERTS, Mr. MACREADY, Mrs. GLOVER, Miss HELEN FAUCIT, Mrs. CLIFFORD

A NEW COMIC OPERA,
CALLED
THE BLACK DOMINO,
Adapted from LE DOMINO NOIR by Scribe, the Music by Auber,
Will be brought forward with all possible expedition.

A NEW FARCE,
IN WHICH
Mr. POWER, Mr. BARTLEY and Mrs. GLOVER
will appear, is in preparation.

Vivat Regina. No Money returned. W. S. JOHNSON, "Nassau Press," 60, Nassau Street, Soho

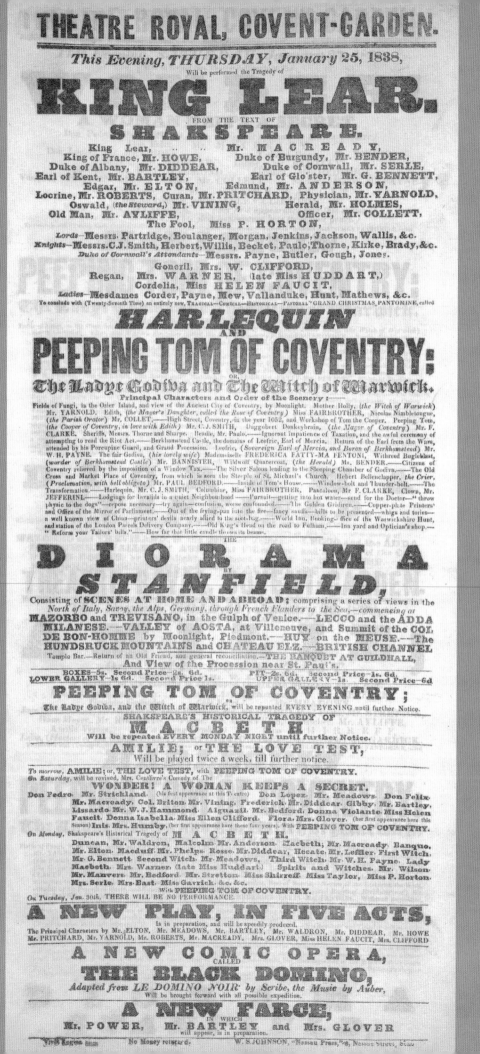

Chapter 7

'He is return'd': The Revision and Restoration of *King Lear*

Lucy Munro

On 25 January 1838, London playbills advertised a forthcoming performance by William Charles Macready in *The Tragedy of King Lear*. The revival was, at first glance, unremarkable. The leading Shakespearean actor of his day, Macready had already played Lear in a clutch of well-received performances in 1834. Yet sharp-eyed readers may have noticed something odd about the playbill: not only did it declare (apparently superfluously, to modern eyes) that the play was 'FROM THE TEXT OF SHAKSPEARE', but its cast included 'The Fool, Miss P. HORTON'. The Fool? This was a novelty. As early as the Restoration, audiences had begun to demand greater plausibility, sentiment and decorum in tragedy, and Shakespeare's plays were regularly adapted to suit their tastes. *King Lear* began to show its age, and in 1681 Nahum Tate took radical action. Describing the play as 'a Heap of Jewels, unstrung and unpolisht', he refurbished its narrative and characters: Lear's daughter Cordelia and Gloucester's son Edgar, the two faithful children, fell in love; Lear was allowed to retire happily at the end of Act 5; and Lear's sardonic companion, the Fool, disappeared entirely.

While Tate's *King Lear* is an example of a standard process of revision, it is also among the most successful adaptations ever made: it dominated the stage for at least 150 years. Even when Tate's alterations themselves fell victim to changing tastes, they were only gradually rolled back. David Garrick reintroduced selected lines from Shakespeare's play in performances of *King Lear* between 1756 and 1776; George Colman removed the Cordelia-Edgar affair in his 1768 adaptation but kept the happy ending; and Edmund Kean

OPPOSITE
Shakespeare's text returned to the stage: playbill for *King Lear* at the Theatre Royal, Covent Garden, 25 January 1838.
British Library Playbills 124a

temporarily restored Shakespeare's final scene in 1823. Yet elements of Tate persisted – notably some of his reordering of key scenes – and the Fool still remained offstage. Macready's 1838 production therefore made a decisive step towards restoring a *King Lear* that Jacobean audiences would have recognised, and its impact tells us a great deal about expectations of Shakespeare in performance in the early to mid-nineteenth century.

The Fool in King Lear

Macready's own 1834 production had restored much of the fabric of Shakespeare's text, but it did not take the final step of reinstating the Fool. Writing in the *New Monthly Magazine*, John Forster hailed Macready's restoration of 'the unalloyed language and severe passion of Shakspeare' but accused him of denying spectators that 'which would have touched our hearts most nearly, and moved most sensibly our pity'. Exclaiming 'Ah! Mr. Macready, why did you omit the Fool?', Forster made a case over five closely argued pages for the character's dramatic and theatrical impact.

Macready listened, and his plan to reintroduce the Fool was the subject of gossip in early 1838. Hostile towards Macready and a partisan supporter of his rival, Kean's son Charles, *Figaro in London* printed a cruel but vivid sketch of the 'great tragedian' in his preparations:

> Macready is dashing and splashing about in all directions, with a desperation that is pitiable. … When we heard the *Fool* was to be played in 'King Lear', we confess we did not think it a novelty, as Macready himself has already played the fool in 'King Lear' on more than one occasion. It appears, however, that he thinks *one fool* not enough in the play, and he has consequently fished up another from the text of Shakspeare.

Macready agonised about the production, which was fraught with textual and other problems. Helen Faucit initially refused to play Cordelia, but eventually consented 'very ungraciously' to act the role; with rehearsals under way, Macready was still complaining to his journal about her 'discontented tone'. The Fool also troubled him. He originally cast Drinkwater Meadows, an actor then in his thirties who had played Shakespearean roles such as Launcelot Gobbo in *The Merchant of Venice* and Shallow in *The Merry Wives of Windsor*, but was unhappy with the effect, writing on 4 January, after the first rehearsal:

> My opinion of the introduction of the Fool is that, like many such terrible contrasts in poetry and painting, in acting representation it will fail of effect; it will either weary and annoy or distract the spectator. I have no hope of it, and think that at the last we shall be obliged to dispense with it.

Priscillia Horton as Ariel in *The Tempest*, painted by Daniel Maclise, 1838.

The following day, he discussed the problem with John Wilmott, his prompter and, later, stage director, and George Bartley, the actor playing Kent:

> … mentioning my apprehension that with Meadows, we should be obliged to omit the part, I described the sort of fragile, hectic, beautiful-faced, half-idiot-looking boy that it should be, and stated my belief that it never could be acted. Bartley observed that a woman should play it. I caught at the idea, and instantly exclaimed: 'Miss P. Horton is the very person.' I was delighted at the thought.

Priscilla Horton, then aged 20, had joined Macready's company in 1837, playing Mopsa in *The Winter's Tale* and the Boy in *Henry V*; later in 1838 she was to play Ariel in *The Tempest*, a role in which she was painted by Daniel Maclise. With Horton on board, the production received its first performance before a packed house on 25 January. Later that evening, Macready wrote: 'I scarcely know how I acted the part. I did not satisfy myself. We shall see the papers to-morrow, which I suppose will set us right on the question. Was occasionally pretty good, but I was not what I wished to have been.' He was perhaps his own harshest critic: the papers, when they appeared, were almost universally positive about Macready's performance, the reintroduction of the Fool and the sets and costumes, which drew on images of ancient Britain.

Perhaps the most enthusiastic response was – unsurprisingly – Forster's. Writing in the *Examiner*, he claimed that Macready had 'restored to the stage Shakspeare's true *Lear*, banished from it, by impudent ignorance … we shall be glad to hear of the actor foolhardy enough to attempt another restoration of the text of Tate!' He also noted the impact of particular lines, such as: 'And my poor fool is hanged' (Act 5, scene 3), describing:

> the sublime pathos of the close, when *Lear*, bending over the dead body of all he had left to love upon the earth, connects her with the memory of that other gentle, faithful, and loving being who had passed from his side – unites, in that moment of final agony, the two hearts that had been broken in his service.

While other reviewers could not match Forster's rapture, they generally approved of both Macready's decision to include the Fool and Horton's performance. *The Times* declared that the role was 'very cleverly acted with a happy mixture of archness and silliness', while the *Theatrical Observer* thought that Horton 'executed her difficult task with great tact and judgment, and sang her snatches of songs most sweetly'. Some critics voiced objections, however. The *Spectator* had a completely different conception of the character from Macready, arguing that Horton's was 'a complete, but we conceive a mistaken character: she gave us an arch, simple-witted, sportive boy, rather than the shrewd, searching Fool of King Lear'. The *Morning Post*, in contrast, still thought the character impossible to stage with any tragic decorum:

> we do not think that former managers were injudicious in the omission of the character … the audiences of a theatre have not a nice apprehension of the deep yet delicate lights and shadows of feeling which are brought out in such a character as *Lear's Fool*, and it does seem upon the stage rather an inharmonious appendage to the thrilling incidents and solemn grandeur of the play.

Reviewers' responses to the play were clearly influenced by their own preconceptions about both the play and the extent to which it might be staged convincingly.

Nonetheless, the Fool was here to stay. In the next major revival, at Sadler's Wells in 1845, Samuel Phelps cast Henry Scharf – a comic actor who also played Touchstone and Feste – and was attacked by some reviewers for offering the 'shrewd, searching Fool' described by The *Spectator* in 1838. By the 1850s, even burlesque versions of *King Lear* were registering the change. Charles James Collins and Joseph Halford's *King Queer and his Daughters Three*, staged at the Strand Theatre at Easter 1855, starred Rebecca Isaacs as a

Cordelia who disguises herself as the Fool, and Frederick Marchant's 'Musical Extravaganza' *Kynge Lear and Hys Faytheful Foole*, performed at Samuel Lane's New Britannia Theatre in Hoxton, East London, in June 1860, featured Ruth Edwin as the Fool.

     Although some theatre historians have hailed the casting of Scharf as the 'true' restoration of the character, the Fool continues to be one of the few male roles in Shakespeare that are regularly played by a woman. In addition, Macready's conception of the Fool as – in his words – a 'fragile, hectic, beautiful-faced, half-idiot-looking boy' has also shaped some of the most important adaptations of *King Lear*. Grigori Kozintsev's Russian-language film, *Korol Lir* (1971) creates an impression almost of symbiosis between Jüri Järvet's physically vulnerable, bird-like Lear and Oleg Dal's shaven-headed Fool; they first appear together, heralded by the sound of the Fool's bells, and the Fool does not disappear in Act 3, but returns in the heat of battle

Oleg Dal as the Fool in Grigori Kozintsev's Russian-language film *Korol Lir* (1971).

in Act 5 to play his pipe for the convalescent Lear. At the end of the film, the bodies of Lear and his daughters are carried away slowly; the procession moves past the sobbing Fool, a soldier kicking him out of the way. Producing his pipe, the Fool begins to play, whereupon Kozintsev cuts first to the peasants who are already trying to put things back in order, putting out fires and collecting debris, and then to Edgar. He looks at the camera and moves towards it, apparently on the point of delivering the play's last speech, but eventually he simply blinks and moves out of the frame, suggesting Kozintsev's reluctance to endorse even the hollow consolation of Shakespeare's final lines. Akira Kurosawa's *Ran* (1985) gives the jester Kyoami one of the film's longest speeches, spoken over the body of his master, Hidetora: 'Are there no gods? … If you exist, hear me! You are mischievous and cruel! Are you so bored up there you must crush us like ants?' Recalling Gloucester's 'As flies to wanton boys are we to th' gods; / They kill us for their sport' (Act 4, scene 1), the nihilism of this speech invokes both the film's title, which translates as 'madness' or 'chaos', and the word Kurosawa places at the end of his published screenplay: 'San!' – 'disaster' or 'wretchedness'. When the Fool not only re-enters the play but also survives his master, the tragedy becomes bleaker yet.

Macready's Druid Circles

Posterity has generally focused on the textual originality of Macready's production, but contemporaries also hailed his innovative sets and costumes. James Barry's painting *King Lear Weeping over the Dead Body of Cordelia* (1786–8) had introduced ancient Britain into the play's visual tradition: his giant, almost monolithic Lear, clutching his head in one hand and the body of Cordelia in the other, looms in front of a monument resembling Stonehenge, itself positioned halfway up a lofty mountain. Half a century later, Macready created his own primitive past with mostly new scenery and carefully designed special effects. *John Bull* described the impact in vivid terms:

> The castles are heavy, sombre, solid; their halls adorned with trophies of the chase and instruments of war; druid circles rise in spectral loneliness on the heath; and the 'dreadful pother' of the elements is kept up with a verisimilitude which beggars all that we have hitherto seen attempted. Forked lightnings, now vividly illumine the broad horizons, now faintly coruscating in small and serpent folds, play in the distance; the sheeted element sweeps over the foreground, and then leaves it in pitchy darkness; and wind and rain howl and rush in 'tyranny of the open night'.

A mid-nineteenth-century engraving of Macready and Faucit represents the mountains, rocks, trees and tents of the final scene; like Barry's painting, it portrays a Lear dwarfing his Cordelia as

Macready gestures to the heavens, his robe with ermine trim signifying the deposed king's royal status. Macready has the piercing eyes and distinctive features noted by contemporaries. The actor-manager John Coleman, who first met Macready in the mid-1840s, offers an intense description of his physical presence:

> His features appeared irregular and corrugated. He had a spacious brow and delicately pencilled eyebrows, but the nose beneath was of a most composite order – a mixture of Grecian, Milesian, and snub, with no power of dilation in the nostrils. His eyes were dull and lustreless by day, but at night, as I afterwards discovered, they were orbs of fire. His mouth though small, was well cut and decided; the lower jaw, which was firm and massive, was very much underhung. His closely shorn and blue-black beard imparted a grim and saturnine cast to his features.

The ermine robe also appears in another image of the production, a sketch by George Scharf, in which Kent and the Fool anxiously try to prevent Lear from removing it; behind them Edward Elton's Edgar gestures towards the king. Edgar wears a loose tunic and holds a staff, costume conventions that had survived from the eighteenth century,

Engraving of James Barry's 1786–8 painting *King Lear Weeping over the Dead Body of Cordelia*. The backdrop and composition of the painting may have influenced Macready's staging of the scene.
British Library 85/Tab.599.c

while the Fool reflects Macready's conception of a childishly naïve figure; Horton wears a stylised coxcomb over her long hair, and her tunic has a frieze of animals around the sleeves and hem.

In his detailed historical setting, Macready set a pattern for later productions. In 1858, his old bête noire, Charles Kean, by that time noted for his meticulous re-creations of the periods in which Shakespeare's narratives were set, had problems with the lack of detailed evidence about life in ancient Britain, and therefore decided to set the play in the year 800. Henry Irving's 1892 production, shaped in part by the artist Ford Madox Brown, portrayed a period 'shortly after the departure of the Romans, when the Britons would naturally inhabit the houses left vacant', the *Glasgow Herald* commenting that purely ancient British costumes 'would probably be a somewhat trying experience to Lyceum audiences'. Since the mid-twentieth century, productions and adaptations of *King Lear* have often rejected historical realism, instead mingling various periods to create something timeless or temporally hybrid, or finding alternative contexts for the narrative: feudal Japan in *Ran*; the American Midwest in Jane Smiley's 1991 novel *A Thousand Acres*. Nonetheless, the settings chosen for *King Lear* continue to have meaning, and to affect the ways in which the narrative is received.

Rewriting Shakespeare; Shakespeare Rewriting

For his contemporaries, Macready's 1838 *King Lear* was a point of fulfilment, nothing less than the restoration to the stage of Shakespeare's play. Yet its status is less clear-cut than its reception might suggest. Earlier productions had also been hailed as restoring the play 'as Shakespeare wrote it', but with hindsight each looks like only a partial reconstruction. Moreover, Macready's was not wholly 'the text of Shakespeare', as some reviewers claimed. The indecorum of the Fool was tolerated, and Shakespeare's tragic ending retained, but other moments of violence and incongruity were not: following late eighteenth- and early nineteenth-century practice, the blinding of Gloucester – dubbed 'so unpleasing a circumstance' by the dramatist George Colman – was removed, along with the moment in Act 4 at which Edgar makes Gloucester think that he has fallen from the cliff at Dover. Even as he restored Shakespeare's text, therefore, Macready continued to embody a tradition of adapting *King Lear* to contemporary tastes and sensibilities.

More seriously, perhaps, the very idea of an 'original' *King Lear* becomes increasingly troubled the more closely we look at Shakespeare's play. *Lear* derives from two different sources: the sixteenth-century historian Raphael Holinshed's *Chronicles* and an anonymous play, *The True Chronicle History of King Leir and His Three Daughters*, probably first performed in the late 1580s. And Shakespeare's play itself survives in not one but two early authoritative texts. The first, in cheap, small-format quarto, was published in 1608 as *M. VVilliam Shake-speare, his True Chronicle History of the Life and Death of King Lear, and his Three Daughters*;

THE True Chronicle Hi-ftory of King LEIR, and his three daughters, Gonorill, Ragan, and Cordella.

As it hath bene diuers and sundry times lately acted.

LONDON,
Printed by Simon Stafford for Iohn Wright, and are to bee fold at his fhop at Chriftes Church dore, next Newgate-Market. 1605.

ABOVE
The anonymous precursor to Shakespeare's *Lear*: *The True Chronicle History of King Leir and His Three Ddaughters, Gonorill, Ragan, and Cordella* (1605).
British Library C.34.L.11

OPPOSITE
William Charles Macready as Lear and Helen Faucit as Cordelia, pictured in the final scene of the play.
British Library 2300.h.5

MR MACREADY as KING LEAR.

"O, thou wilt come no more, never, never, never, never."

ACT 5. SCENE 3.

JOHN TALLIS & COMPANY LONDON & NEW YORK

the second appeared in the 1623 First Folio. There are numerous changes in the First Folio text: some scenes disappear, such as Lear imagining putting his daughters on trial, and the report of Cordelia's response to her father's hardship; lines are reassigned, such as the final speech of the play, now given to Edgar rather than Albany; and numerous lines are added or revised. For much of the play's history, editors treated the quarto and First Folio texts as two imperfect versions of a lost original play, and generally conflated them to produce one longer, hybrid text. Recent scholars have argued, in contrast, that the folio text is a deliberate revision of the quarto, possibly undertaken after Shakespeare's death by one of his successors, but more probably his own.

Although Tate's revisions were billed as 'alterations', his version of *King Lear*, with its happy ending and romance plot, also restored an earlier, pre-Shakespearean version of the narrative: *The True Chronicle History of King Leir and His Three Daughters* has a happy ending, a tragicomic narrative in which various trials and hardships are overcome, and a more extended treatment of the relationship between Cordelia and her husband. In the preface to his adaptation, Tate identifies some of the factors that made the tragedy incompatible with Restoration tastes and continued to trouble later actors, writers and spectators. He argues that introducing the Cordelia–Edgar relationship makes Cordelia's resistance to her father and Edgar's disguise plausible, while also heightening the emotional impact or 'Distress', as he terms it. The ending troubles Tate on moral and aesthetic grounds, and he prefers to make his story 'conclude in a Success to the innocent distrest Persons' – i.e. end happily for Edgar and Cordelia: 'Otherwise I must have incumbred the Stage with dead Bodies, which Conduct makes many Tragedies conclude with unseasonable Jests'. Finally, *Lear*'s outmoded language poses problems – should Tate imitate the style of the old play, or risk incongruity by inserting modern idioms into it? These issues – genre, emotional impact, characterisation and language – have recurred throughout the history of *King Lear* in its many different versions. The play's progress has not been a linear process of steady revision or a circular movement from original to revision and back to original. Instead, writers, theatre-makers, filmmakers and artists have all found different ways of recasting its narrative. Even though it rejected most of Tate's innovations, Macready's 1838 *Lear* did not stand apart from this process, but was embedded in it.

Rewriting Tragedy

The story of Lear and his daughters has appeared in a variety of forms. In Holinshed's *Chronicles*, the husbands of Gonorilla and Regan dethrone Leir, only to be defeated in battle by Cordeilla and her husband, the Prince of Gallia; Leir is restored and reigns for another two years, to be succeeded after his death by Cordeilla. Adapting this narrative in the 1580s, *King Leir* ends with Leir's

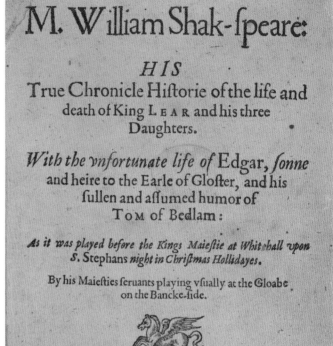

The first quarto edition of Shakespeare's *King Lear* (1608).
British Library C.34.k.18

restoration. However, Holinshed continues – as chronicles must – and describes the reign of Cordeilla, her deposition at the hands of her nephews, who 'disdeig[n] to be vnder the gouernement of a woman', and her suicide in prison. If Shakespeare read his Holinshed beyond the end of the story dramatised in *King Leir*, he would have found a narative of renewed violence and disintegration that may have influenced his own, tragic conception of the story.

Nonetheless, Shakespeare may himself have been uncertain about the effect of his tragedy on spectators. In addition to reassigning the final lines of the play from Albany to Edgar, the First Folio version of *King Lear* also reconceives the moment of Lear's death. In the quarto, Lear's final words are 'Break, heart, I prithee break' (Scene 24). The Folio reassigns these lines to Kent, and gives Lear two new lines, 'Do you see this? Look on her. Look, her lips. / Look there, look there', with a new stage direction indicating that he dies at this moment (Act 5, scene 3). In the quarto, Lear dies broken-hearted; in the folio, he appears to see something – perhaps a glimmer of life – on Cordelia's lips.

This was the version restored to the stage in the nineteenth century by Edmund Kean and, later Macready, and reviewers commented on its capacity to move spectators to tears. According to the *European Magazine and London Review*, 'many a tearful eye bore testimony to the power with which [Kean] represented the agonies of a broken heart', while the *Herald* spotted 'many a handkerchief in requisition amongst the crowded auditory in the galleries' at Macready's 1838 revival. But spectators had been weeping along with Lear since the days of David Garrick; indeed, a much-repeated epigram about the relative successes of Garrick and Spranger Barry – both of whom performed Tate's ending – reads:

> The town has found out diff'rent Ways
>   To Praise the diff'rent Lears;
> To Barry they give loud Huzzas,
>   To Garrick only Tears.

The epigram suggests two distinct ways in which the play might work on spectators, either arousing admiration for the technical virtuosity of the performer or provoking a more purely emotional response.

Garrick seems to have tinkered with the play regularly between 1756, when his revival was billed as 'With RESTORATIONS from SHAKESPEAR', and his retirement in 1776. Two snapshots of his *King Lear* survive: a promptbook based on a 1756 edition of Tate's *Lear*, purchased by the British Library at Sotheby's in 1979, with annotations in Garrick's hand; and the text printed in *Bell's Edition of Shakespeare's Plays*, which claims to be taken from the Drury Lane promptbook. Garrick's impact was perhaps strongest in the Act 1 speech in which Lear curses Goneril – well into the nineteenth century, theatre critics would watch for 'the curse' and its effect on spectators – and he sought to repeat its success by inserting additional, Shakespearean lines into the emotionally charged

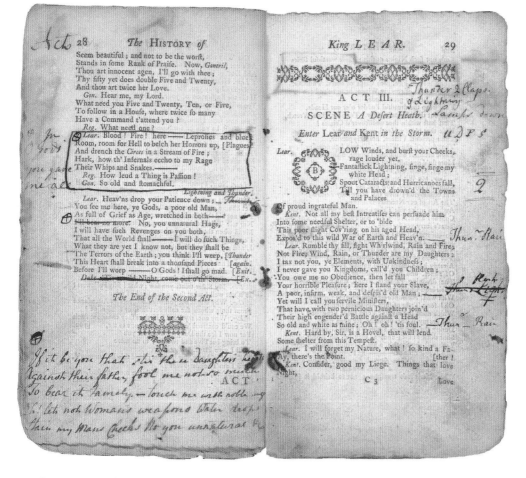

confrontation with Goneril and Regan in Act 2. After both daughters
refuse to support his retinue, and Regan declares 'My Sister treats
you fair', Garrick adds in the margin:

> Lear. O heavens I gave you all. Reg. And in good time you gave
> it. Thunder Lear. Made you my Guardians, my repositories;
> what must I come to you with five & twenty, Regan said you
> so. Reg. Even so.

On the following page he adds further lines from Shakespeare:

> If it be you that stir these daughters' hearts
> Against their father, fool me not so much
> To bear it tamely – touch me with noble anger.
> Oh! let not woman's weapons waterdrops
> Stain my man's cheeks.

Garrick was strongly criticised, and equally strongly defended, for
crying at the end of the curse in Act 1; here, he seems to have sought
a similar effect.

King Lear has also moved spectators in less expected ways.
In spring 1940, the Old Vic Theatre in London reopened with a
production of *King Lear* starring John Gielgud and directed by
Lewis Casson with substantial assistance from the renowned

Shakespearean actor and director Harley Granville Barker. Gielgud commented in a letter to his father, 'Nothing but such a master as Barker and a mighty work like *Lear* could have kept one so concentrated these ten days with such a holocaust going on around us. One must be very grateful for such work at a time like this.' Although the production was well received, Gielgud appears to have had doubts about the value of theatrical performance during wartime, and to have articulated them in comments during his curtain-call after at least one performance. Among his papers is a letter from Irene Blackman of West Humble, Surrey, whose sons, then aged 20 and 21, were on active service. Blackman saw *Lear* on 21 May and was moved to write to Gielgud the next day, telling him:

> I don't think you can possibly know what an enormous help a play as perfect as last night's can be, or you would not have any doubts such as you expressed then. Last night was like a gift from the gods to me – to get away even for a little from present troubles, not to forget but to take fresh heart of courage from great words grandly spoken, & to realise that after all we individually are not important – that is a far better tonic than any doctor can prescribe & I do thank you most wholeheartedly for giving it to us so lavishly. … Thank you more than I can say for an unforgettable experience that will give me heart & courage to face whatever the future may hold both for me & for my two sons in the services. I only wish they could have been with me last night.

Horribly enough, Blackman's older son, Ralph, was to be killed when his ship, the *Thomas Connolly*, went down on 17 December 1940; something of the tone of her letter to Gielgud is captured, however, in a notice published in *The Times* on 18 December 1944: 'In happy and constant memory of our darling son … and of those of his shipmates who went with him. "Say not good night, but in some brighter clime / Bid me good memory"'. The last lines quote from Anna Laetitia Barbauld's poem 'Life'.

Rewriting Lear's Daughters

In 1838, reviewers were keen to praise Macready for rejecting Tate's story of Cordelia and Edgar. However, from Holinshed's *Chronicles* to Smiley's *A Thousand Acres* and beyond, the characterisation of Lear's daughters has consistently been revised and reinterpreted. Even representations of Cordelia, the 'good' daughter, have been unstable. In Holinshed, she appears in one illustration as 'Cordeilla Queene', a muscular crowned figure, grasping her sceptre like a weapon. When she is imprisoned by her nephews and kills herself, Holinshed describes her as 'a woman of a manly courage', and this moment is represented in a second illustration: richly dressed, and seated on the end of a lavishly decorated bed, Cordeilla guides a dagger into her breast.

body was buried at Leycester in a channel of the Riuer of Soze beneat
Cordeilla Queene.

10

In contrast to Holinshed's resolute and martial Cordeilla, *King Leir* presents Cordella as wholly innocent and Gonorill and Ragan as purely, gleefully malignant. Tate follows suit: because his Cordelia is in love with Edgar, she cannot marry the King of France and return with an army to aid her father, and he instead stresses her sexuality and vulnerability. In one of his interpolated scenes, Cordelia and her maid, Arante, are attacked by ruffians sent by Edmund. Cordelia cries 'Help, Murder, help! Gods! some kind Thunderbolt / To strike me Dead', but instead Edgar appears with a quarterstaff, with which he drives the 'Bloud-hounds' offstage. The popularity of this scene is reflected in Peter van Bleeck's painting *Mrs. Cibber in the Character of Cordelia*. Susanna Cibber's Cordelia – a role that she regularly played opposite the Lears of Garrick and James Quin in the 1740s and -50s – is accompanied by Arante, with the ruffians cowering to the left as Edgar emerges, staff in hand, on the right.

Shakespeare's own Cordelia is intriguingly ambivalent, a quality intensified by changes in the First Folio. In the very first scene, the revised text stresses her resistance to Lear by supplementing a crucial moment in the exchange between them. After Cordelia says that she can say 'Nothing my Lord' in response to Lear's demand that she profess her love for him to earn a share of his kingdom, the Folio adds two lines: Lear asks 'Nothing?', to which Cordelia replies 'Nothing'. Lear's response, 'Nothing will come of nothing', thus leads to a repetition of the word 'nothing' five times in four lines. Simultaneously, the sentimental description

Peter Van Bleeck Pinxt 1755.

Mrs Cibber in the Character of Cordelia.

Play of Lear. Act IIId.

of Cordelia's response to her father's hardship in Act 4 is cut. Twentieth-century adaptations of *Lear* built on this ambiguity. The Cordelia of Edward Bond's play *Lear* (1971) – who is not Lear's daughter but his political opponent – changes from helpless victim to ruthless guerrilla leader and totalitarian ruler in a rare restoration of Holinshed's military figure. In *Ran*, Kurosawa plays with the gender assumptions of the original story still further by making the children of Lord Hidetora his sons rather than his daughters, although he retains the play's polarised depictions of women in the dynamic and unscrupulous Kaede and the gentle and forgiving Sué. While Bond and Kurosawa do little to shake the patriarchal perspective of Shakespeare's *Lear*, Smiley's *A Thousand Acres* reorientates the story by using Ginny, Goneril's equivalent, as the first-person narrator. Larry Cook, Smiley's Lear, oppresses and sexually abuses his elder daughters, Ginny and Rose; they protect Caroline, the youngest, but his actions drive an irreversible wedge between older and younger siblings, to the extent that towards the end of the novel Caroline argues that her sisters 'seek out bad things. They don't see what's there – they see beyond that to something terrible, and it's like they're finally happy when they see that!' Focusing on the hidden histories of family and environment, Smiley reframes *King Lear* from a feminist perspective.

Rewriting Language

The language of *King Lear* has been as unstable as its representation of Cordelia, shaped by the forces of modernisation, translation and censorship. Bond's *Lear* presents a radical new vision of the play, written in boldly contemporary language. He sums up its perspective in his *Theatre Poems and Songs*:

> In scene one Lear suffers the Great Vice
> Fear
> And so commits the Three Great Crimes
> Cruelty arrogance and rhetoric

In *Lear*, the king's 'Cruelty arrogance and rhetoric' colour his attitudes towards both his realm and his daughters. He vigorously defends building a wall to protect his kingdom – 'When I'm dead my people will live in freedom and peace and remember my name, no – venerate it! … They are my sheep and if one of them is lost I'd take fire to hell to bring him out' – and equally vigorously condemns his daughters for marrying his enemies, sounding very like Shakespeare's Lear in doing so:

> You talk of marriage? You have murdered your family. There will be no more children. Your husbands are impotent. … Where will your ambition end? You will throw old men from their coffins, break children's legs, pull the hair from old women's heads, make young men walk the streets in beggary

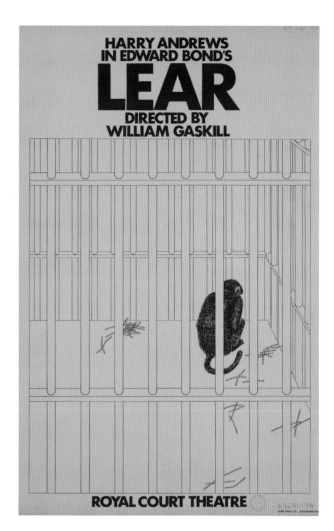

Poster for Edward Bond's *Lear*, first staged at the Royal Court Theatre, London, in 1971.
Victoria & Albert Museum

and cold while their wives grow empty and despair – I am ashamed of my tears! You have done this to me.

Bond's suspicion of Shakespeare's rhetoric also emerges in moments at which he responds directly to the text of *King Lear*. For example, where Shakespeare's Lear declares in the mock-trial scene (present only in the quarto), 'let them anatomize Regan; see what breeds about her heart' (Scene 13), Bond turns rhetoric into stage spectacle, as Lear's daughter Fontanelle is shot and dissected on stage.

Around the same time as Bond was working on *Lear*, Peter Brook's film of *King Lear*, finally released in 1971, was going through a long process of development. Taken with non-Anglophone adaptations of Shakespeare's plays such as Kurosawa's *Throne of Blood* (1957), an adaptation of *Macbeth*, and Kozintsev's adaptation of *Hamlet* (1964), Brook explored the idea of 'translating' *Lear* into modern English, and commissioned a screenplay by the poet Ted Hughes. 'I've got myself involved in a major piece of sacrilege', Hughes wrote to John and Nancy Fisher in October 1968; but he agreed with Brook that the imagistic language of Shakespeare's verse would clash with the visual language of film. His draft version of Lear's first speech thus radically simplifies the language:

> Give me the map there.
> We are growing old
> it is time we unburdened ourselves
> of all these cares of government
> and prepared ourselves for death.

In the event, the project did not work out – Hughes wrote, 'I got completely sick of it, had bad dreams about it etc' – and Brook returned to the Shakespearean text. However, he marries it with a visual style marked by disjunctive cuts and extreme angles, creating a distinctively disorientating response to the play, in which almost all perspectives are uncertain.

Other responses to the play's language have been informed by prevailing attitudes towards blasphemy and, especially, obscenity. In his 1818–19 lectures on Shakespeare, Samuel Taylor Coleridge pioneered a new mode of 'particular and practical Criticism', focusing more closely on the details of language than his contemporaries. Facilitating this approach, he made notes on blank pages interleaved in his copy of Samuel Ayscough's 1807 edition of Shakespeare's works. In these notes, Coleridge praises Shakespeare's use of the opening lines of *King Lear* to set up the character of Gloucester's illegitimate son Edmund, and explores the way in which the son is forced to listen to his father's 'degrading and licentious Levity' about the circumstances of his birth. However, if Coleridge had used another 1807 edition, Thomas and Henrietta Maria Bowdler's hugely popular *Family Shakspeare*, he would have known nothing of these lines, because nearly all of them were cut in order to preserve the innocence of readers. Here, Gloucester does not pun in a heavily jocular fashion on Kent's use of the word 'conceive', and he does not joke that there was 'good sport' at Edmund's 'making' or describe him as a 'whoreson' (Act 1, scene 1).

Theatrical censorship, which persisted in Britain until 1968, had its own preoccupation with indecency. Gordon Bottomley's verse drama *King Lear's Wife*, performed at the Birmingham Repertory Theatre in 1915 with costume and set designs by Paul Nash, depicts Lear's queen, Hygd, on her deathbed, exploring her relationships with her husband and daughters. Goneril is a pensive adolescent huntress and Cordeil an irritating daddy's girl, condemned by Hygd as 'My little curse', conceived only 'To keep her father from another woman'; Lear is secretly starving his wife and conducting an affair with her waiting woman, Gormflaith. The complexities of the narrative and its relationship with Shakespeare's *King Lear* did not much concern the censor; after a plot summary, the bulk of G. S. Street's report focuses on language. Describing the play as 'a strong thing on the whole' and conceding that 'the author must be allowed some plainness

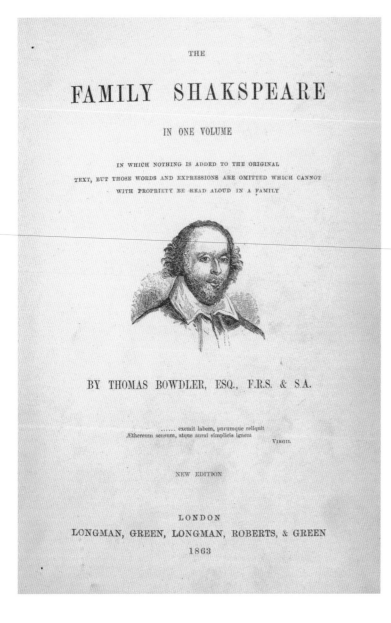

THE

FAMILY SHAKSPEARE

IN ONE VOLUME

IN WHICH NOTHING IS ADDED TO THE ORIGINAL
TEXT, BUT THOSE WORDS AND EXPRESSIONS ARE OMITTED WHICH CANNOT
WITH PROPRIETY BE READ ALOUD IN A FAMILY

BY THOMAS BOWDLER, ESQ., F.R.S. & S.A.

...... exemit labem, purumque reliquit
Æthereum sensum, atque aurai simplicis ignem
VIRGIL.

NEW EDITION

LONDON
LONGMAN, GREEN, LONGMAN, ROBERTS, & GREEN
1863

The Family Shakspeare was first published in 1807. Thomas Bowdler claimed (not entirely truthfully) that 'nothing is added to the original text; but those words and expressions are omitted which cannot with propriety be read aloud in a family'. Bowdler's sister, Henrietta Maria, is not credited for her part in the collaboration lest it be known that she had read the 'improper' original version.

of phrase', Street nonetheless objected strongly to the 'revolting' words sung absentmindedly by an old serving-woman as she and her companion lay out Hygd's corpse:

> A louse crept out of my lady's shift –
> Ahumm, Ahumm, Ahee –
> Crying 'Oi! Oi! We are turned adrift;
> The lady's bosom is cold and stiffed,
> And her arm-pit's cold for me.'
> …
> The lady's linen's no longer neat –
> Ahumm, Ahumm, Ahee;
> Her savour is neither warm nor sweet;
> It's close for two in a winding sheet,
> And lice are too good for worms to eat;
> So here's no place for me.

Thinking the song 'needlessly offensive to modern taste' and recommending that it 'might be cut out', Street also thought that 'the audience might be spared any gruesome details in the business of the laying out'. Accordingly, the Lord Chamberlain's Office wrote to the manager of the Birmingham Repertory Theatre, stating that the 'dirge' would 'be found to be somewhat revolting and hardly presentable matter on the stage'. In particular, the reference to the louse and the words 'armpits' and 'savour' were to be omitted. The censor was not wholly out of tune with public opinion: the *Times Literary Supplement* thought that Bottomley had indulged in ugliness 'for the sake of ugliness, as if it were interesting in itself'. Nonetheless, *King Lear's Wife* pioneered a trend for freer and more exploratory adaptations of Shakespeare's plays.

The product of adaptation, revision, addition and erasure, Shakespeare's *King Lear* has become subject to the same processes, providing creative stimulus for a host of artists, filmmakers, theatre-makers and writers. While commentators in 1838 may have thought that Macready was restoring 'Shakspeare's true *Lear*', it is more accurate to view his production as one adaptation among many. However, his decisive step in returning the Fool to *King Lear* continues to leave its mark on our understanding of both the play and its numerous offspring.

Chapter 8

'The revolution of the times': Peter Brook's *A Midsummer Night's Dream*, 1970

Peter Holland

Watching the Revolution

On 27 August 1970 Clive Barnes, the theatre critic of the *New York Times*, attended the first night of Peter Brook's production of *A Midsummer Night's Dream* for the RSC. It is striking enough that he travelled to Stratford-upon-Avon to see it. But the opening of the review, published the next day, was an extraordinary statement:

> Once in a while, once in a very rare while, a theatrical production arrives that is going to be talked about as long as there is a theatre, a production which, for good or ill, is going to exert a major influence on the contemporary stage. ... If Peter Brook had done nothing else but this 'Dream', he would have deserved a place in theatre history.

Barnes, notoriously and frequently acerbic, capable of closing a show with a bad notice, is here brilliantly acute and plainly exhilarated. He identifies, wittily and concisely, exactly what Brook had achieved:

> Brook has approached the play with a radiant innocence. He has treated the script as if it had just been written and sent to him through the mail. He has staged it with no reference to the past, no reverence for tradition. He has stripped the play down, asked exactly what it is about. He has forgotten gossamer fairies, sequined eyelids, gauzy veils and whole

OPPOSITE
Mary Rutherford as Hermia hanging from a trapeze in Peter Brook's *A Midsummer Night's Dream*.
RSC

forests of Beerbohm-trees. He sees the play for what it is –
an allegory of sensual love, and a magic playground of lost
innocence and hidden fears.

In many ways Barnes's celebration of Brook is a misunderstanding of
what Brook was doing. The 'radiant innocence' was in fact assumed.
Brook was deeply knowledgeable about the play's stage tradition, and
every innovation in the production is less a refusal to reference the
past than a direct response to, and alteration of, its characteristics.
It is not that Brook had forgotten those gossamer fairies but that
he wanted to construct a performance world in which they could
be forgotten. His audiences would quickly be able to at least half-
forget them, to see their absence and to value what was revealed by
replacing the traditional view of what fairies look like with men and
women dressed, as the production's images now suggest, in outfits
just right for a slightly hippie forest-world of Indian music and the
open sexiness of summers of peace and love.

But in one respect above all Barnes was right: in Brook's
approach to *A Midsummer Night's Dream*, the most radical of his

Poster for the RSC's
1970 production of
*A Midsummer Night's
Dream* directed by
Peter Brook. The poster
features Sally Jacobs's
famous white-box set
design. In this abstract
world, Titania's bower
is a giant feather and
long coils of wire stand
in for the forest while
the fairies look on
from above.

Shakespeare productions to that date, he had created something that would be profoundly influential and would remain in the awareness of theatregoers over more than forty years. Images of individual actors are familiar to many, but few productions have ever formed images that have so frequently been reproduced, so often been quoted, so quickly attained iconic status. Asked to think of 'Brook's

Poster for the Japanese leg of the world tour of Peter Brook's *A Midsummer Night's Dream*, 1973.

Dream' and most will recall photographs of Sally Jacobs's white box of a set, of the trapezes and Titania's giant red ostrich-feather bower, of the colour-blocks of the costumes and the vast spiral of wire that, like a monstrous Slinky, could be used by the far-from-benign fairies to trap the lovers in its coils, of the spinning plates and stilts that came from the Chinese circus that influenced Brook's thinking. Only those who saw the production will recall the evocative sounds of the play, especially the Free-Kas, then-trendy plastic tubes that, whirled around by the fairies, hauntingly formed the soundscape of the wood.

The materials out of which Brook made audiences dream a new *Dream* had no place in the contemporary conventions of Shakespearean production. Now they appear familiar tropes of performance, so superbly right did they seem then to so many – though by no means all – and so influential did they become. It is not, I think, overstating the case to see in that production a paradigm shift, a fracturing and reforming of the nature of classical theatre production. Tens of thousands saw Brook's *Dream*, in Stratford-upon-Avon and London and then on its year-long world tour encompassing three cities in the UK, fourteen across Europe (including Berlin, Belgrade, Bucharest and Budapest), three in the United States (Los Angeles, San Francisco and Washington), four in Japan (Tokyo, Osaka, Kobe and Nagoya) and three in Australia, ending in Sydney. More people, it was claimed, saw the Brook *Dream* than had ever seen any other production of a Shakespeare play.

And however much those who never saw it are aware of it, talk of it, perceive its influences, they cannot have that memory of an emotion that, for me at least, the production created then and which remains with me. I remember vividly the experience of seeing it in the autumn of 1970 – more vividly indeed than dozens of productions seen in the last few years – and recall not only the details of the performance but above all the feelings it fired in me. Driving 100 miles to Stratford-upon-Avon to see a matinee, I was running late, could not find a parking spot and left the car where I was sure it would be ticketed. Settling into my seat three minutes before curtain-up, I could not imagine why I had wanted to see this most childish of Shakespeare's plays. I came out three hours later, dancing across the lawn in front of the Royal Shakespeare Theatre, filled with more joy than any other theatre performance has given me, before or since.

And, no, I did not get a parking ticket.

The First Revolution

There is little record of Brook's *Dream* on film (unless a copy of the supposedly destroyed Japanese film of it surfaces one day), partly because Brook resisted proposals to film it:

> I always refused because the essence of Sally Jacobs' imagery was a white box. The invisible, the forest, even the darkness

of night were evoked by the imagination in the nothingness
that had no statement to make and needed no illustration.
… [P]hotography is essentially naturalistic and a film based
only on whiteness, least of all a soiled and blotchy one, was
unthinkable.

The white box was the crucial part of the concept, even if it
reminded some of a squash court, for Brook wanted to work
with less and less, not the opulent more and more of traditional
productions. 'I only knew what the *Dream* mustn't be … That was the
starting point. This white box started from the sense of elimination.
What's the purest version of elimination? White.' Though Jacobs and
Brook probably had no idea of its origins, their space was not a new
idea. In 1915 Harley Granville Barker had this to say to an interviewer
during the New York run of his production, which had opened at the
Savoy Theatre the previous year: 'These modern theatres with their
electric lights, switchboards and revolving stages are all well enough
but what is really needed is a great white box. That's what our theatre
really is.'

Between 1912 and 1914 Barker directed three brilliant and
controversial Shakespeare productions at the Savoy: *The Winter's
Tale, Twelfth Night* and *Dream*. Audiences were surprised, even
shocked, by his approach. For some critics Barker's *Dream* was 'never

Illustrations of
characters from
Harley Granville
Barker's production
of *A Midsummer
Night's Dream* from
the *Illustrated London
News*, 11 April 1914.
Though Barker's
production moved
towards modernism in
some respects, it was
still incredibly lavish,
with fairies covered in
expensive gold leaf.
British Library NEWS75

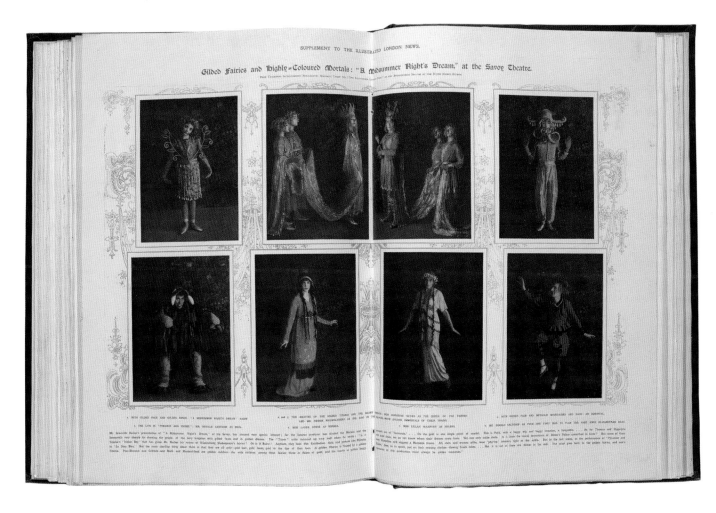

Shakespeare's "Dream"'; for others it was precisely the reverse, a *Dream* 'according to Mr. Granville Barker. And, let it be said at once, according to Shakespeare'.

What provoked the responses – and, liked or hated, the production could certainly not be ignored – was in part something as simple as the unusual nature of the production's soundscape, for this was a *Dream* without a trace of Mendelssohn. Barker thought this Romantic aural overlay irrelevant to the play's world and instead worked with Cecil Sharp to create a score based on English folk music and only played when the text explicitly required it. The Englishness of the music was echoed in the costuming of Puck, played, unusually for the time, by a man (Donald Calthrop): a hobgoblin dressed in scarlet with red berries in his yellow hair which, as the *Times* reviewer said, 'stream[ed] like a comet behind him'. There was no lush underscoring and no lush realism to watch. On the small stage of the Savoy, Barker and his designer, Norman Wilkinson, made no attempt to create a realistic forest, instead using silk curtains, not drop-cloths, the drapes painted with abstractions of woodland and moving in the breeze, all backing a bare stage.

But it was the fairies that most astonished. By this point in the tradition of performances, everyone knew exactly what fairies were supposed to look like: either a female *corps de ballet* dressed in long tutus (the style derived from the ballet *Les Sylphides*), or a cast mostly of children costumed in something vaguely Greek with gauze wings. That was the kind of image of the fairy world that Herbert Beerbohm Tree had offered in his spectacular production at Her Majesty's Theatre in London in 1900 – famously with a set that included live rabbits in the wood. It was the kind that Clive Barnes was still alluding to in 1970 ('whole forests of Beerbohm-trees') and which fell into the trap Sally Jacobs wanted to avoid, of 'illustration' or 'overpictorialisation'. Not a trace of that for Barker, who costumed his fairies in gold, with their faces and hands gilded, at great cost, with sheets of gold leaf that had to be applied each day meant that, on matinee days, the fairies could not wash between (performances). They were, as an American reviewer commented, 'not ethereal, but solid as gilt statues, and stiff like statues, too, moving with quaint, automatic motions'. The theatre critic Desmond MacCarthy thought they were 'ormolu fairies, looking as though they had been detached from some fantastic, bristling old clock', but A. B. Walkley was nearer the mark when he asked, 'Is it Titania's Indian Boy that has given Mr. Barker his notion of Orientalizing Shakespeare's fairies? Or is it Bakst? Anyhow they look like Cambodian idols and posture like Nijinsky.' No wonder he thought the score should have been by Stravinsky.

Between Revolutions

One might have expected Barker's brilliant reimagining to have changed productions of *A Midsummer Night's Dream* forever. But traditions die hard. It was hardly surprising that, when Hollywood

turned to the film in 1935, it should have kept close to the Beerbohm Tree style. It is more disappointing that, when Tyrone Guthrie, a director usually innovative in style, turned to the play for the Old Vic in 1937, he should have wanted to pay homage more to Tree than to Barker.

The Warner Brothers production was Hollywood's most spectacular Shakespeare film to date in the era of the talkies. It was prompted by the huge success of Max Reinhardt's production at the Hollywood Bowl in September 1934, one of three productions of the play he directed in California that year. Reinhardt was, to say the least, obsessed with the *Dream*: he directed it some thirteen times between 1905 and 1934, mostly in Germany but also in Florence, Oxford and New York. The productions did not radically change in their view of the play as a neo-Romantic, opulent and decidedly safe vision, fully equipped with large casts, vast sets and plenty of Mendelssohn. Fixed in outline long before Barker's production, Reinhardt's *Dream* was ripe for Hollywood treatment, the great showman director and the wonders of studio soundstages naturally meeting.

Still from the 1935 Warner Brothers film of *A Midsummer Night's Dream* directed by Max Reinhardt.

As the 'Making of' featurette *A Dream Comes True* (1935) proudly announced, the forest set included giant redwoods, cut down and transported to the Warner Brothers lot. There were sixty-seven truckloads of trees and shrubbery brought in, covering more than 6,100 square metres (66,000 square feet) of studio. The studio spared no expense – or so their hype would have us believe – and they certainly scoured their list of studio players, casting a newcomer like Olivia de Havilland (Hermia) alongside great stars such as James Cagney (Bottom), Mickey Rooney (Puck) and Joe E. Brown (Flute). An ensemble with no one lead, the cast was enough to rival MGM's slogan 'More stars than there are in heaven'. Oberon and Titania could enter with enough attendants to overpopulate the screen, the former with bat-winged henchmen, the latter with dozens of glittering women and children, while the forest had a goblin orchestra, a unicorn and every special effect then known in order to make the fairy world magical. This is anything but a space of the imagination: audiences could sit back and see the reality of fairyland, a space of balletic dance choreographed by Bronislawa Nijinska, especially in a lengthy dance sequence, accompanied by Mendelssohn's 'Nocturne', showing the war in which the creatures of moonlight were overcome by the figures of the night. As if Mendelssohn's score was inadequate for the task, it was reworked, even more extravagantly, by Erich Korngold. The film was directed by Reinhardt with William Dieterle, who, as Wilhelm Dieterle, had acted for him in Europe. While its view of the play is far from bland – not least in the dark power of Oberon (Victor Jory) or Bottom's terror at discovering himself transformed with the ass's head, something that Shakespeare does not suggest – all is constricted by the demands of studio filming. Its assumption is that spectacle is really all the

Headdress worn by Vivien Leigh as Titania in Tyrone Guthrie's 1937 production of *A Midsummer Night's Dream*, which recalled the pictorial tradition of the Victorian era. The headdress was designed by Olivier Messel using cheap materials such as cellophane and metallic paper to create the illusion of opulence from a distance.

Victoria & Albert Museum

audiences wanted, and spectacle is what Reinhardt was delighted to give them, in what he envisaged as 'a *Gesamtkunstwerk* [total work of art] for the masses'.

At the Old Vic, Guthrie tried his best to create stage images that might rival Reinhardt's film. Theseus had Nubian slaves, fairies flew, and Ninette de Valois, director of the Vic-Wells Ballet, choreographed a proper *'corps de Sylphides'* to (of course) Mendelssohn's music. For all the excellence of the cast – especially Ralph Richardson as Bottom and Robert Helpmann as Oberon – Guthrie had nothing new to say about the play. Spectacle was all that mattered, as it was when the company's 1954 production, directed by Michael Benthall, toured to New York with an orchestra of sixty, twenty-four dancers and thirteen tons of scenery. As if to pinpoint what really mattered, Helpmann, a fine actor as well as dancer, was now partnered not by Vivien Leigh as Titania but by Moira Shearer, who was best known as a dancer, not least from the film *The Red Shoes* (1948). It was in such a context that Peter Brook was already making his mark as a director by disdaining tradition and reimagining Shakespeare.

Towards a Revolution

Peter Brook was born in London in 1925, the son of Russian Jews who had emigrated from Latvia. His first production of *Hamlet* was a childhood performance using puppets at home for family and friends, with a script headed '*Hamlet* by William Shakespeare and Peter Brook'. As Brook's biographer Michael Kustow reports, Brook 'made the puppets, pulled their strings and spoke everyone's lines'. When the show was over, he wanted to begin again 'with a different version'. It is too easy – but still irresistible – to see the proto-director as puppet-master, string-puller, co-author. More useful, though, is the dissatisfaction with what has been achieved, the need to do it again but differently. And, as a distant echo, there is the presence of the great theatre theorist Edward Gordon Craig (1872–1966), whose concept of 'the actor as *Übermarionette*' was designed to enable the actor to be totally under the control of the artist-director.

After a degree at Oxford, Brook quickly found himself directing for Sir Barry Jackson at the Birmingham Repertory Theatre in 1945. Jackson was so impressed that he chose him to direct *Love's Labour's Lost* at the Shakespeare Memorial Theatre in Stratford-upon-Avon the following year, making Brook the youngest ever to direct there. Brook chose to make Shakespeare's Navarre a pastoral idyll from Watteau, because, he wrote later,

> every one of Watteau's pictures has an incredible melancholy. And if one looks, one sees that there is somewhere in it the presence of death, until one even sees that in Watteau (unlike the imitations of the period, where it's all sweetness and prettiness) there is usually a dark figure somewhere, standing with his back to you.

A play which usually hardly made for decent box office was a triumph and packed the house. The production managed two things at once, making both Brook's reputation as the most brilliant young director of the time and the play's reputation as not simply theatrically viable but theatrically exhilarating. It was a remarkable achievement.

In 1947 Brook directed *Romeo and Juliet* at Stratford, wanting, he said, to break away from the popular conception of *Romeo and Juliet* as a pretty-pretty, sentimental love story, and to get back to the violence and the passion of the stinking crowds, the feuds, the intrigues, to recapture the poetry that arises from the Veronese sewer and to which the story of the two lovers is merely incidental. He stripped the play of its usual lyricism and replaced it with an overwhelming atmosphere of Italian heat, something now so familiar in productions of *Romeo* that it is difficult to imagine how shocking that might have been. The reviews were terrible.

In 1950 came *Measure for Measure* with John Gielgud as an icily vicious Angelo. Memorably, near the end, immediately after Mariana had pleaded with Isabella to join her in trying to save Angelo's life and before Isabella's response, Brook placed a pause. Not just a brief moment, the pause stretched out further and further: thirty-five seconds on opening night, as much as two minutes later in the run. Brook wanted Barbara Jefford as Isabella to hold the pause until she felt that the audience could stand no more. For Brook this was no piece of actor's bravado but the creation of a space in which the core of the play's meaning could be apparent: 'a silence in which all the inevitable elements of the evening came together, a silence in which the abstract notion of mercy became concrete for that moment to those present'.

In 1953 he made an extremely short *King Lear* for CBS television, starring Orson Welles (then aged 38) and cut to a running time of seventy-three minutes. Then, in 1955 came a Stratford production of *Titus Andronicus*, the first ever there, starring Laurence Olivier as Titus and Vivien Leigh as Lavinia. For Brook, '[e]verything in *Titus* is linked to a dark flowing current out of which surge the horrors, rhythmically and logically related – if one searches in this way one can find the expression of a powerful and eventually beautiful barbaric ritual'. The 'real appeal' of the play 'was obviously for everyone in the audience about the most modern of emotions – about violence, hatred, cruelty, pain – in a form that, because *unrealistic,* transcended the anecdote and became for each audience *quite abstract and thus totally real*'. As the theatre critic Kenneth Tynan commented:

> This is tragedy naked, godless, and unredeemed, a carnival of carnage in which pity is the first man down. We have since learned how to sweeten tragedy, to make it ennobling, but we would do well to remember that *Titus* is the raw material, 'the thing itself', the piling of agony on to a human head until it splits.

OPPOSITE
Vivien Leigh as Lavinia in the RSC's 1955 production of *Titus Andronicus*. Peter Brook abstracted the violence in the play, using red streamers to symbolise blood, as seen here hanging from the stumps of Lavinia's severed hands.
British Library Add MS 80731

The movement towards abstraction as a means to achieve the most 'real' was especially marked in Brook's extraordinary representation of the raped and mutilated Lavinia. Reports spoke of audience members fainting and of a St John's Ambulance crew always on duty, but the production photographs show not some horrifying hyperrealism of blood and gore, but of extreme abstraction: Leigh clutched in her hands long streamers of red cloth and gripped another in her mouth. There was no blood at all, only a sign of what could not be shown: theatre at its most abstract and metaphoric but also at its most terrifying in this representation of the limits of suffering. As with *Love's Labour's Lost*, this was the rescue of a play. As the critic Jan Kott put it, 'Mr Brook did not discover *Titus*. He discovered Shakespeare in *Titus*. Or rather, in this play he discovered the Shakespearian theatre, the theatre that had moved and thrilled audiences, had terrified and dazzled them.' It was Brook's greatest triumph in Shakespeare production to date.

The Tempest, again with Gielgud in the lead, was at Stratford in 1957, and Brook returned to the play once more for the *Tempest* exercises/workshop at the Roundhouse, London, in 1968. But there was also Peter Weiss's *Marat/Sade* (1964) and the devised anti-Vietnam War piece *US* (1966). And there was *King Lear* twice more, first onstage for the RSC in 1962 and then on film in 1970. For the theatre historian David Williams, the RSC *Lear* marked 'a major crossroads in [Brook's] career':

> … the end of romantic fantasy and decoration of any kind, of lighting effects and fixed set designs … the genesis of ensemble concerns, work on the actor as supreme creator, the primary source in an empty space: starkness and provocation, clarity and visibility at every level: the uneasy fusion of Artaud, Beckett and Brecht in search of a prismatic density of expression and form: a truer reflection of the spirit of our age.

Paul Scofield as King Lear in Peter Brook's 1970 film of *King Lear*.

And it required an emptied stage space. If the stills in the RSC archives now make the stage look almost conventional in its bareness, one needs to reinflect the image with an awareness of how shocking that was. A New York critic complained: 'It puts a strain on me to have to imagine where I am.' There was nothing except for two flats and a backcloth, 'all painted', Albert Hunt wrote, 'in a subtle whitish, chalky grey – geometrical straight lines only broken by dangling squares and triangles of painted metal (for the palace) and three corroded metal thunder sheets (for the storm)'. The light was unremittingly strong and white. The choices were made for meaning: as the Shakespearean theatre historian Marvin Rosenberg commented, 'the bareness of Brook's stage was metaphysical, as well as actual. … The fierce illumination banished any shadows of divinity, mystery, or superstition.' The house lights were up when the first actors came on to the stage. They went up again at the interval, taken very late, with the blinded Gloucester still on stage. Brook had cut the conversation of the servants who want to help the blinded man: 'I'll fetch some flax and whites of eggs / To apply to his bleeding face.'

Scene from Peter Brook's 1962 stage production of *King Lear* at the RSC.

Now, heaven help him!' (Act 3, scene 7). Instead, the servants clearing the stage buffeted him about, uncaring, without the slightest sign of compassion, more concerned with their work than his suffering. It was a device that Brook would recall at the interval of *US*, when actors, with paper bags over their heads, came into the audience, asking for help to find their way out of the auditorium, seeking, often unsuccessfully, for a small gesture of common humanity.

As Kenneth Tynan saw, for Brook

> his production is amoral because it is set in an amoral universe. For him the play is a mighty philosophic farce in which the leading figures enact their roles on a gradually denuded stage that resembles, at the end, a desert graveyard or unpeopled planet. It is an ungoverned world; for the first time in tragedy, a world without gods, with no possibility of hopeful resolution.

In such a context judgement was both difficult and demanded of the audience. This was not the nice, kindly, much-abused old man version of Lear that had, for instance, been Charles Laughton's performance in the play's previous production in Stratford in 1959. Scofield's grizzled, angry king left Goneril's home after encouraging his knights to wreck the place, as they devastatingly, exuberantly and dutifully did.

It took nearly a decade for Brook to film the play, at first working with the poet Ted Hughes on a new version of the text, stripped down and simplified. In the event, Brook did not use Hughes's version; the language in the film is Shakespeare's. The first word of the film is Lear's 'Know' (Act 1, scene 1) but 'Know' emerges into the soundscape of the film after one of the most extraordinary openings of any film. The opening shot, slow and prolonged, pans across a group of men, all standing, motionless, filmed in black and white, in a state of mute expectation. It takes a while to realise that something else is unusual about the sequence: the complete absence of sound. There will be no non-diegetic sound at any point in the film – no sound whose source is not visible on screen; it is almost the only film I know without any underscoring, another aspect of cutting out the inessential. Then, finally, there is a cut to a new shot, a massive room, ordered and symbolic; again after an awkwardly long rhythm of waiting, a door to the room can be seen to be closing, the first on-screen movement, and then, at last, the first sound is heard, the thud of the door now shut. Cut again to a man's head, slumped, slightly twisted, as if it might be after a stroke, shaded and withdrawn, and speaking out of the side of his mouth a single syllable: 'Know'. But we cannot know that the sound is 'Know'; it could just as easily, perhaps even more probably, be heard as 'No'. Only when, after a pause, the sentence continues – 'that we have divided' – can we parse the first sound as an instruction to know and not a principle of negation, though the latter will be in many respects even more dominant in the film than any movement towards knowledge.

Filmed in the icy wastes of Jutland in northern Denmark, which provided for Brook a landscape that looked 'like the England of a thousand years ago' in the way that no part of the English countryside now does since it 'has transformed itself into an artificial countryside', this *Lear* is unremittingly as bleak as its first moments. After the shoot, after the choice to work 'with an elimination of as much period detail as possible', Brook edited in ways that sought 'to interrupt the consistency of style, so that many-levelled contradictions of the play can appear', as he wrote to the Russian film director Kozintsev, whose own bleak film of *King Lear* appeared a year later.

Creating a Revolution

While some of Brook's methods in the 1970 *Dream* now seem part of theatre's vocabulary, they were startling then. Where Shakespeare productions had tended towards a kind of representational world, using techniques that belonged to the conventions of classical theatre, Brook replaced them or, better, conjoined them with ideas drawn from radically different traditions. John Kane, who played Puck, was, to say the least, surprised when Sally Jacobs, the production's designer, showed him her sketch of his costume:

> a drawing of a curly-headed character wearing a one-piece-baggy-panted-luminous-yellow-jump-suit and a moonlight-blue skull-cap. I found it impossible to relate the picture I held in my hand to any conception I may have had of the part of 'Puck' up to that time. Peter explained. Recently both he and Sally had witnessed a Chinese circus in Paris and had

OPPOSITE
Costume design for Puck by Sally Jacobs, 1970. In this circus-inspired production, Puck walked on stilts and spun a plate which he used to enchant other characters instead of the usual magic flower.
RSC

Puck - John Kane and
Robert Lloyd

Midsummer Nights Dream
R.S.C.

Sally Jacobs '70

been struck by the difference between our performers and theirs. When the occidental acrobat performs, his costume emphasizes his physique. … Peter's Chinese acrobats hid the shape of their bodies with long flowing silk robes and performed their tricks with delicacy and speed, so that it seemed the most natural thing in the world for them to spin plates, or walk on stilts.

No longer a matter of representation, objects became symbolic. What does a magic flower look like? It can be a plant representing whatever botanical specimen a director believes to be the true form of 'love-in-idleness' but which never seems especially magical. Bringing the flower to Oberon (Alan Howard), Kane's Puck entered (Act 2, scene 1), high above the stage, swinging on a trapeze; his response to 'Hast thou the flower there?' was to reach into his pocket and take out a silver plate, spin it on the end of a Perspex rod and tip it to Oberon, who took it, still spinning, on his wand, another Perspex rod, all accompanied by the eerie sound of a finger running round the rim of a wine glass. As Peter Thomson, reviewing the production, put it, 'the plate does not *become* the flower. Instead, the act of passing it becomes the *magic* of the flower'.

In such a world, the fairies, all adult actors (here often malevolent spirits and known to the company as the Audio-Visuals since they made strange sounds and moved objects around), dropped great coils of wire, enmeshing Hermia in these mobile but resisting cages. Here Titania's bower could become a gigantic red ostrich

Designer Sally Jacobs and cast members practising the art of plate-spinning. Each day of rehearsals began with circus skills.
RSC

feather suspended over the stage. Here the sounds of the forest were bangs and crashes, rasps and rattles, and, above all, the strange whoosh of the Free-Ka tubes. It was no surprise that these fairies lulled Titania to sleep by sitting cross-legged on trapezes singing a distinctly Indian chant. As well as magic, these fairies could be comic helpers: when Bottom is still asleep, alone on stage, at the end of the forest scenes (Act 4, scene 1), a fairy arm appeared from the side of the stage holding out an alarm clock ringing his awakening.

In such a world, too, the rather chaste and prudish view of love could become something radically different. In Brook's theatre, love was not a platonic emotion divorced from the sharpness of sexual desire. Titania's love for the transformed Bottom was unquestionably the desire for sex with him and, though she spoke the line 'Tie up my love's tongue, bring him silently' (Act 3, scene 1), the moment was anything but silent. Instead, Bottom, braying like an ass, hoisted on a fairy's shoulder with the fairy's arm raised as an erect ass's phallus between his legs, left the stage triumphantly, with the watchers throwing dozens of paper-plates and streamers, Oberon swinging from side to side on a trapeze, equally triumphant in his revenge on his erring queen, and, at massive volume, the sound of Mendelssohn's 'Wedding March', originally written as part of his incidental music to the play, blaring in ironic solemnity on this impossible and lust-filled 'marriage'. No longer the sound for the Athenian triple wedding, the march now celebrated the complex meanings of this act of desire.

The stage space itself had no hint of palace or forest in its set design. The action took place on, above and around the giant

Annotated promptbook
for Peter Brook's
*A Midsummer Night's
Dream*, 1970.

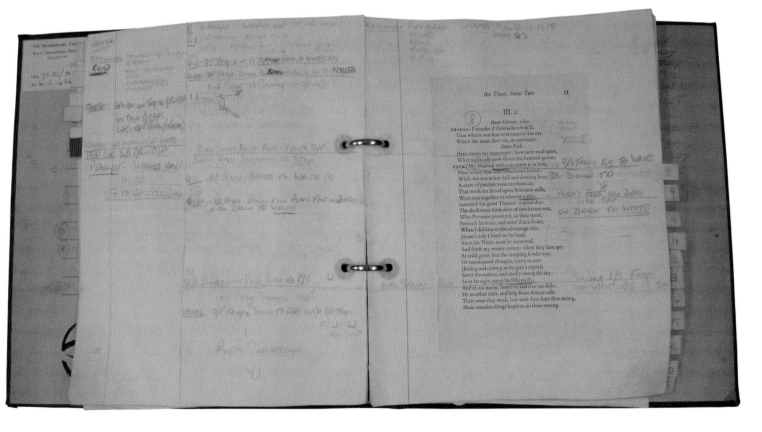

Sara Kestelman as
Titania with Alan
Howard as Oberon
(left) and John Kane as
Puck (right).
RSC

white box, making the long night in the wood, in this greatest
of all comedies of the night, something we imagined rather than
something we saw conjured up by the effects of stage lighting. More
than 3.5 metres (12 feet) above the stage floor, on the top of the three
sides of the box, ran a platform where actors not in a scene stood and
watched, like us, sharing the spectacle of performance.

Brook's project was to find the play's heart, its thematic unity,
not by finding the right analogue external to the theatre but instead
by celebrating theatre itself. The answers lay within the space of the
rehearsal room, not by imposing a concept. In the white box, with
these colourful abstract costumes, to the strange palette of music
and sounds created by Richard Peaslee, the production could be an
apparently limitless investigation, a free examination of what might
be found in the play. Brook wrote that, 'at the centre of the *Dream*,
constantly repeated, we find the word "love"', but at the centre of the
production lay the collaborative act of imagination that is theatre.
If *A Midsummer Night's Dream* had seemed to be the Shakespeare
play most suited to children, the meaning of that now lay not in
a cute exposition of an adult's view of fairies but instead through
reinvesting the play with the qualities of the child's imagination,
sometimes happy, often troubled, always ranging unexpectedly
across the playfulness of all play.

The accounts of the rehearsal process, especially in David
Selbourne's day-by-day diary of the weeks of work, are often
descriptions of actors in despair, with Brook's outbursts of anger at
their failure to find new modes of performance driving them further
and further into a space of insecurity. Early in the rehearsal process,
Brook's major complaint was that the actors were doing too much
analysing. Over and over again Brook could be heard accentuating,
as Shomit Mitter wrote in his study of Brook's rehearsal practices,
'the need to pursue bodily work entirely independently of analytical
interference'.

If the preparation was for some traumatic and others revelatory, it transferred something of both outcomes into the play's most complete investigation of the making of theatre, the workers' performance of *Pyramus and Thisbe*. Where productions have usually treated this as the opportunity for endless gags, unlimited mockery and a contempt shared between the onstage and theatre spectators, Brook showed utter respect for their endeavours. Perhaps nothing typified this serious comedy more than the lion's mask, a wooden cabinet that Snug had made as a skilled carpenter ('joiner') and here made by the actor (Barry Stanton) himself, with its front suggesting a lion's face but with two neat doors that he could open to show his own face within in order to reassure the 'ladies' who might otherwise 'quake and tremble here' (Act 5, scene 1).

One of the most imitated of Brook's devices for the play has been the doubling of Titania/Hippolyta, Oberon/Theseus and Puck/Philostrate. The doubling was not so much thematised as dramatic meaning as enjoyed for its theatrical virtuosity. Confronted with the rapid change from fairy world to human world in Act 4, where Fairy King and Queen exit and Athenian Duke and future Duchess enter immediately, Brook's solution was, as throughout the production, to make the mechanics of the transformation, the reality of performance, completely visible. The two actors walked upstage in one role, turned and walked downstage in the other, donning cloaks to define the difference. The doubling is not a problem for theatre: if we accept Alan Howard and Sarah Kestelman as one pair we can equally accept them as the other a moment later. As Jay Halio comments, 'What had once been regarded as a difficult if not impossible doubling now looks, thanks to imaginative and simple staging, perfectly natural.' It is the collocation of 'imaginative and simple' that defines Brook's method, turning what seems intellectually problematic into the easily acceptable theatrical solution.

Shakespeare's play ends with Puck's request for applause: 'Give us your hands, if we be friends' (Act 5, scene 1). Brook's actors, having played out the last sequence of the play in a downbeat way, did not ask us to clap but instead to reach out our hands and grasp theirs as they left the stage and moved among us (and John Kane could be heard up in the circle calling 'Author, author!'). For the one and only time in my playgoing, I did reach out my hands, not threatened by the breaking of the barriers between actors and audience but instead thrilled to be able to join with them physically, as we had all joined together throughout the performance. As Brook wrote, 'there is only a practical difference between actor and audience, not a fundamental one'. If we must always regret that only tiny fragments of his *Dream* were filmed, it also seems only right that this most theatrical of productions was never transferred to the wrong medium. Instead, the still photos recall this energetic production, memories preserve traces of its sound, and the production goes on being talked about 'as long as there is a theatre'.

Chapter 9

'The wheel is come full circle': *Twelfth Night* at Middle Temple Hall and Shakespeare's Globe, 2002

Farah Karim-Cooper

In 2002 an all-male cast dressed in a dazzling array of Renaissance clothing performed Shakespeare's comedy *Twelfth Night* at Middle Temple Hall. The choice of venue was designed to commemorate the 400th anniversary of the play's first recorded performance there in 1602, as documented in the diary of the law student John Manningham. This unique event demonstrated Shakespeare's Globe's distinctive commitment to the origins of Shakespearean performance, a continuing theme of Mark Rylance's residency there as founding Artistic Director. After a short run in the Elizabethan hall, the company of actors moved the production into the reconstructed Globe Theatre and played there through the summer of 2002 before embarking on a brief American tour in August 2003. In the Middle Temple Hall performances, Mark Rylance played Olivia and Eddie Redmayne played Viola in a production deliberately recalling one of the chief practices of early modern theatre: only men and boys played on the commercial stage. The production was staged in the hall as it might have been in 1602, with audiences in risers sitting along each wall and the actors performing along a 'corridor' stage in the middle of the hall. The great timber screen provided two doors that enabled easy entrance and exit points, while the musicians were placed on the second level of the screen above the actors. The hall was candlelit for the event. The experience of watching this production in fact began before the play started. As the Shakespeare critic David Nicol comments:

> Upon arrival at the building, each spectator was presented with a cardboard box containing Elizabethan snack food:

OPPOSITE
Eddie Redmayne as Viola/Cesario in Shakespeare's Globe's 'Original Practices' production of *Twelfth Night*, 2002.

ginger and prunes on a stick, an 'aniseed cracknell' (which
was very tasty indeed), and a bread roll called a 'manchet'
(which contained many ingredients but tasted of nothing at
all). We were then directed toward the great hall itself, where
Elizabethan music could be heard, and mulled wine was being
served. But before we could enter, we had to walk through
the actors' dressing room, where we were invited to watch the
cast apply their make-up and lace their doublets …

Audiences were given an Elizabethan 'experience' as part of the
pre-show in an attempt to re-create the atmosphere as well as the
staging practices of a sixteenth-century theatrical event. The beauty
of the clothing was enhanced by the audience's sensory engagement
with the dressing room itself. The production enabled audiences to
interact with the company in multiple ways within an aesthetically
pleasing and intimate setting, candlelit for the performances, its
stained-glass windows and Elizabethan portraiture offering a direct
connection to John Manningham's day. In his review Nicol remarked
that, 'the Globe's *Twelfth Night* was a fascinating investigation into
how the play might have looked and functioned in one of its original
performance spaces'.

Mark Rylance as the
Countess Olivia in
Shakespeare's Globe's
'Original Practices'
production of *Twelfth
Night*, 2002.

Exactly ten years after its first performance, this Olivier and Tony Award-winning production, comprehensively revived, transferred from Shakespeare's Globe to theWest End and eventually to Broadway, where it captured the imaginations of American audiences and critics alike. The theatrical style that the production exemplified – 'Original Practices' – has had a lasting influence on the way that audiences, critics and scholars imagine performance in Shakespeare's original theatres. The practices generated in the first ten years of performance at the reconstructed Globe were in part shaped by the absence from that theatre of modern lighting design and sound amplification. The artists of the Globe have tended to shun the term 'authenticity', recognising that the idea that it might be possible to perform 'authentically' in an 'authentic' theatre space is a fantasy. Instead, 'Original Practices' – a term coined by Mark Rylance in 1997 to describe the theatrical experiment he felt should be the core mission of Sam Wanamaker's reconstructed theatre – was created to show in a new light the significance of Shakespeare's language in relation to the theatre space, the actor's body, the audience, the clothing that actors wore and the role of music in early modern performance.

Edgar Playford as the Queen and 'Master A. Bartington' as Ophelia in William Poel's all-male production of *Hamlet* at the Carpenters' Hall, London, in 1900.
British Library 11795.t.85

Reconstruction

Sam Wanamaker – the most successful of reconstructors – was not the first to dream of a reconstructed Shakespearean theatre. In the 1880s and 1890s, the theatre director William Poel set out in pursuit of Shakespeare's original stagecraft, his interest specifically in the re-creation of the stage, costume and performance style of the Elizabethan theatre. In his own words, Poel stated that his 'original aim was just to find out some means of acting Shakespeare naturally and appealingly from the full text as in a modern drama' – 'naturally' being a concept defined in changing ways across time. In 1881 Poel began his quest to recover Elizabethan stage practices with a production of *Hamlet*, which was based on the so-called 'bad' or 'short' quarto. It was performed at St George's Hall in London and was staged entirely in Elizabethan costume. This was the first of many attempts to capture something of the past in performance, an endeavour that came to be known as the 'Elizabethan revival'. Significantly, in 1888 an important drawing was discovered that would support some of the theories Poel held about how performances in Elizabethan playhouses were staged. The only surviving illustration of the interior of an Elizabethan amphitheatre, a sketch of the Swan Theatre, provided visual evidence – partial but fascinating – of the kind of stage on which Shakespeare's actors might have worked. The drawing is a contemporary copy of the original sketch (now lost) by Johannes de Witt, a Dutch tourist who visited London in the 1590s. Operated by the impresario Francis Langley, the Swan was one of the first theatres in Southwark. It was built in 1595 and described by De Witt in his *Observationes londinienis* as 'the finest and biggest of the London theatres'. Although the

William Poel's 1893 production of *Measure for Measure,* in which he unsuccessfully attempted to create the stage of the Elizabethan Fortune Theatre within a Victorian proscenium-arch auditorium.

drawing arguably raises more questions than it answers, theatre historians consider it one of the most important pieces of visual evidence about sixteenth-century amphitheatre architecture.

Poel's motivation for reviving Elizabethan theatre practice was fuelled partly by the evidence that had come to light in the course of the previous 100 years. Another influential theatrical document, the Fortune contract, set out the agreement between Philip Henslowe and Peter Street, a carpenter, to build the Fortune Theatre on the north side of the Thames. This contract was discovered in 1790 and, with the Swan drawing, it provided a basis for Poel's 'Fortune fit-up' in 1893. This portable structure had a *frons scenae* or stage wall, a balcony and two doors at stage level; there was an inner stage (which scholars refer to now as the 'discovery space'), a 'heavens' or stage roof and two 5.5-metre (18-foot) pillars to support it. The 'fit-up' enabled Poel to test some of his theories, but his system of staging was nonetheless heavily shaped by the need to hide some of the action and business behind curtains. The pillars provided, Poel surmised, a mid-stage location for curtains, which would be opened and closed; theoretically, a scene would be played behind the pillars with the curtains open and then, immediately afterwards, another scene played in front of the pillars with the curtains closed. This method enabled the stage-hands and actors to hide business such as the movement of props on and off the stage. But, as theatre historians suggest, this technique was misinformed and did not reflect the practices which we now understand

Photograph of a model
created at the request
of William Poel for a
proposed new theatre
in the style of the
original Globe.

British Library 11795.t.85

characterised Elizabethan staging. Reactions to Poel's endeavours
were mixed. His company, the Elizabethan Stage Society, performed
many productions on the Fortune fit-up stage, including *Measure
for Measure* in 1893. The *Times* review of this production found
the clashes between the small details of accuracy and the 'striking
anachronisms' too incoherent. Significantly, in 1897 Poel decided to
stage *Twelfth Night* in Middle Temple Hall. Although he too attempted
to create an Elizabethan atmosphere in the hall, presumably because
it was a sixteenth-century venue and an original Shakespearean
performance space, Poel somewhat perversely brought his Fortune
fit-up into the space rather than exploiting the Elizabethan
architecture already in place.

Eventually, Poel drew up plans for a Globe Theatre, and a
model based on these plans was constructed and displayed in 1902 at
a meeting of the London Commemoration of Shakespeare League,
fuelling discussion about ways to commemorate Shakespeare and
debate about the extent to which a reconstruction of an Elizabethan
playhouse might be possible. Shortly thereafter, in 1912, the
'Merry England' Exhibition at Earl's Court in London saw the first
reconstruction of the Globe based on the drawing by Poel and the
subsequent small-scale model. The 1912 Globe was seen by O. S. E.

Keating, who later went on to endorse a reconstructed Globe for the 1933–4 World's Fair in Chicago, Illinois. Although the Chicago Globe had some glaringly inaccurate features – it had a roof, it lacked a yard for standing 'groundlings' and it was much smaller than the original – it did provide Fair-goers with an approximate sense of what it might have been like to perform without a proscenium arch. Without the Chicago Globe, arguably, there would be no Globe in London today, for Sam Wanamaker himself was at the World's Fair and seems to have been inspired by the idea of reconstructing Shakespeare's theatre.

Wanamaker's project to reconstruct the Globe began nearly forty years later in 1970, when he proposed that the Greater London Development Plan for Southwark should include the theatre as its centrepiece. Assembling scholars and theatre artists to advise on the reconstruction, Wanamaker and his lead architect Theo Crosby set out to build the most 'authentic' version of the Globe possible. Wanamaker and Crosby believed that their ambitious project would not only regenerate the depressed and neglected Bankside but would advance the knowledge of Shakespearean theatre for actors, scholars, university students and schoolchildren. At the heart of Wanamaker's vision was that the Globe should function not only as a working theatre but also as a location providing new opportunities for teaching and learning, a policy exemplified by his appointment as Director of Education of Patrick Spottiswoode in 1984, thirteen years before the theatre was complete. Wanamaker faced much resistance to the idea of authenticity, and those who knew him report how uncompromising this principle became for him as time went by. The aim was to build the theatre using the materials and techniques of early modern carpentry, which required a deep understanding and detailed knowledge of historical timber framing on the part of the theatre's makers. The prospect of a building made entirely of timber was a major concern for the Southwark District Surveyors. After Wanamaker's structural engineers proved that English oak was a good fire-resistant material, however, it was clear that the principle of 'no compromise' would not stand in the way of actual construction. In a letter dated 27 August 1982, Theo Crosby confirmed what he had managed to agree with the council, that the theatre would be built entirely of English oak and that it would as a result not be a fire hazard:

> We agreed a timber structure for the Globe with a one hour fire rating. I also agreed we would omit the thatch roof and substitute plain (clay) tiles. All soffits would be plastered, as would both sides of the external wall. Balustrades and railings all of solid oak. In general it would be a heavy Tudor oak structure and would be constructed in the old way: joints, pegs and so on, as authentically as we can.

By tackling the building regulators one issue at a time, Crosby and Wanamaker were able to ensure the building would be constructed in green oak and, eventually, with a thatched roof. Basing the reconstruction on the 1599 Globe (rather than the second, built in 1614) and with the support of scholars Andew Gurr and John Orrell, Wanamaker was insistent that the roof over the galleries should be made of English thatch. He rejected suggestions of any kind of all-encompassing roof (plastic and glass were suggested to him) to shelter standing audiences from the rain and fought for thatching despite the concerns of the fire authorities. The walls of the theatre would be made of lath and plaster, also constructed in the 'old way', using a plaster mix consisting of lime putty, sand and animal hair. In addition to rejecting modern materials and techniques where he could, Wanamaker insisted that the building materials be acquired in England. The entire project took over three decades, with vast amounts of fundraising, educating and campaigning. Sadly, neither Wanamaker nor Crosby survived to see the completed theatre, but both would have been thrilled with the extraordinary success of Shakespeare's Globe as a working theatre, education centre and one of the finest examples of historical craftsmanship in London.

Because there are no surviving plans of the original Globe to tell us its exact specifications or reveal exactly where, for instance, the stage pillars were located, evidence for the 1599 Globe had to be recovered from a wide range of sources, including the Swan drawing and the Fortune contract, and also the 'long view' of London by Wenceslaus Hollar, dated to 1647 but based on earlier sketches. This drawing shows a Globe Theatre – the second, 1614 Globe Theatre, that is, given the date of the drawing. The second theatre was reconstructed on the original foundations after the 1599 Globe burned down during a summer 1613 production of Shakespeare and

The second Globe Theatre pictured in Wenceslaus Hollar's 'Long View of London from Bankside', 1647. The Globe and the bear-baiting pit were mistakenly labelled the wrong way round: the theatre was to the left.
British Library Maps 162.h.4

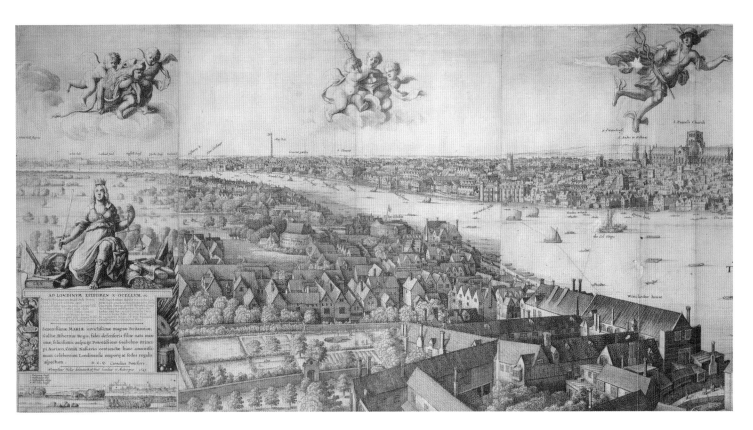

John Fletcher's *Henry VIII: or, All Is True*. The play texts themselves also provided useful evidence about the features of the stage, such as how many doors there should be and where to place the inner stage or 'discovery space'. What resulted is a building made entirely of English green oak, with a thatched roof, lime-plaster panelling, three levels of galleries, a central yard where the 'groundlings' stand, an elaborately painted *frons scenae* (or tiring-house wall) with a central opening and two flanking doors leading to the 'tiring house', a stage roof or 'heavens', an upper stage gallery, including a musicians' room/gallery, and two traps, one in the stage roof and the other on the stage floor. All of the features in the reconstructed Globe have a reference point either in a piece of documentary evidence, a contemporary drawing or in the plays themselves. There are still some features in the Globe that may not be accurate, but in the absence of a blueprint or surviving architectural plans, complete accuracy could never have been achieved. While the theatre is only a best guess, it is perhaps the most academically rigorous of reconstruction projects and, in terms of the construction methods used, the most attentive to Elizabethan practices.

Interior of the current Globe on the South Bank, London, where the 'groundlings' are very close to the stage and eye contact between actors and audience members makes for a dynamic relationship between the two groups.

'Original Practices' at Shakespeare's Globe

The principles of 'research, materials and craft' that underpinned Sam Wanamaker's reconstruction of the Globe Theatre prompted its first Artistic Director, Mark Rylance, and the team of artists he assembled – Claire van Kampen (founding Director of Theatre Music), Jenny Tiramani (founding Director of Theatre Design and creator of the School of Historical Dress) and Tim Carroll (Associate Director) – to respond to the building using these principles as artistic guidelines. Rylance has referred to the Globe as 'the most experimental theatre space in England' because the architecture itself in effect proposed a new way of staging Shakespeare. Rylance's notion of experimentation was crucial to the development of staging at the Globe. The relationship of the performances to the space was an absolute priority for Rylance and his fellow artists. Rigorous research into Renaissance clothing and period music in particular and, as Rylance suggests, a process of learning to play *with* rather than *to* or *at* or *for* a highly visible audience characterised the process of creation of an 'Original Practices' production. Although the first full production at the new theatre during the 1996 'Prologue' season was done in modern dress – which could in any case itself be considered an 'Original Practice' given that actors in Shakespeare's time for the most part wore contemporary clothing – it was decided that each season thereafter would stage at least one production that experimented with the practices of Shakespeare's original theatre company. While other theatres and companies were creating productions using various experiments such as original rehearsal techniques (at for example the Blackfriars Theatre in Staunton, Virginia), all-male casting (the theatre company Propeller) and performing on Elizabethan-style stages, nowhere else in the world were artists conducting such extensive academic research with a view to reproducing in the most accurate approximation to the circumstances of the first Globe Theatre the aesthetics and practices of original Shakespearean performance.

The experiment, therefore, was bold – in some ways outrageously so – and while the production was lauded by some critics and won Olivier Awards, not everyone understood the world that was being portrayed. For example, after attending a performance of *Twelfth Night* in Middle Temple Hall (2002), Nicol reflected on the experience as alienating:

> With their strange haircuts (very short at the front, very long at the back), their faces caked in make-up, and their skinny legs sticking from voluminous trunks, the siblings [the twins Viola and Sebastian, who are at the centre of the play's action] looked like bizarre life-forms from an alien zoo rather than attractive, androgynous young humans.

The tight-fitting doublets, the wigs that approximated Elizabethan hair styles and the make-up designed to reflect the Renaissance beauty ideal of a white complexion and rose-coloured cheeks were strange to the audiences; the clothes the Globe actors wore did not look anything like the looser and more familiar but largely inauthentic costumes actors wore in contemporary films such as *Elizabeth* (1996) or *Shakespeare in Love* (1998). By 2013, however, most theatre critics would embrace the experiment. Writing for the *New York Post* about the revival on Broadway, Elisabeth Vincentelli explained to her readers, 'They kick it old-school [at Shakespeare's Globe]: with an all-male cast in period 17th-century costume. ... The result, directed by Tim Carroll, is a feast for the senses.' Going from 'bizarre life-forms' to 'a feast for the senses', the 'Original Practices' experiment at Shakespeare's Globe made a distinctive mark in the cultural and theatrical landscape of the later twentieth and early twenty-first centuries and has shaped our understanding of early modern performance.

Jenny Tiramani refers to the outfits worn by actors in the context of 'Original Practices' performance not as 'costume' but as 'clothing'. One reason for this is again the principles that govern this performance style. After detailed research that involves examining surviving clothes or fragments of clothing from the sixteenth and seventeenth centuries and a sampling of Renaissance portraits, Tiramani and her team of craftspeople and makers design and construct clothing using period patterns (both patterns of surviving garments and patterns drawn by tailors of the period), techniques and materials. Therefore, for Tiramani, they make clothes, not costumes. Another reason for referring to the garments the actors wear as 'clothes' is that acting companies in Shakespeare's time would have spent large amounts of money on what they wore on stage, sometimes purchasing entire outfits from servants, who had inherited their masters' clothes but were unable to wear them because of 'sumptuary' legislation that forbade people of the lower social classes to wear rich, expensive textiles. Actors in the sixteenth- and seventeenth-century theatre companies were often, in other words, wearing real clothes, not costumes.

The gown worn by Mark Rylance in his role as the Countess Olivia in the 2012 production of *Twelfth Night* is one such item of 'clothing'. Designed by Tiramani, cut by Luca Costigliolo (a designer and maker and a member of the Globe's wardrobe department 1999–2005) and made by Sarah Stammler and Debbie Watson, Olivia's outfit is a reproduction of a sixteenth-century Italian noblewoman's dress. It was made by hand, using sixteenth-century techniques and fabrics. The gown made for the 2012 production, constructed from a length of cut and uncut black silk velvet with a strapwork design and hand-woven by Giuseppe Gaggioli in Genoa, was only the top layer of the actor's clothing. It was worn over a white linen smock, a pair of boned silk bodies (corset) and layers of skirts, including a Spanish farthingale and a silk petticoat. Rylance's Olivia also wore stockings and garters underneath the skirts. Like any noblewoman in 1602, Olivia also wore accessories, carefully researched and made using the same principles of construction. The lace cuffs pinned to the sleeves are essential to the outfit's overall aesthetic and help further the illusion of femininity, as Rylance was able to make small

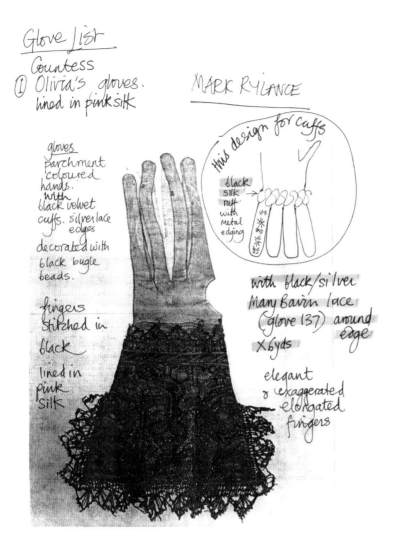

Glove design by
Jenny Tiramani for
Shakespeare's Globe's
2002 production of
Twelfth Night.

Shakespeare's Globe

gestures with his hands, hiding their masculine attributes behind the elaborate lace. The large starched linen and lace neck ruff was not only a key component of the Elizabethan noblewoman's outfit but helped to reflect light upon the face. In Rylance's case, the ruff was useful in disguising other distinctive male features such as his Adam's apple. Other important accessories included a rich, textural forepart tied around the petticoat that gave the illusion that Olivia was wearing two expensive gowns, a lace hat, a black veil, a coronet and a jewelled head-tire – all worn at different points in the play as the language or setting required.

All the outfits in this production were made according to the same historical guidelines, including the outfit that Viola wears when she is disguised as the Duke Orsino's boy, Cesario. The most striking element of Cesario's look is the beautifully crafted silk thread wig(s) worn by Michael Brown in the 2002 Globe production and by Johnny Flynn (Globe, Apollo West End) and Samuel Barnett (Broadway) in the 2012 revival. Drawing upon contemporary portraits, the designers in Tiramani's team created a look for Sebastian and Cesario that closely resembled the fashions for young gentlemen around the year 1600. The effect of wearing Renaissance clothing made to

Mark Rylance being dressed as Olivia. The dressers would begin to help the actors into their costumes an hour before the performance was due to begin.

historically accurate specifications has been instructive for many Globe actors, who have reported the impact upon their bodies. The way one stands, sits, walks, dances and gestures is affected by the fact that these clothes 'fit' in a way that clothes do not today, that is, extraordinarily tightly. This experiment in historical dress has taught us not only a great deal about the clothes worn by Elizabethans, but also about bodily movement on the Shakespearean stage and the rules of deportment in the early modern social world.

Although the Globe artists had been experimenting with 'Original Practices' since their 1997 production of *Henry V*, in some ways the 2002 *Twelfth Night* can be viewed as a culmination of the rigorous investigation that characterises these productions. For this production, the team decided to start using original make-up in order to create the full effect of Renaissance femininity, but they were forced to compromise because materials found in sixteenth- and seventeenth-century cosmetic paints were largely poisonous. For the most part, they stuck to the principle of using only materials available in Shakespeare's time. The white base consisted of a mixture of plain chalk crushed with pure pigment and with a little rose or almond oil. To create darkened eyebrows, they dipped a brush into water and then into a pot of black lamp soot. Moroccan clay pots were used for the red in the lips and pink-coloured chalk to create the blush in the cheeks. The idea was to create a simulacrum of the Renaissance beauty ideal, which consisted of pale skin, pinkish/rose-coloured cheeks, dark eyes and small ruby lips. While in Shakespeare's time there were very mixed views about make-up, some seeing it as sinful, hypocritical and disgusting ('slibber sauces', as it was colourfully described by the puritan Philip Stubbes), the acting companies of the time made great use of cosmetics for special

Mark Rylance applying cosmetics made (mostly) using ingredients that would have been available in Shakespeare's time.

effects, using them to create the pallid complexion of a ghost, to paint the faces of boys to look like women and, for *Twelfth Night*, to create the illusion of identical twins. When, in the 'Original Practices' production, Cesario and Sebastian simultaneously entered from each of the two flanking doors of the Globe stage towards the end of the play, the similarity between them was dizzying, an effect created not only by the identical outfits they were wearing but also by their wigs and make-up.

The other distinctive feature of 'Original Practices' productions is the historical approach developed to create music for the performances. The founding Director of Theatre Music at the Globe and current Globe associate for Early Modern Theatre Music, Claire van Kampen, decided it was important to 'look at the practice of Renaissance music, and, working with early music practitioners … us[e] only reconstructed period instruments without using amplification or electronic aids'. Crucial to van Kampen's method, then, was a return to original 'sources and references', as she puts it, which means searching for evidence of songs and music that might have been available to musicians and actors in the sixteenth and seventeenth centuries. Like Tiramani, van Kampen also draws on evidence from the particular year a play is set or was staged, because musical trends and fashions had a tendency to change rapidly, as they do now. *Twelfth Night* is a particularly musical play, and there are several surviving period songs that proved to be appropriate for the songs in the play text itself, such as 'Ah Robin', sung by Feste as 'Hey Robin', a song by William Cornysh that can be found in the Henry VIII Manuscript of around 1510–20. Because the evidence for instrumentation can be rather fragmentary, van Kampen selected music from a range of sources to create her compositions and to

shape the cues for the instrumental music in the productions. The early music practitioner Keith McGowan arranged most of the compositions for the 2002 production of *Twelfth Night*. The music for the production changed radically, however, when it moved from the Middle Temple Hall (which used an indoor 'mixed consort') to the Globe Theatre, which required the shawms (double reed instrument), sackbuts (an early version of the trombone) and drum of the outdoor playhouse. When it transferred to the Apollo Theatre in the West End, the music was further rearranged, van Kampen adding a cornett and sackbut ensemble; the same music was adapted to a shawm and sackbut ensemble for its Broadway run, where the same company of actors and musicians played *Twelfth Night* in repertory with *Richard III*.

Perhaps most importantly, van Kampen is particularly sensitive to Shakespeare's dramaturgy when she is arranging and composing music and shaping the cues for an 'Original Practices' production. This attentiveness to the play text is common to all the artists assembled by Rylance in the first ten years of performance at Shakespeare's Globe. The language, verse and story are organically tied to the methods and material practices of these productions, staged to showcase the extraordinary capacities of the reconstructed Globe itself. This theatrical experiment has not only brought to light new possibilities for our understanding of the look, feel and sound of Shakespearean performance in its original moment, but has also demonstrated to us, as audiences, our own desire to share a space intimately with actors – whether a genuinely original space such as Middle Temple Hall or a reconstruction such as the Globe – so that we become not only a part of, but also contributors to, the meaning of a Shakespeare play in performance.

OPPOSITE
Michael Brown as
Viola/Cesario and Rhys
Meredith as Sebastian
in *Twelfth Night* at the
Globe, 2002.

THE ♛ WOOSTER ♛ GROUP

HAMLet

BY WILLIAM SHAKESPEARE

Chapter 10

'Look here, upon this picture': Theatrofilm, The Wooster Group *Hamlet* and the Film Industry

Judith Buchanan

The Wooster Group *Hamlet*, directed by Elizabeth LeCompte, opened in Paris and Berlin in November 2006. In early 2007 it played in St Ann's Warehouse back in the company's native New York and it has since been revived, to enthusiastic acclaim, in Amsterdam, Los Angeles, Athens, Gdansk, Bucharest, Sarasota, Dublin, Santiago and São Paulo. Its most recent run was at the Lyceum, Edinburgh, in August 2013 as part of the Edinburgh Festival. The Wooster Group stage *Hamlet* incorporates into its live performance an older film of *Hamlet* starring Richard Burton, generating from this a bravura performed conversation between on-screen and off-screen action. Taking the Burton film as the hub around which its own production revolves, The Wooster Group actors sometimes emulate the on-screen action precisely and sometimes riff off it in witty and percussive ways. Since the Burton film (or 'theatrofilm', as it was marketed) was made from a stage production, inviting the film to spill back into a live stage production is, The Wooster Group jokes, a process of 'reverse theatrofilm'. This twenty-first-century, mixed-media *Hamlet* is the pivotal production for this chapter. However, it comes into sharpest focus if we first understand the significance of the older film that inspired it. Looking at the provenance of that film takes us back from the present moment, 2016, in which we commemorate the 400th anniversary of Shakespeare's death, to 1964, the 400th anniversary of Shakespeare's birth.

OPPOSITE
Poster for The Wooster Group's *Hamlet*, designed by the artist Richard Prince. The pile of editions signals the production's interest in the legacy of prior *Hamlets*.
Photo by Richard Prince

Richard Burton's *Hamlet*, the Theatrofilm and its Precedents

As part of the 1964 Shakespeare commemorative events, a high-profile stage production of *Hamlet* was mounted that played in Toronto, Boston and at the Lunt-Fontanne Theatre on Broadway. With Sir John Gielgud directing and Richard Burton in the title-role, the production's credentials were impeccable. As Gielgud explained to his cast on the first day of rehearsals, his central idea for the production was that it should court the appearance of a final run-through, 'in rehearsal clothes, stripped of all extraneous trappings'. Sets and properties were minimal in order not to 'cramp the imagination and the poetry' and the mode of vocal delivery paid heed to poetic form while privileging a freshness of thought and a conversational naturalism. In both visual and vocal style, therefore, it was strikingly low-key. Despite the production's relative understatement, it brought together a series of highly sellable elements which ensured capacity audiences and significant media attention throughout its run. Gielgud's Shakespeare pedigree, Burton's star status and vigorous charisma as an actor, the celebrity glamour of Elizabeth Taylor in supportive attendance and the commemorative import of the Shakespearean moment proved a combination the market could not resist. The production's significant cultural capital was both illustrated and consolidated by Burton's appearance as Hamlet on the cover of *Life* magazine in April 1964. Cultural capital translated satisfyingly into record-breaking box office and the show's top-priced tickets sold for an unprecedented $9.90. Moreover, the stage production's success prompted the suggestion that a film be made of it. Audiences beyond Broadway should be enabled to share in the experience, it was thought, and, given its popularity, the commercial case for doing so seemed sound.

Many previous celebrated Shakespearean productions had been adapted for the screen to bring a lauded performance to wider audiences. In fact the history of Shakespearean cinema had begun in September 1899 – just four years after the Lumière brothers' pioneering cinematograph screening in Paris – when the actor-manager Herbert Beerbohm Tree had arranged for a few short scenes from his lavish London stage production of *King John* to be shot on film by the British Mutoscope and Biograph Company. These filmed excerpts were then shown as part of the Biograph moving-picture programme in variety halls and elsewhere as, in effect, a teaser-trailer for the stage production itself, which was, as the film's programme entry announced with topical force, 'now playing at Her Majesty's Theatre'.

The film was, therefore, both a sample record of, and a contemporary advertisement for, the stage production. The short fragment of the film that survives depicts a poison-wracked John (played by Tree) writhing in pain, earnestly mouthing inaudible words, spurning comfort, clutching at his chest, desperately stretching out his arms as if in a direct appeal to the camera and then collapsing histrionically back into his chair on the point of death. Despite the surviving scene's brevity and the extravagance of Tree's performance style in it – so alien to contemporary performance

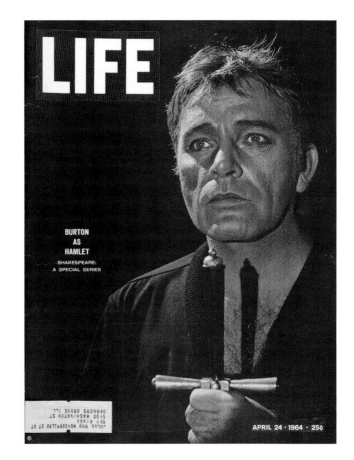

Richard Burton as
Hamlet on the cover of
Life magazine, a special
edition to celebrate
the 400th anniversary
of Shakespeare's birth
in 1964.
British Library

tastes – this surviving film fragment is valuable for the rare access it provides to a Shakespearean stage actor of significant moment from the late nineteenth century.

　　　Many later Shakespeare films were autonomously conceived as works of cinema rather than originating in a stage production. In general, such films told their stories more accessibly to picturegoers and with more energy in their cinematography than was the case for films derived from theatrical productions. Nevertheless, other theatre practitioners followed Tree's lead in seeking greater prominence and longevity for a stage production by making a film of it.

Johnston Forbes-Robertson as Hamlet. Forbes-Robertson had played Hamlet many times on the stage before working with Cecil Hepworth and Hay Plumb on the 1913 *Hamlet* film.

Photo J. V. L. Caswall Smith, 1897

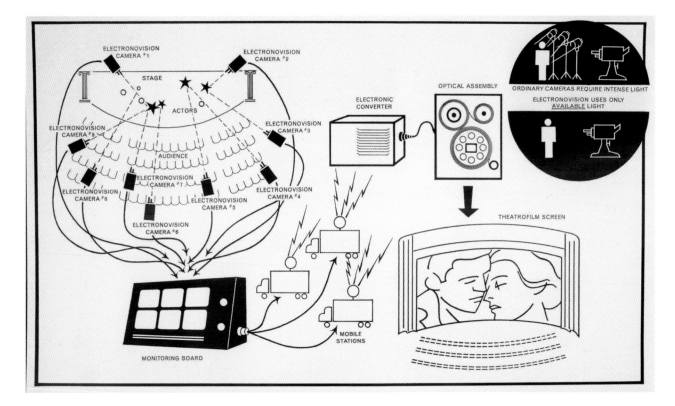

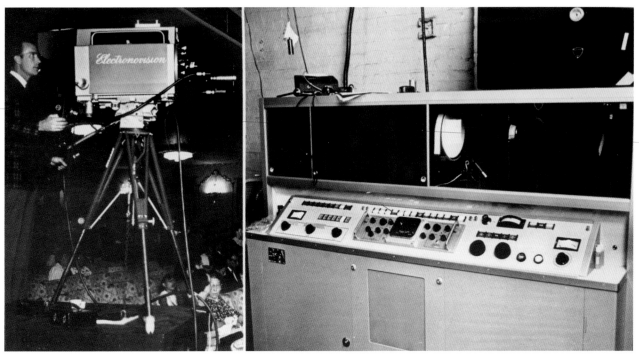

Sir Johnston Forbes-Robertson, an old-school man of the classical London stage with patrician tastes, however, had little enthusiasm for the newfangled business of filmmaking. It was, in fact, a mark of the actor's timeless distinction not to be tarnished by the modern, the material or the modish either professionally or personally. Despite his own inbuilt preferences on this score, in 1913 Forbes-Robertson temporarily overcame his prejudices to be filmed as Hamlet by Hay Plumb and Cecil Hepworth in a production that emerged directly from his much-praised Drury Lane staging of *Hamlet*. The high-profile film that resulted was given a sparkling opening night to rival that of a West End theatre production and received a significant international distribution (though tellingly it received no mention at all in Forbes-Robertson's autobiography). In the film's prefatory sequence, Forbes-Robertson as Hamlet and his wife Gertrude Elliott as Ophelia are introduced in gently animated cameos with a quotation from the play displayed below each film 'portrait': 'My tables – meet it is I set it down' (Act 1, scene 5) for Hamlet; 'There's rosemary, that's for remembrance' (Act 4, scene 5) for Ophelia. These oddly chosen and incomplete introductory quotations make little sense on their own, serving rather to signal the film's broader priorities: archivally to 'set down' (record), as was deemed 'meet' (appropriate), this celebrated piece of theatre, and in a form explicitly intended to aid 'remembrance'. Despite its transplanted location in a series of beautiful settings and rebuilt sets on the Dorset shore, the film introduced by these stylised vignettes then predominantly unspools as a scrupulously archived account of the acclaimed stage performances it cinematically 'remembers'.

The suggestion in 1964 to make a film from the celebrated Gielgud–Burton stage *Hamlet* was, therefore, certainly not in itself new. The specific proposal in this case, however, was radically innovative: in effect, it was an early anticipation of live-cast cinema. Using the inventive but short-lived process known as Electronovision, producer-entrepreneur H William (Bill) Sargent Jr, working with film director Bill Colleran and the distribution arm of Warner Brothers, arranged for the filming of the Burton stage *Hamlet* on seven cameras (not seventeen, as The Wooster Group asserts) across the scheduled live shows of 30 June and 1 July 1964. Edited partly during production itself ('through the miracle of Electronovision'), the resulting film was then rented out to nearly a thousand 'specially selected' cinemas across the United States and Canada, under very strict conditions of exhibition. The film was to play in cinemas in September, a month after the theatrical run had finished. Given its significant prestige value, Warner Brothers urged all exhibitors to be both energetic and fastidious in thinking how best to 'host' this unique Shakespearean work. An exhibitors' pack of marketing instructions was sent to all participating film theatres.

> 'HAMLET' is a FIRST – as an attraction, as a Broadway hit
> brought to your own community, and as entertainment
> in a new kind of electronic-optical process … [G]ear your

OPPOSITE
An infographic mapping the Electronovision process that enabled stage productions to be filmed live from multiple cameras, edited into a streamlined production and subsequently disseminated to cinemas. Photographs of the film cameras and editing suite employed proudly showcased the company's cutting-edge technology.
British Library, Laurence Olivier Archive Add MS 80611

thinking to terms of PRESTIGE, IMPORTANCE and STATUS … 'HAMLET' and Richard Burton are BIG NEWS. Get every advantage you can out of this favorable circumstance.

To sustain a sense of the cultural loftiness of the film and of the event, exhibitors were exhorted to pay particular attention to 'Dressing the House for "Hamlet"': the lobby was to be decorated with fresh flowers; an event-specific booth covered in black velvet was to be set up from which tickets for this show only could be sold; foyer staff were to wear their *Hamlet* medallions; and as for the washrooms, they should be 'clean and freshly stocked – very important'. In among the exacting (and entertaining) pedantry of all this, the two central aims were clear: to court an air of distinction for the theatrofilm *Hamlet* that set it apart from other cinema releases and, in doing so, to generate a real sense of occasion for the 'performances' (as they were termed) of this distinguished film.

By contractual agreement, there were four (and only four) synchronised film show times for the Burton *Hamlet* across North America. These took place on the afternoons and evenings of 23 and 24 September 1964. Thereafter, all prints were to be returned and destroyed. These stipulations, advertised ahead of time and rigorously adhered to, were intended to boost sales by impressing

The idealized saleswoman and salesbooth for the theatrofilm *Hamlet*, together with a Richard Burton cardboard medallion. These items were distributed to cinemas participating in the special screenings of *Hamlet* on 23 and 24 September 1964.

British Library, Laurence Olivier Archive Add MS 80611

upon the public the time-bounded nature of the opportunity to experience this history-making Shakespearean performance moment in the life of the nation. It was a daring, even a visionary, attempt to capture a sense of liveness, to generate a shared and synchronous cultural experience for those attending even in locations remote from each other, and to evoke in a recorded medium something of the evanescent properties of theatre. As Burton himself expressed it in a straight-to-camera piece for the film's trailer:

> This has never happened before. The immediacy, the sense of *being there,* is unlike any experience you have ever known. This is the theatre of the future, taking shape before your eyes today. And you'll be there, part of this historic first. I hope you'll join me, and the distinguished New York cast, as *Hamlet* bursts upon the twentieth century through the miracle of Electronovision.

The film was marketed as offering the chance to be 'part of' something, and to *be there,* at a highly celebrated 'live' Shakespeare 'performance' from Broadway itself. 'For the first time in history,' the trailer continued, 'you'll see a live Broadway hit in your own motion picture theatre.'

For Gielgud (who was quoted in the *New York Times* as saying 'I deplore the tendency of actors to try to immortalize everything they do'), the result was a miserably compromised hybrid that 'can't be very cinematic and … is not the theater'. The film fared little better with the critics, who were scathing about the quality of the photography, lighting and sound. It had been a brilliant idea, and it carried with it a strikingly charismatic central performance and some other properly memorable ones – notably Hume Cronyn (who won a Tony Award for his Polonius) and Eileen Herlie (who reprised the role of Gertrude that she had played in Laurence Olivier's 1948 film). It was, moreover, an idea accompanied by some impressively ambitious marketing initiatives. The imperfectly developed technology of its moment, however, fell short of being able to do full justice to the visionary brilliance of the conception. In the wake of the reception of the Burton *Hamlet* theatrofilm, Olivier, who had been considering enlisting the same technology to disseminate his own National Theatre stage production of *Othello*, dropped the idea in favour of the more conventional Olivier *Othello* film production we know today.

Theatrofilm was an idea ahead of its time. It was a vision of event cinema whose moment would come fifty years later with NT Live, Live from Stratford-upon-Avon and comparable live theatre-broadcasting programmes. For these more recent initiatives, an intimate and evocative account of the stage show they are relaying is offered to cinema-going audiences in ways beyond the reach of Electronovision. Moreover, the proudly advertised 'liveness' of the event can now mean exactly that, rather than being an aspirational marketing term used to refer to a production actually filmed two months previously. The way we experience Shakespeare is changing: when we watch an NT Live performance, for instance, we become part of an audience that is far bigger than the local. What's more, there is a phenomenon of 'being there' which is created with others from across the globe, nurtured and fuelled by the geographically spread, but hashtag-bonded, community of the Twittersphere.

Warner Brothers and Bill Sargent Jr almost certainly believed they were doing something unprecedented in recalling and destroying the prints of this Shakespeare film after its theatrical run. Like the legendary Roman King Tarquin, invited to buy unique works of prophecy from the Sybil before she tossed them on the fire, audiences were made to feel the urgency of seeing the film before it was destroyed forever. In this respect, however, the Burton *Hamlet* was once again unknowingly treading in the footsteps of innovative filmmakers from the silent era. As far back as 1911, in a well-advertised marketing ploy, all prints of the Herbert Beerbohm Tree–William Barker film of Shakespeare's *Henry VIII* (adapted from Tree's successful London stage production) had been recalled after a six-week run. In a striking piece of theatricality that self-consciously displayed the flammability of film, the recalled prints were then all publicly and ceremonially burned by Barker himself, in line with the publicised arrangements on this score. The aim had been to generate publicity, and enhanced revenue, by creating an imperative to see the film in the limited period in which it was extant. And however painful the knowledge of that strategically choreographed blaze may be to those of us from a subsequent generation now deprived of the film, judging from the success of the six-week run that preceded it, as a marketing ploy it clearly worked.

Although there is no evidence that any of the *Henry VIII* prints survived the 1911 fire, at least two copies of the Burton *Hamlet* escaped the later cull: one was donated to the British Film Institute by Burton himself; another was discovered in his garage after his death. As a result, this flawed *Hamlet* film – emerging as it did from a distinguished Broadway stage production and from a filming, distribution and exhibition project distinctly ahead of its time – was available to be cannily appropriated by The Wooster Group.

The Wooster Group *Hamlet*

The Wooster Group is a New York-based experimental theatre company with a track record of recycling and repurposing archival materials into innovative performance modes. For *Hamlet*, they digitised a version of the celebrated Richard Burton film, re-edited it to suit their own purposes and then choreographed and synchronised their own performed interactions with it. The production emerged as a mêlée of live and recorded performance, an encounter between the on-screen and off-screen, the then and the now, the long gone and the vibrantly present. In inviting the two planes of action to bump up against each other in this way, the production became a celebration and exploration of the reciprocal relationship between contemporary performance and the historical archive.

To some extent, this made conspicuous something that is in

any case true of all Shakespeare performances, and of none more so than performances of *Hamlet*. Since there is no such thing as a virgin interpretation of an established play, all new productions consciously or otherwise mediate between the present moment of performance and a set of preceding interpretations of that work. The actor Steven Berkoff has described the experience of assuming a role previously inhabited by the greats as a constant process of 'boxing with ghosts', the ghosts of past inhabitants of the role seeming reluctant to cede place too easily to the newcomer. Every actor who steps out on to the stage as Hamlet, therefore, has to negotiate his (or her) own relationship – combative, concessionary or both – with the famous Hamlets who have preceded him (or her). The actor can steer a path through these by emulation, accommodation, adjustment

Kate Valk, Casey Spooner, Scott Shepherd and Ari Fliakos in The Wooster Group's *Hamlet*.
Photo: © Paula Court

and/or resistance. Part of The Wooster Group project is to summon a
representative of those past ghosts in the form of the Burton *Hamlet*
and to make that legacy, implicit in all productions, explicitly visible
in this one. As the actors themselves announce in production, they
are committed to 'channeling the ghosts of the 1964 production'.
What we might call the 'rehearsal room mechanics' by which any
performance and production comes to be – partly through imitative
engagement with a set of prior performance practices, partly through
a partial or more substantial rejection of them – is literalised as part
of The Wooster Group's *Hamlet* performance itself. It is a production
that, in effect, shows its working.

The version of the Burton film seen in back projection in The
Wooster Group *Hamlet* is grainy, jerky and incomplete. Its projection
speed is also manipulated in full sight of the audience, being fast-
forwarded through some sections, negotiating little jump-cuts in
others. This variable film speed prompts a comparable, impressively

Scott Shepherd in
gestural alignment
with Richard Burton
in The Wooster
Group's *Hamlet*.
Photo: © Paula Court

seamless and quasi-comic adjustment in the style and pace of the contemporary cast's movements as they fall (literally) into step with the older production. Scott Shepherd, who plays The Wooster Group Hamlet, also acts as an extra-dramatic interpreter, helping the audience navigate some of the presentational complexities of the production. As the audience's perceptual field is rarely focused in a singular way, making sense of the production is a teasingly intricate business. Pieces of stage furniture are constantly being moved forwards and backwards in order to adjust the audience's proximity to the action, in witty emulation of the changed focal lengths in the film. And in his mediator role, Shepherd even physically repositions fellow actors on occasions to ensure that the onstage film camera can pick them up on the live-feed, onstage mini-screen for an appropriately framed close-up designed to mimic the action of the back projection.

As an introductory prologue, Shepherd offers a gently humorous, meta-theatrical commentary on the show's production process. As he explains, individual characters from the back projection will sometimes fade from view – airbrushed out of a continuing scene, in effect – in order not to detract unduly from the live action. Despite the declared intention to minimise distraction, the disappearance of characters from the back projection – and the frequent erasure of Burton's Hamlet in particular – becomes in itself a significant eye-draw. For audiences, this further complicates the focus of attention: should one watch the absent place on screen to await the return of the missing character, or ignore the backdrop film to concentrate on the imitative live action whose own idiosyncratic progress craves the referent of the film to make sense stylistically, or flick between planes of action to create a dynamic synthesis between the two? In the process, the audience reflects not only upon what is present in the production but also on what is absent. Showcasing the disappearance of certain characters from the cinematic back projection forms part of The Wooster Group's playful exploration of the relationship between contemporary performance and the legacy of past performances which all actors have to negotiate.

We might have expected that the live actors' gesturally harmonised engagements with the on-screen actors would have revitalised the performances we see on the film, drawing those actors from a past age more closely into the orbit of the audience through the act of mediation. The actual effect of the striking visual (and vocal) alignment of the doubled bodies is, however, quite often the reverse: the three-dimensional bodies in our space emphasise the remoteness of the two-dimensional ones. Juxtaposed with the potency of contemporary living bodies, the filmed bodies seem yet more like weathered runes from another age. In fact the closer the synchronicity in action between the two planes of action, the more emphatically marooned in a distant time and place the grainy two-dimensional figures then seem. And their eclipsing is confirmed as strategy, not just happenstance, by their intermittent erasure from the screen. Acts of performative emulation and even homage, the production seems to declare, are always disruptive and always regenerative: pure recovery is neither a worthwhile nor a feasible project.

The Wooster Group *Hamlet* is simultaneously a tribute to, pastiche of and competitive engagement with the Burton *Hamlet*. In enlisting the film as a ghost presence within its own production, it incidentally demonstrates some kinship with the ways in which acts of haunting inhabit its own Shakespearean source. Not only is *Hamlet* underpinned by a necromantic imperative (summoning the ghost of the old king), it is also dramatically propelled by an imperious act of speaking from beyond the grave into the present (the ghost's instruction to revenge). The significance of the eruption of the past into the present therefore drives both the mode of delivery for The Wooster Group *Hamlet* (past production in the space of the present one) and the plot of the play itself (dead king haunting the space of the living). And as part of the line of legacy and regressive dependencies that quietly characterise all productions, it points backwards to something that was true also of the Burton *Hamlet*.

Just as the relationship between past and present is key for The Wooster Group, so it was also for the Burton–Gielgud production. Gielgud cast Eileen Herlie to reprise the role – Gertrude – that she had played in the much-celebrated and highly influential 1948 film of *Hamlet* by Laurence Olivier. Moreover, that it was Gielgud directing connected the Broadway production to a long performance history of *Hamlet*s. Gielgud had played the prince several times in his career, and always to great acclaim: of his Hamlet at the Haymarket for the 1944–5 season, the British critic James Agate declared that Gielgud's was, and was likely to remain, 'the best Hamlet of our time'. When Kenneth Branagh, in turn, cast Gielgud as a distressed Priam (in dramatised illustration of the player king's speech) in his 1996 film of *Hamlet,* he did so specifically to make reference to this Hamletian performance legacy. This film sequence is itself then absorbed as an additional back projection into the generously acquisitive Wooster Group production. In a similar way, Michael Almereyda included footage of Gielgud's 1944 Hamlet in his *Hamlet* film of 2000. To point up his own symbolic significance in the Burton *Hamlet*, Gielgud took the singular step of casting himself as the ghost. In this production, the ghost appeared only as a pre-recorded voice accompanied by a shadowy projection on the back wall – that is, it 'appeared' in ways not actually requiring an in-person appearance at all. Thus, well before itself becoming a projected 'absence' within The Wooster Group's production, the Gielgud–Burton staging had already made apparent the significance of absence within the performance history of *Hamlet*. Any production of *Hamlet* must, after all, deal with questions of presence, of absence and of the meaning of an interaction between the two: Shakespeare's story of a dead father's ghostly commission, a living son's sense of obligation to that commission, and a dialogue between the two that perplexes those on stage (for whom Hamlet seems to converse 'with the incorporal air', Act 3, scene 4) makes this inevitable. In this context, and given the film's history and symbolic freighting,

Richard Burton as Hamlet with Eileen Herlie as Gertrude and Hume Cronyn as Polonius in John Gielgud's production at the Lunt-Fontanne Theatre, Broadway, 1964.

what more eloquent choice of work could there be than the Burton–Gielgud *Hamlet* to drive and anchor The Wooster Group's exploration of past and present, absence and presence, archive and performance?

The Wooster Group cast enacted their exploration of the meanings of presence and absence in *Hamlet* with virtuosic energy. Their production was not, however, the first to consider the relationship of the on-screen to the off-screen in a Shakespeare show. Live lecturers mediating between picturegoers and the pictures themselves had been a common feature of the early cinema period and particularly recommended for Shakespeare films; and for a short time actors were employed in some venues to add voices to a production from a hidden position behind the projection screen. But the most savvy and entertaining engagement with these questions, before the Wooster Group production, came in 1916, the tercentenary of Shakespeare's death, when J. M. Barrie (of *Peter Pan* fame) turned the on-screen/off-screen relationship into a zany pre-show for the premiere of his parodic Shakespeare film.

The Film Industry and the 1916 and 2016 Shakespeare Centenaries

By 1916 cinema was technically proficient and globally networked, and its practitioners were well rehearsed in debates about its own cultural placement. The medium was not, however, considered sufficiently culturally weighty or artistically respectable to be included in the line-up of art forms selected to fête Shakespeare as part of the official tercentenary commemorative events in Britain. Smarting at the exclusion, Barrie responded to the snub by releasing a skittish film entitled *The Real Thing at Last* that contrasted the making of a British and an American film of *Macbeth*. Among its satirical targets (and there were many), it specifically caricatured cinema's conspicuous exclusion from the Shakespeare celebrations. The 'real thing' that was supposedly 'at last' being delivered here was a 'proper' version of Shakespeare with which to celebrate the tercentenary. In this tongue-in-cheek version of 'proper' Shakespeare, however, few proprieties were observed and much absurdity was let loose.

The narrative was based upon the entertaining juxtaposition of two hypothetical productions of *Macbeth*, one an underplayed British period version, the other a brasher American updated one. The comparative structure enabled the film to trade upon comically stereotyped contrasts. In the British version, Lady Macbeth rubbed at one 'very small spot of blood'; in the American one she was 'covered in gore'. In the British production, the cauldron was 'very small', the acting style contained and the plot recognisably Shakespearean; in the American one, the cauldron was huge, the action exaggeratedly melodramatic and the potential for both goriness and sexuality enhanced. The British version ended with predictably coy understatement: 'The elegant home of the Macbeths is no longer a happy one'. The American version blithely opted for closure of another kind: 'The Macbeths repent and all ends happily'.

In sum, the British film industry emerges with a marked preference for the modestly performed, the materially spare, the appropriately historical and the fractionally dull; the American film industry for the overblown, the sensationalised, the gory, the updated and, however improbable in plot terms, the happily resolved. These were reputations that proved both delightfully amenable to parody and resilient over time.

The Real Thing at Last was first exhibited at the London Coliseum on 7 March 1916 as part of a fundraising Royal Command performance for the troops. For its premiere, Barrie choreographed an event-specific preface that self-consciously and skittishly demonstrated the film's intricate relationship to live theatre. A stage set of a picture-house frontage was erected on the stage. Before the lights went down and the projection began, the entire cast filed up on to the stage from their front-row seats, to be seen as their three-dimensional, substantive selves before then disappearing through a door in the set marked 'STAGE DOOR' as if themselves entering the picture-house ready to perform in the film to follow. Left behind on stage, Irene Vanbrugh (a bit-part actress in the film) touched a barrel with a wand, out of which large amounts of tightly jammed-in film

Theda Bara as Juliet in Fox Film's silent motion picture of 1916, released to coincide with the tercentenary of Shakespeare's death.

then exploded on cue. By this symbolic act of cinematic 'release' (the sort of literalising pun that delighted Barrie), the just-seen, real-world actors could cede to their shadowy projected counterparts and the screening could begin. To sustain the effect of live and projected action working in dialogue with each other, Edmund Gwenn (who played both Macbeth and the American film producer in the film), 'distinctly overdressed and smoking a large cigar', assumed the role of showman to supply a live commentary on each scene 'in an exaggerated American accent'. While the impression was given that most of the cast had stepped *on to* the canvas from their previous position in the stalls and on the stage, Gwenn's on-screen character had apparently stepped *off* the screen on to the apron of the Coliseum in order to act as impresario and extra-cinematic commentator. 'Reverse theatrofilm' – staging a conversation between off-screen and on-screen Shakespeare – had had its proponents in the pre-sound era too.

The British Library's 2016 Shakespeare exhibition's choice to devote its final Act to filmed Shakespeare suggests a level of establishment recognition for the dissemination of Shakespearean work through the screen that had eluded the industry in 1916. Despite its exclusion from the official celebrations, however, Shakespearean filmmaking boomed in 1916, fuelled in part by the increased interest that the tercentenary brought with it. Feature-length Shakespeare films to emerge that year included the Thanhouser Company's *King Lear* (starring Frederick Warde), the Triangle-Reliance *Macbeth* that Herbert Beerbohm Tree made in Hollywood at D. W. Griffith's invitation, and two big-budget American versions of *Romeo and Juliet*. The Metro release starred Beverly Bayne and Francis X. Bushman, Hollywood's premier screen idols of the moment; in an unexpected but commercially savvy piece of casting, the Fox version starred

A pre-release still frame, ahead of post-production artwork, from the 2016 feature film of *Macbeth* directed by Kit Monkman with Mark Rowley as Macbeth and Al Weaver as Banquo.
© GSP Studios

Poster for Laurence
Olivier's film of
Henry V (1944) shot
in technicolor.
Olivier's film used
the Shakespeare
play partly as a filter
through which to
express the concerns
and aspirations of its
wartime moment for a
home front audience.

the sexually charged screen vamp Theda Bara, whose Juliet was, as she herself explained, 'no Sunday school girl'. A hundred years on, the film industry seems similarly energised by the 2016 celebrations. One only has to scan the current release schedule for feature-length productions and offshoots of *Macbeth* to catch the scale of the current creative interest: Michael Fassbender in Justin Kurzel's production, Sean Bean in Vincent Regan's, Kenneth Branagh in Martin Scorsese's, Mark Rowley in Kit Monkman's. To say nothing of the myriad short films, digital mash-ups and experimental reflections and refractions by which our many platforms of consumption are now populated.

In among these creative energies, there is an increasing appetite, in tune with The Wooster Group project, to understand our Shakespearean engagements as part of a historical trajectory and larger cultural story. In the credit sequence for *Prospero's Books* (1991), Peter Greenaway dramatises the process of textual and interpretative transmission across generations in which the film itself participates by showing an old book being passed carefully from hand to hand, read by some, passively passed on by others. In the Kit Monkman film of *Macbeth* (scheduled for release in spring 2016), the unspooling and secret viewing of an early, almost unknown silent version of *Macbeth* from 1909 punctuates the present-time action. The witches in this production know what they know, it transpires, because they have seen the film: being unplaced historically gives them access to the tale's cultural currency across time. In the opening sequence of the draft screenplay for Laurence Olivier's carefully planned, but finally unmade, film of *Macbeth* from the 1950s, a young, vigorous Macbeth stares down into a pool from where he sees an anguished version of his older self staring back up at him. The script returns to this image of the reciprocal gaze across time for the closing moments of the proposed film, framing its story with an arresting image simultaneously of foresight and hindsight.

Characters from within a dramatic world, and the productions that carry them, look forwards and backwards through a range of mechanisms to try and help place themselves: gazing into prophetic pools, falling into synchronised step with actors from another era, summoning antecedents in acts of cultural necromancy, receiving a multiply inflected book from a line of predecessors, clandestinely viewing cans of knowledge-imparting silent film. And of course, those productions that do not carry an image explicitly illustrating a cross-temporal gaze are certainly not without one: working with legacies of interpretation and performance is part of the business of playmaking and filmmaking.

As well as looking across time, Shakespeare films are also invested in, and eloquent about, their own specific moment. Barrie's *The Real Thing at Last* tells us not only its own impish tale of cultural comparison, but also of an establishment prejudice against cinema *per se* in 1916. Asta Nielsen's 1920 *Hamlet* gives us not only a beautifully wry and knowing central performance but also showcases both the gleeful opportunities and the emotional complexities of a 1920s modish androgyny. Olivier's 1944 *Henry V*, a cinematic pageant of Technicolor, rousing verse-speaking and stirring music, speaks also of an urgent wartime need to believe in a just war, to see its prosecution as admirable and its enemies as defeatable. Grigori Kozintsev's *Hamlet* uses the play as an above-suspicion mouthpiece for articulating political dissent in 1964 Soviet Russia. Julie Taymor includes multiple time frames in *Titus* (1999) to show how vulnerable any historical moment can be to the emergence of theatres of cruelty. The film closes on an act of rescue of the vulnerable from the uncompromising brutality of those arenas in ways that spoke at the time of the war in Bosnia and Herzegovina but that assumes renewed piquancy, at the time of writing, in relation to the current Syrian refugee crisis.

Afterword: A Future for Shakespearean Filmmaking?

The imminent death of cinema in the wake of other technologies and other patterns of entertainment has been announced many times. But as the writer and critic Raymond Bellour reminds us, the much-heralded end of cinema is 'un fin qui ne finit pas de ne pas finir' (an end which is never done with not being done). And Shakespearean filmmaking certainly shows no signs of diminishing in popularity. Cinema is, however, changing. It is, for example, no longer confined by the formal properties and architectural bounds that used to contain it: it has escaped those to percolate into the rhythms and the spaces of our daily life. Cinema is among us, in both our public spaces and in the intimacies of our day: the town square, the school room, the halls of commerce and of art, our living rooms, and, most potently of all, the palm of our hand. Yet everywhere, Shakespeare must jostle for our attention and, significantly, for that of the next generation, alongside dizzying arrays of competition.

What, in this context, is the future for Shakespeare on screen? It would seem to be bi-fold, embracing both enhanced complexity and enhanced simplicity in different strands of its evolution. On the one hand, filmmakers deploy a complex wealth of reference beyond the immediate context of the film in order to participate in the conceptually crowded landscape of a heavily mediatised world. On the other, they pare away as much of the fuss of design, technological innovation and cross-reference as possible in order to rediscover and privilege the simple telling of the tale. At the moment in which I write, this latter approach is best exemplified, in extreme form, by Forced Entertainment's recent surprising smash-hit internet project 'The Complete Works: Table-Top Shakespeare'. In this series of live-streams, each of which is shot in a single take from a static camera, Shakespeare's plays are intimately retold to an assembled audience world-wide on a simple table-top, using everyday objects such as salt and pepper pots, scouring pads, batteries, margarine tubs and ketchup bottles to represent their characters. Both the densely referential and the starkly simplified approaches can be properly stimulating. As we contemplate a range of possible futures for screen Shakespeare, however, the singular success of the second is also somehow heartening.

Further Reading

Prologue: Beginnings of a Life in Performance

Jonathan Bate, *The Genius of Shakespeare* (Oxford: Oxford University Press, 1998)

Jonathan Bate, *Soul of the Age: The Life, Mind and World of William Shakespeare* (London: Viking, 2008)

Katherine Duncan-Jones, *Ungentle Shakespeare: Scenes from His Life* (London: Arden Shakespeare, 2001)

Stephen Greenblatt, *Will and the World: How Shakespeare Became Shakespeare* (New York: Norton, 2004)

Charles Nicholl, *The Lodger Shakespeare: His Life on Silver Street* (London: Viking, 2008)

Charles Nicholl, *The Reckoning: The Murder of Christopher Marlowe* (New York: Harcourt Brace, 1992)

Eric Rasmussen, *The Shakespeare Thefts: In Search of the First Folios* (London: Palgrave, 2011)

David Riggs, *The World of Christopher Marlowe* (London: Henry Holt, 2004)

James Shapiro, *A Year in the Life of William Shakespeare: 1599* (New York: HarperCollins, 2005)

Chapter 1 'A hit, a very palpable hit': *Hamlet* at the Globe, c. 1600

David Bevington, *Murder Most Foul: Hamlet through the Ages* (Oxford: Oxford University Press, 2011)

E. K. Chambers, *The Elizabethan Stage* (Oxford: Oxford University Press, 1930)

Barry Day, *This Wooden 'O': Shakespeare's Globe Reborn* (Ottawa: Oberon Press, 1997)

Margreta de Grazia, *Hamlet without Hamlet* (Cambridge: Cambridge University Press, 2007)

Stephen Greenblatt, *Hamlet in Purgatory* (Princeton, NJ: Princeton University Press, 2001)

Andrew Gurr, *Playgoing in Shakespeare's London* (Cambridge: Cambridge University Press, 1987)

Thomas J. King, *Casting Shakespeare's Plays: London Actors and Their Roles 1590–1642* (Cambridge: Cambridge University Press, 1992)

Chapter 2 'Into something rich and strange': *The Tempest* at the Blackfriars Playhouse c. 1610–11

Paul Brown, '"This Thing of Darkness I Acknowledge Mine": *The Tempest* and the Discourse of Colonialism', in *Political Shakespeare: New Essays in Cultural Materialism*, ed. Jonathan Dollimore and Alan Sinfield (Manchester: Manchester University Press, 1985), pp. 48–71

Martin Butler, 'Prospero in Cyberspace', in *Re-Constructing the Book: Literary Texts in Transmission*, ed. Maureen Bell et al. (Aldershot: Ashgate, 2001), pp. 184–96

Andrew Gurr and Farah Karim-Cooper (eds.), *Moving Shakespeare Indoors: Performance and Repertoire in the Jacobean Playhouse* (Cambridge: Cambridge University Press, 2014)

Peter Hulme and William H. Sherman (eds.), *'The Tempest' and Its Travels* (London: Reaktion Books, 2000)

Gordon McMullan, *Shakespeare and the Idea of Late Writing: Authorship in the Proximity of Death* (Cambridge: Cambridge University Press, 2007), pp. 331–7

Mary M. Nilan, 'Shakespeare, Illustrated: Charles Kean's 1857 Production of *The Tempest*', *Shakespeare Quarterly* 26 (1975), pp. 196–204

William Shakespeare, *The Tempest*, ed. Virginia Mason Vaughan and Alden T. Vaughan (London: Arden Shakespeare, 1999)

Tiffany Stern, '"A Ruinous Monastery": The Second Blackfriars Playhouse as a Place of Nostalgia', in Gurr and Karim-Cooper (2014), pp. 97–114

Chapter 3 'The wide world': Shakespeare across the Globe

James C. Bulman (ed.), *The Oxford Handbook of Shakespeare and Performance* (Oxford: Oxford University Press, 2016)

Thomas Cartelli, *Repositioning Shakespeare: National Formations, Postcolonial Appropriations* (London: Routledge, 1999)

Andrew Dickson, *Worlds Elsewhere: Journeys around Shakespeare's Globe* (London: The Bodley Head, 2015)

Barbara Hodgdon and William B. Worthen, *A Companion to Shakespeare and Performance* (Oxford: Wiley-Blackwell, 2005)

Margaret Jane Kidnie, *Shakespeare and the Problem of Adaptation* (London: Routledge, 2009)

Sonia Massai, *World-Wide Shakespeares: Local Appropriations in Film and Performance* (London: Routledge, 2005)

Martin Orkin, *Local Shakespeares: Proximations and Power* (London: Routledge, 2005)

Chapter 4 'Do you not know I am a woman?': The Legacy of the First Female Desdemona, 1660

Tony Howard, *Women as Hamlet* (Cambridge: Cambridge University Press, 2007)

Elizabeth Howe, *The First English Actresses: Women and Drama, 1660–1700* (Cambridge: Cambridge University Press, 1992)

Joanne Lafler, 'Theatre and the Female Presence', in *The Cambridge History of British Theatre, Volume 2: 1660 to 1895*, ed. Joseph Donohue (Cambridge: Cambridge University Press, 2004)

Gail Marshall, *Shakespeare and Victorian Women* (Cambridge: Cambridge University Press, 2012)

Clare McManus, 'Women and English Renaissance Drama: Making and Unmaking "The All-Male Stage"', *Literature Compass* 4.3 (2007), pp. 784–96

Fiona Ritchie, *Women and Shakespeare in the Eighteenth Century* (Cambridge: Cambridge University Press, 2014)

Chapter 5 ''Tis mad idolatry': *Vortigern*, the Ireland Forgeries and the Birth of Bardolatry

Paul Baines, *The House of Forgery in Eighteenth-Century Britain* (Aldershot: Ashgate, 1999)

Angela Carter, *Wise Children* (London: Chatto & Windus, 1991)

Vanessa Cunningham, *Shakespeare and Garrick* (Cambridge: Cambridge University Press, 2008)

Christian Deelman, *The Great Shakespeare Jubilee* (London: Michael Joseph, 1964)

Michael Dobson, *Making of the National Poet: Shakespeare, Adaptation and Authorship* (Oxford: Oxford University Press, 1992)

Martha W. England, *Garrick's Jubilee* (Columbus, OH: Ohio State University Press, 1964)

Jeffrey Kahan, *Reforging Shakespeare: The Story of a Theatrical Scandal* (Bethlehem, PA: Lehigh University Press, 1998)

Jeffrey Kahan (ed.), *Shakespeare Imitations, Parodies, and Forgeries, 1710–1820*, Volume III (Abingdon: Routledge, 2004)

Patricia Pierce, *The Great Shakespeare Fraud: The Strange True Story of William-Henry Ireland* (Stroud: Sutton, 2004)

James Shapiro, *Contested Will: Who Wrote Shakespeare?* (London: Faber & Faber, 2010)

Chapter 6 'Haply, for I am black': The Legacy of Ira Aldridge

Anon, *Memoir and Theatrical Career of Ira Aldridge, the African Roscius* (London: *c.* 1848; available online)

Delia Jarrett-Macauley (ed.), *The Diverse Bard* (London: Routledge, 2016)

Bernth Lindfors (ed.), *Ira Aldridge: The African Roscius* (Rochester, NY: University of Rochester Press, 2007)

Bernth Lindfors, *Ira Aldridge: The Early Years, 1807–1833* (Rochester, NY: University of Rochester Press, 2011)

Bernth Lindfors, *Ira Aldridge: The Vagabond Years, 1833–1852* (Rochester, NY: University of Rochester Press, 2011)

Bernth Lindfors, *Ira Aldridge: Performing Shakespeare in Europe, 1852–1855* (Rochester, NY: University of Rochester Press, 2013)

Herbert Marshall and Mildred Stock, *Ira Aldridge: The Negro Tragedian* (London: Rockliffe, 1958)

Paul Robeson, *Here I Stand* (New York: Beacon Press, 1958)

Paul Robeson Jr, *The Undiscovered Paul Robeson: An Artist's Journey, 1898–1939* (New York: Wiley & Sons, 2001)

Paul Robeson Jr, *The Undiscovered Paul Robeson, Quest for Freedom, 1939–1976* (New York: Wiley & Sons, 2010)

Ayanna Thompson (ed.), *Colorblind Shakespeare: New Perspectives on Race and Performance* (New York and London: Routledge, 2006)

**Chapter 7 'He is return'd':
The Revision and Restoration of *King Lear***

Vanessa Cunningham, *Shakespeare and Garrick* (Cambridge: Cambridge University Press, 2008)

Richard Foulkes, '"How Fine a Play was Mrs. Lear": The Case for Gordon Bottomley's *King Lear's Wife*', *Shakespeare Survey* 55 (2002), pp. 128–38

Peter Holland (ed.), *Shakespeare Survey*, Volume 55: *King Lear and Its Afterlife* (Cambridge: Cambridge University Press, 2002)

Alexander Leggatt, *Shakespeare in Performance: King Lear* (Manchester: Manchester University Press, 2nd edn 2004)

W. Moelwyn Merchant, 'Costume in *King Lear*', *Shakespeare Survey* 13 (1960), pp. 72–80

Roger Paulin (ed.), *Great Shakespeareans*, volume 3: *Voltaire, Goethe, Schlegel, Coleridge* (London: Continuum, 2010)

Marvin Rosenberg, *The Masks of King Lear* (London: Associated University Presses, 1972)

Gefen Bar-On Santor, 'Shakespeare in the Georgian Theatre', in *The Oxford Handbook of Georgian Theatre 1737–1832*, ed. Julia Swindells and David Francis Taylor (Oxford: Oxford University Press, 2014), pp. 213–28

Richard Schoch (ed.), *Great Shakespeareans*, volume 6: *Macready, Booth, Irving, Terry* (London: Continuum, 2011)

J. C. Trewin (ed.), *The Journal of William Charles Macready 1832–1851* (London: Longmans, 1967)

**Chapter 8 'The revolution of the times':
Peter Brook's *A Midsummer Night's Dream*, 1970**

Peter Brook, *The Empty Space* (London: MacGibbon & Kee, 1969)

Peter Brook, *The Quality of Mercy: Reflections on Shakespeare* (London: Nick Hern Books, 2013)

Peter Brook, *The Shifting Point* (London: Methuen, 1988)

Christine Dymkowski, *Harley Granville Barker: A Preface to Modern Shakespeare* (Washington: Folger Library, 1986)

Barbara Hodgdon, *Shakespeare, Performance and the Archive* (Abingdon and New York: Routledge, 2015)

Russell Jackson, *Shakespeare Films in the Making* (Cambridge: Cambridge University Press, 2007)

Michael Kustow, *Peter Brook: A Biography* (London: Bloomsbury, 2005)

Glenn Loney (ed.), *Peter Brook's Production of William Shakespeare's 'A Midsummer Night's Dream' for the Royal Shakespeare Company* (Chicago: Dramatic Publishing Company, 1974)

David Selbourne, *The Making of 'A Midsummer Night's Dream'* (London: Methuen, 1982)

David Williams, *Peter Brook: A Theatrical Casebook* rev. edn (London: Methuen, 1991)

Gary Jay Williams, *Our Moonlight Revels* (Iowa City: University of Iowa Press, 1997)

**Chapter 9 'The wheel is come full circle':
Twelfth Night at Middle Temple Hall and Shakespeare's Globe, 2002**

Christie Carson and Farah Karim-Cooper (eds.), *Shakespeare's Globe: A Theatrical Experiment* (Cambridge: Cambridge University Press, 2008)

J. R. Mulryne and Margaret Shewring (eds.), *Shakespeare's Globe Rebuilt* (Cambridge: Cambridge University Press, 1997)

Marion O'Connor, *William Poel and the Elizabethan Stage Society* (Cambridge: Chadwyck-Healey, 1987)

Paul Prescott, 'Sam Wanamaker', in *Great Shakespeareans*, Volume 15: *Poel, Granville Barker, Guthrie, Wanamaker*, ed. Cary M. Mazer (London: Arden and Bloomsbury, 2013)

Simon Smith, 'Music at Shakespeare's Globe: Claire van Kampen, Original Practices and Theatrical Experimentation' (2013/2014). http://www.shakespearesglobe.com/uploads/ files/2014/07/music_at_the_globe.pdf (last accessed 15 June 2015)

**Chapter 10 'Look here, upon this picture':
Theatrofilm, the Wooster Group *Hamlet* and the Film Industry**

Jennifer Barnes, '"Posterity is Dispossessed": Laurence Olivier's Macbeth Manuscripts in 1958 and 2012', *Shakespeare Bulletin* 30.3 (2012), pp. 263–98

Raymond Bellour, *La Querelle des dispositifs: cinéma-installations-expositions* (Paris: POL, 2012)

Judith Buchanan, *Shakespeare on Film* (Harlow: Longman-Pearson, 2005)

Judith Buchanan, *Shakespeare on Silent Film: An Excellent Dumb Discourse* (Cambridge: Cambridge University Press, 2009)

Mark Thornton Burnett, *Shakespeare and World Cinema* (Cambridge: Cambridge University Press, 2012)

Christie Carson and Peter Kirwan (eds.), *Shakespeare and the Digital World: Redefining Scholarship and Practice* (Cambridge, Cambridge University Press, 2014)

Thomas Cartelli and Katherine Rowe, *New Wave Shakespeare on Screen* (London: Polity, 2007)

Luke McKernan, 'A Scene – King John – Now Playing at Her Majesty's Theatre', in *Moving Performance: British Stage and Screen, 1890s–1920s*, ed. Linda Fitzsimmons and Sarah Street (Trowbridge: Flicks Books, 2000), pp. 56–68

Luke McKernan and Olwen Terris (eds.), *Walking Shadows: Shakespeare in the National Film and Television Archive* (London: British Film Institute, 1994)

Emma Smith, '"Sir J. and Lady Forbes-Robertson left for America on Saturday": Marketing the 1913 Hamlet for Stage and Screen', in Fitzsimmons and Street (2000), pp. 44–55

Richard L. Sterne, *John Gielgud Directs Richard Burton in Hamlet* (London: Random House, 1967)

W. B. Worthen, 'Hamlet at Ground Zero: The Wooster Group and the Archive of Performance', *Shakespeare Quarterly*, 59.3 (Fall 2008): pp. 303–22

Illustration Credits

Index